The Good Muslim

Reflections on Classical Islamic Law and Theology

MONA SIDDIQUI
University of Edinburgh

CAMBRIDGE
UNIVERSITY PRESS

CAMBRIDGE
UNIVERSITY PRESS

Shaftesbury Road, Cambridge CB2 8EA, United Kingdom

One Liberty Plaza, 20th Floor, New York, NY 10006, USA

477 Williamstown Road, Port Melbourne, VIC 3207, Australia

314–321, 3rd Floor, Plot 3, Splendor Forum, Jasola District Centre, New Delhi – 110025, India

103 Penang Road, #05–06/07, Visioncrest Commercial, Singapore 238467

Cambridge University Press is part of Cambridge University Press & Assessment, a department of the University of Cambridge.

We share the University's mission to contribute to society through the pursuit of education, learning and research at the highest international levels of excellence.

www.cambridge.org
Information on this title: www.cambridge.org/9780521740128

First published 2012

A catalogue record for this publication is available from the British Library

Library of Congress Cataloging-in-Publication data
Siddiqui, Mona.
The good Muslim : reflections on classical Islamic law and theology / Mona Siddiqui.
p. cm.
Includes bibliographical references and index.
ISBN 978-0-521-51864-2 (hardback) – ISBN 978-0-521-74012-8 (paperback)
1. Religious life – Islam. 2. Islam – Doctrines. 3. Islamic ethics. 4. Islamic law.
5. Islam – Essence, genius, nature. I. Title.
BP 188.S575 2012
297.2–dc23 2011033316

ISBN 978-0-521-51864-2 Hardback
ISBN 978-0-521-74012-8 Paperback

THE GOOD MUSLIM

In this unusual, thought-provoking, and beautifully written book, Mona Siddiqui reflects upon key themes in Islamic law or theology. She has selected these topics, which range through discussions about friendship, divorce, drunkenness, love, slavery, and ritual slaughter, in part because they are of particular interest to her, and in part because they reveal fascinating insights into Islamic ethics and the way in which arguments developed in medieval scholarly discourse. These pre-modern religious works contained a richness of thought, hesitation, and speculation on a wide range of topics, which were socially relevant but also presented intellectual challenges to the scholars for whom God's revelation could be understood in diverse ways. These subjects of course remain very relevant today, both for practicing Muslims and for scholars of Islamic law and religious studies, and the book shows just how these debates resonate in contemporary Islamic thought. Mona Siddiqui is an astute and articulate interpreter who relays complex ideas about the Islamic tradition with great clarity. These are important attributes for a book which, as the author acknowledges, charts her own journey through the classical texts and reflects upon how the principles expounded there have guided her own thinking and impacted on her teaching and research.

Mona Siddiqui is Professor of Islamic and Interreligious Studies at the Divinty School, University of Edinburgh. She is the author of *How to Read the Qur'an* (2007) and editor of *Islam, Volumes 1–4* (2010).

In fondest memory of my friend Norman Calder

Contents

Contents

Acknowledgements

I began this book while working at the University of Glasgow's Department of Theology and Religious Studies. During this time a conversation with Marigold Acland at Cambridge University Press became the initial inspiration behind this book; her support throughout has been constant. My thanks also go to the entire team at Cambridge for their help in bringing this book to its completion. I would also like to extend my gratitude to the anonymous reader whose comments helped sharpen some of the technical content. The cheerful encouragement of my family, who have been hearing the word 'Cambridge' endlessly for the last few months, lies at the core of all my endeavours; to them a big thank you.

Mona Siddiqui

Acknowledgements

Introduction

> Modern scholars have sometimes noted that attitudes towards the nature of truth and the extent to which truth is to be disseminated among society at large were very different in medieval Islamic society from what they are in the Modern West. Medieval Muslim thinkers of various schools, both orthodox and heterodox, tended to think that society was inevitably divided into an elite which was capable of understanding the full truth and a majority of persons who were not capable of such understanding.
>
> (Nikki Keddie)[1]

An interesting question about the Islamic intellectual tradition is who were the scholars of the formative and classical period writing for? Maybe just for each other, maybe there was no one audience, or maybe this is a very modern question. Modern understanding of scholarship inquires after originality, sources, and influence. Very often the modern audience is assumed to be secular and liberal, rather than confessional or literalist. In the Western academic tradition we delineate disciplines of scholarship, as much as for establishing the parameters of scholarly excellence as for our own sense of epistemological direction and focus. In addition to this question, we must also ask how was the knowledge and learning of early Muslim scholars imparted? Since the 1980s there has been much progress regarding the question of oral and written transmission of knowledge in early Islam, that is, the first three centuries of Islam. Drawing upon the works of several Western scholars, Sebastian Günther explains how the scholarly sessions (*majālis*) held by Muslim scholars for the purpose of teaching their students, relied largely on oral and aural instruction.[2] Written materials in the form of collections of data and 'lecture scripts' were

[1] Nikki R. Keddie, 'Symbol and Sincerity in Islam', *Studia Islamica*, 19, 1963, pp. 27–63.

[2] Sebastian Günther, 'Assessing the Sources of Classical Arabic Compilations: The Issue of Categories and Methodologies', *British Society for Middle-Eastern Studies*, 32:1, 2005, pp. 75–98.

used as memory aids and, in the course of time, these collections came to be fixed in memory and writing. However, the concept of a book did not gain shape in early Muslims scholarship, although scholars exercised authorial creativity through their selection and arrangement of themes as well as displaying a sophisticated method of internal referencing in various written forms. They produced different kinds of written collections and notes, many of which were used by their students for the composition of their own works. Günther writes, 'Interestingly enough, these lecture scripts and written collections of data from the first three centuries of Islam seem to make up the majority of the "sources" used by authors of later times when composing their often voluminous compilations.'[3]

Faith always requires scholarly expression. The Qur'ān was not only to be read liturgically but also scholastically. The intellectual debates of the formative period flourished during the classical era of Islamic thought (*c.* 1000–*c.* 1500/*c.* 1600)[4] and reflected their intellectual interests through particular literary genres. These were notably exegesis (*tafsīr*), philosophy (*falsafa*), theology (*kalām*), mysticism (*taṣawwuf*), and jurisprudence (*fiqh*). *Kalām* is the word that comes closest to theology in Islam, meaning 'words' or 'discussion', and the science of *kalām* became the science of discussing all things divine. The scholarly search for the roots of Islamic theology continues to divide scholars. There are those who see certain themes in early Islamic thought develop largely in response to an encounter with Christianity. Others peceve an original, inner development of Muslim thought.[5] Many of the theological issues arose from religious and political issues faced by the early Muslim community including the relationship between free will and predestination, sin and salvation, the nature of ethical values such as right and just, and the concept of the creation of the Qur'ān. In addition, the whole epistemology of knowledge itself, divided broadly between divine knowledge and human knowledge, focused on the kind of knowledge God created in humankind. Theologians could be broadly divided into rationalist and traditionalist. The rationalists were those who stressed the primacy of reason over revelation in case of any contradiction between the two. The traditionalists were those thinkers who relied on the Qur'ān, the *sunna*, and the consensus of the scholars first and foremost as the basis of their theology.[6] Philosophy developed

[3] Günther, 'Assessing the Sources', p. 78.

[4] I have used these dates as reflective overall of the pre-modern world though the historical periods of classical and medieval are subject to difference of opinion.

[5] Josef Van Ess, 'The Beginnings of Islamic Theology', in John E. Murdoch and Edith Dudley Sylla, eds., *The Cultural Context of Medieval Learning*, Dordrecht/Boston: Reidel 1975, pp. 87–111.

[6] See Binyamin Abrahamov, 'Theology', in Andrew Rippin, ed., *The Blackwell Companion to the Qur'ān*, Oxford: Blackwell, 2006.

under the ʿAbbāsids with the translations of Greek philosophy and science, and while it retained its non-Islamic origins, ʿAbbāsid rule witnessed the appearance of distinguished Islamic philosophers such as al-Kindī (d. 870), al-Fārābī (d. 950), and Ibn Sīnā (d. 1037). They claimed a rightful stake in knowledge of the divine and became leading intellects of the philosophical world, combining theology, philosophy, and politics in their works.

The major Islamic science however was *fiqh*, knowledge or understanding, translated as jurisprudence and generally absorbed within the concept of Islamic law. Although the concept of God's ideal law is encapsulated in the word *sharīʿa* it was the juristic discipline of *fiqh* that came to dominate the legal world and where one finds some of the greatest intellectual and literary achievements of Muslim scholarship. Joseph Schacht described Islamic law as the 'epitome of Islamic thought'.[7] It is generally thought that while ethics and law are distinct disciplines in Islamic thought, the former was obscured by the growth of the latter. Ethics can be defined as a practical science that seeks to know right from wrong, how one arrives at ultimate principles, but law, which was also concerned with expressing divine will, was based on the premise of determining right action. Sunnī Islam recognises four sources through which Islamic law is derived. These are the Qur'ān, the *sunna* of the Prophet, the consensus (*ijmāʿ*) of the community, and analogical reasoning (*qiyās*), a method of discovering new judgments from what God had already commanded or forbidden. It is worth mentioning here, albeit briefly, that in recent years a number of scholars have questioned the origins of Islamic jurisprudence and broken with this traditional historiography. Key among these scholars was Joseph Schacht, whose theories are summarised aptly by the late Norman Calder, sceptical but broadly in agreement with Schacht:

> Joseph Schacht, following the methodological and historical presuppositions of Goldziher, in his study of early Muslim jurisprudence (1950), broke the historical link between *ḥadīth* and *fiqh*. He argued, against the implications of the Muslim hermeneutical tradition, that the structures of *fiqh* were initially independent of (and so, in time, provoked) the major corpus of *ḥadīth* literature. The real origins of *fiqh*, for him, lay in the living tradition of local schools, ie in a juristic adaptation of real social norms, which was only gradually transformed into the structures of the classical hermeneutical nexus.[8]

The traditional linear understanding of the development of Muslim jurisprudence remains a critical and contested academic debate, with scholars both

[7] Joseph Schacht, *An Introduction to Islamic Law*, Oxford: Clarendon Press, 1964, p. 1.
[8] Norman Calder, *Studies in Early Muslim Jurisprudence*, Oxford: Clarendon Press, 1993, p. vii.

accepting and refuting this revolutionary claim by Schacht. Those questioning Schacht's theories have asked from where is Muslim jurisprudence derived if not from the Qur'ān and *ḥadīth*? Furthermore, what exactly does Schacht mean when he refers to a 'living tradition'?[9] Human reason had to be applied for the elaboration of Islamic law. The best effort applied by each scholar jurist (*faqīh*) to assess and determine any one ruling from the texts of revelation to the norm of law was contained in the concept of *ijtihād*, and legal theory became known as *uṣūl al-fiqh*, the 'principles' or 'roots' of *fiqh*. By virtue of *ijtihād*, a vast body of positive rules came into being defined as the 'branches' of *fiqh* (*furū' al-fiqh*). The books that laid out the scholar's knowledge of the law encompassing in theory all aspects of life and worship, the types of jurists engaged in the thinking, application, and judgment of law (*muftī*, *qāḍī*) are all contributors to the development of 'religious law' in Islamic thought.

However, *fiqh* was never more than a human approximation of a sacred ideal, a product that was ultimately a pious, but human and therefore imperfect, effort. It saw limitless growth at the hands of the jurists whose writing style combined juristic speculation with literary ingenuity. While there were several schools of law in early Sunnī Islam, the groupings of these jurists eventually settled out at four schools (*madhhab*s). According to medieval Islam, these schools were named after their founders, Mālik ibn Anas (d. 796), Abū Ḥanīfa (d. 767), Al-Shāfi'ī (d. 822), and Ibn Ḥanbal (d. 855). Many Western scholars have argued that the founders of the schools were not responsible for establishing the 'schools' named after them – Mālikī, Ḥanafī, Shāfi'ī and Ḥanbalī, rather that it was the pupils of the founders who established the basic elements of the school (*madhhab*).[10] There is no real evidence of any historical consensus as to why only four schools of Sunnī law were accepted, but there were also Shī'ī schools such as the Zaydīs and Ithnā 'Asharīs that developed separately. As the four schools became established, jurists of individual schools wrote according to the methods and disciplines of that particular school despite spatial and temporal differences. There were two ways by which the views of different writers from different eras were established. One was through the exploration of those problems that each generation of jurists inherited from their ancestors, and the other was through the process of citing past authorities. This was the way in which tradition was

[9] Ze'ev Maghen, 'Joseph Schacht and the Origins of "Popular Practice"', *Islamic Law and Society*, 10:3, 2003, pp. 276–347.

[10] See, for example, Joseph Schacht, *The Origins of Muhammadan Jurisprudence*, Oxford: Clarendon Press, 1967, and, more recently, Christopher Melchert, *The Formation of the Sunnī Schools of Law, 9th–10th Centuries*, Leiden: Brill, 1997.

affirmed and embraced, surviving not through inertia but through the active preservation and participation by generations of scholars.

The richness of juristic speculation within each school and across schools is contained in the diversity of juristic opinion (*ikhtilāf*), the central stylistic feature of *fiqh*.[11] The principle of *ikhtilāf* allowed the jurists to put forward various perspectives on a single point of principle by the discussion of options and circumstances. As *fiqh* acquired a technical life in the creative ingenuity of the jurists, these principles often became buried under a mound of detail and formula. The diverse legal opinions are presented through a casuistical approach where priority is given to the creation rather than application of the law. The texts accommodate a selection of viewpoints on a given issue by citing a large number of different authorities. These authorities remain equally important for the formation of the argument and speculation over the issue at hand.

It is this fundamental concept of argument that I wish to portray in this book. I have tried to show the nature of *fiqh* and *kalām* writing through distinct themes. This book is not a conventional monograph. It is a collection of seven chapters, each of which is devoted to discrete topics of Islamic law or theology; the themes of the chapters reflect the author's personal choice. One could well ask the rationale for such a collection if there is no overarching theme or coherence in the conventional sense. The short response is simply that this book is a personal quest in which I wanted to explore these particular themes in greater detail. The longer response is that it is increasingly important in our modern world to be reminded that Muslim texts from the formative to the classical period presented multiple voices at variance with one another. The pre-modern religious works contained a richness of thought, hesitation, and speculation on a wide range of topics. These topics were not just socially relevant but presented intellectual challenges to the scholars for whom God's revelation could be understood in diverse ways and expressed through different intellectual forms. Each of the chapters reflects how debates were conducted in all branches of knowledge (*'ilm*) in the Islamic world and that the discursive logic within these topics illustrates precisely this point. The chapters are not an exercise in some form of deductive analysis of theory or doctrine but illustrate the intellectual creativity that went into presenting an argument across a range of themes.

Too often in Islamic Studies, books are divided according to law, history, theology, politics, or gender studies with interesting overviews of the subject at

[11] It is not within the cope of this introduction to give more than this skeletal framework on Muslim jurisprudence and other intellectual genres but it is hoped that the reader will use this in addition to the glossary of terms to engage with the material in the book.

hand. This book avoids overviews or big narratives about any given subject area. It certainly does not aim to reflect what many understand to be normative Islam. My interest is in discursive Islam. I have divided the chapters broadly into the 'legal' and the 'theological'. In both disciplines I have used to varying degrees non-Islamic sources and anecdotes to situate the subject matter in a broader framework allowing for some comparative reflection of the concept. Some of the chapters begin with a more personal anecdote, and indeed it was often these very anecdotes that gave the initial inspiration for a more detailed study. This book is aimed at an audience that has some knowledge of Islam and key theological and legal concepts. However, all Arabic terms are italicised and explained, if not in the main text, then in the glossary. The non-specialist will be aided by the extensive glossary, which provides meaning and context to some of the more technical vocabulary and names in the chapters.

The legal chapters provide a close reading of a selection of *furūʿ* texts. This has its own appeal in that *fiqh* like *tafsīr* was also a reading of scripture, an exercise in piety. Classical jurists, however, were not prone to being conclusive in the presentation of their arguments, fully aware that acquiring knowledge of God's law was a human exercise and only God knew the truth. Therefore, *fiqh* was always reflective of a certain hesitancy, structured to varying degrees on epistemological hurdles and the elaboration of alternative viewpoints. This was seen as a mercy from God. The more 'theological' chapters reflect a concern with those themes that need to be reassessed in dialogue with other traditions in the modern era.

A SHORT NOTE ON THE CHAPTERS

The aim of the book is to give the reader a glimpse into a kind of legal and theological inquiry that is both a personal reflection and rooted for the most part in traditional sources; the sources are predominantly Sunnī. The fundamental aim of this book is to show that differences of opinion have always been the essence of scholarship especially for the faithful; they are reflective of conversations that were never meant to finish. The scholars were in search of the truth as they saw it but expressed this truth in the intellectual discipline in which they found their literary and intellectual vocation. The chapters focusing on *fiqh* take you primarily through a single *fiqh* text with occasional references to other texts from the same school and try to show the development of arguments on the subject in question rather than providing a broad historical or social narrative around the issue. The textual detail is paramount here and dependent on the basic methodology of close literary analysis of the passages.

The subjects of slavery, ritually slaughtered meat, wine drinking, and the significance of the oral formulae in divorce are not simply the subject of juristic speculation and casuistry. They serve to show how a scholarly community tried to understand the nature of different aspects of the human social and moral order. In the chapter on divorce, the jurists do this not through taking overt ethical stances or admonishing the husband for severing the *nikāḥ* contract. Rather, their interest lies in showing how relevant the verbal formulae were in deciding when a pronouncement could be considered a divorce, as *ṭalāq* itself is a serious legal and contractual matter. Matrimonial relations between husband and wife could not be sustained if the spoken word was understood as desiring and indeed causing divorce. In a religion that has created its own gendered and patriarchal structures, divorce does not seem to incur either stigma or shame on either husband or wife but rather the full financial consequences for both. Thus in the divorce formulae we are not exposed to the wrongs of divorce or the ethical norms of a marriage, but the 'terms and conditions' that are the legally binding effects in the demise of a contract.

Contractual relationships occur in various forms in Islamic law, and an example of a very different kind of relationship is that between master and slave. The historical and anthropological interest in slavery has in recent years become the focus of much scholarly attention. Western scholars are trying to understand the history of slavery and the abolition of slavery from various perspectives including the nature of slavery in the Islamic world. The Qur'ān sees slavery as a social need but an ethical dilemma. Slaves were not legally competent but had rights and exercised a level of personal autonomy. The chapter on slavery examines a wide range of issues in connection with this ancient form of bondage between human beings. The jurists tried to stretch what rights the slave had, especially when boundaries became blurred through marriage or childbirth, whilst recognising that fundamentally slaves were the property of their masters.

The complexities of dietary preferences have surfaced in recent years as a reflection of social freedom and personal choice in most developed societies. But for most Muslims as well as Jews, scriptural prohibitions affect what is eaten and how it is eaten. The prohibition on eating the 'flesh of pig' and meat that has not been ritually slaughtered has become more public knowledge in recent years. Mālikī legal permission and prohibition across a wide range of texts show, however, that the juristic reflection on pig, blood, and slaughtered animals was far more lax than the more puritanical popular sentiment that seemingly affects Islamic dietary laws today. Believers see in the observance of dietary laws a practised piety but also a social and political identity in an increasingly fragmented world. This religious consciousness is not something new but presents itself as a challenge in many Western societies. This is partly because it creates, amongst other things, a real tension between the rights of religious minorities and the legal status of animals in rights discourse.

In a similar vein, the prohibition on consuming alcohol is commonly perceived as a defining feature of Muslim piety. A close reading of Ibn Rushd reflects the gradual unfolding of this outright prohibition. The awareness of the appeal of drinking alcohol in society along with the reluctance to ban all intoxicants emerges in the legal tension between defining intoxicants and intoxicated. This chapter reveals how the jurists relented ultimately to preserving the ideal of personal piety where wine drinking, and indeed all intoxicants, were eventually deemed subversive to the moral order.

One of the most curious yet appealing aspects of teaching Islamic Studies in the context of religious studies is in the choice of theological and philosophical concepts that one chooses to teach. Very often these subject areas emerge as pertinent and attractive not only because of personal research interests but also because of the comparative studies dimension of one's professional context. I have found that my choice of the 'theological' subjects in this book has been influenced to a great extent by two factors. Firstly, by my personal journey as a Muslim who has lived for most of her life in the United Kingdom, and secondly, by the nature of the department in which I work. My colleagues are predominantly Christian theologians or biblical scholars. Conversations with non-Islamicists can take you into different areas of research and reflection. Furthermore, my own growing interest in Christian–Muslim 'dialogue', a term I use as an umbrella for the various kinds of interreligious engagement, has been crucial in inspiring the seeds of a scholarly interest in Christian theology. As a result, concepts such as salvation, redemption, love, and evil, concepts fundamental in Christian thought, became significant in a way they may not have been had I been a 'purist' of Islamic Studies only.

The chapters on evil and love are a reflection of this ongoing engagement and inspiration from Christian theology. I try to explore how these words have been understood in the Qur'ān and Islamic thought as well as in Christian and Western thought. Evil and love can be seen as two sides of the same coin and central in much of Christian theology to the very idea of how human beings have responded to God and how God responds to human beings. Indeed, in comparing how the word love has been used in the New Testament to its mention in the Qur'ān, many Christians argue that this difference is fundamental to the way the two religions understand the very nature of God himself. The two chapters are different in style from the *fiqh* chapters using the Qur'ān rather than a legal text as the main textual base.

Finally, the chapter on friendship arose out of my interest in current political and sociological issues around identity and religion. The bulk of this chapter explores attitudes to friendship in the classical world and through the belletristic literature of prominent Western scholars. This provides a framework for classical and modern for thinking about friendship. However, it seems to me that some Muslims in the West regard the question of friendship as a divisive, theological issue. It is important to see how the Qur'ān and other literary disciplines have regarded friendship. Who we befriend today says as much about our practice and understanding of religious faith as it does about the meaning and significance of friendship in our lives; this is of personal, religious, and political relevance. In short, all these chapters convey a theme that has a present and personal interest for me but with which I engage through the lens of a past discourse:

> Our historical consciousness is always filled with a variety of views in which the echo of the past is heard. It is present only in the multifariousness of such voices: this constitutes the nature of the tradition in which we want to share and have a part.[12]

[12] Hans-Georg Gadamer, *Truth and Method*, ed. and trans. Garrett Barden and John Cumming, London, 1975, pp. 252–3.

1

Spoken, Intended, and Problematic Divorce in Ḥanafī *Fiqh*

When I began my doctoral studies, many of my parents' friends who were of Indian and Pakistani origin were intrigued by my subject of study. After all, the *Fatāwā 'Alamgīrī* was an impressive body of work, familiar by reputation to some of them, and it seemed appropriate in their view for a young Muslim woman to be studying marriage laws. However, when I also mentioned the subject of divorce (*ṭalāq*) to them, there was a distinct sense of disapproval on their part.[1] Clearly this was not an appropriate subject for study; studying marriage laws had a rationale, but what was the gain in studying divorce? For most of them, the sense of unease was tied to their cultural prejudices, the stigma around the very word divorce within the Islamic context. In studying divorce laws, was I thinking of divorce as an option in my own life? When I think back to those years, I cannot remember any of my parents' friends or any of my own relatives being divorced. Divorce was like a taboo word; it was hardly mentioned, and when the word did occasionally come up, the atmosphere was solemn. It was as if respectable people neither divorced nor talked of divorce.

Yet, the Qur'ān does talk of marriage and divorce, and marriage and divorce laws touch upon some of the most significant aspects of human relationships. Indeed, in the Qur'ān many of the verses that refer to women refer to them largely within the context of marriage and divorce. The verb *nakaḥa* and its derivatives are the closest terms used to encapsulate marriage and the different purposes of marriage. Fundamentally the term *nikāḥ* implies a legal contract between a man and a woman, a social institution and the physical act of sexual intercourse. Marriage is referred to in various contexts in the Qur'ān and the Qur'ān orders men to marry 'women of their choice' (Q 4:3) as an option. The Qur'ān affirms human sexual needs and sees marriage as a

[1] I use the word ṭalāq to mean 'divorce', although it will be clear from this chapter that divorce is not the exact meaning of *ṭalāq*.

desirable and permissible remedy for natural passions. There is a Qur'ānic verse that is explicit in urging restraint in circumstances, 'Let those who cannot afford to marry keep themselves chaste until God enriches them from his bounty.' A prophetic *ḥadīth* also emphasises the importance of marriage as a relationship for fulfilling sexual needs, 'Whoever is able to marry should marry for that will help him lower his gaze and guard his private parts [from committing illict sexual intercourse].'[2]

Sexual need, particularly male sexual desire, is considered a dominant reason for marrying as sexual desire is too powerful an impulse and too great a distraction from service to God. In his section on the benefits of marriage, al-Ghazālī writes that one of the benefits of marriage is that it protects against the 'dangers of lust' (*ghawā'il al-shahwa*).[3] In al-Ghazālī's view man has been created weak and cannot be patient when it comes to women. The sexual need can be so powerful that 'Fayāz b. Nājiḥ says when a man's penis stands [erect], a third of his intelligence goes away and some have said, a third of his faith [goes away].'[4] Al-Ghazālī refers to Junaid the Ṣūfī who is reported as having said, " 'Sexual intercourse is as necessary for me like food is necessary for me" and indeed the wife is strictly speaking nourishment and the reason for the purity of the heart.'[5]

Despite long discourses about marriage in theological works, marriage is encouraged though not obligatory in the Qur'ān. Prophetic *ḥadīth*s have however elevated this relationship to achieving the equivalent to one half of faith and the Prophet as saying that one who does not marry is not 'from him' [his followers].[6]

When one looks at the combined ethos of marriage in scriptural and legal texts, marriage is the basis for a legal, moral, and loving relationship between a man and woman or between a man and his wives. Although the primary consequence of a marriage contract is that sexual intercourse between the two becomes licit so they are protected from committing sexual sin, marriage is encouraged because it establishes and nurtures companionship and emotional ties between husband and wife. In this sense the marriage contract is not just a legal agreement but is also a solemn covenant (*mithāqun ghalidūn*

[2] Muḥammad ibn Ismā'īl Bukhārī, *Ṣaḥīḥ al-Bukhārī: The Translation of the Meanings of Ṣaḥīḥ al-Bukhārī, Kitāb al-nikāḥ*, vol. 7, Saudi Arabia: Maktaba Darrussalām, 1997, p. 20.

[3] Abū Ḥāmid Muḥammad b. Muḥammad al-Ghazālī, *Kitāb Adāb al-Nikāḥ* in *Iḥyā 'Ulūm al-Din*, vol. 2, Damascus: Ālim al-Kutub, 1992, p. 25. Further references to this work will appear in the footnote beginning with *nikāḥ*.

[4] Ghazālī, *Nikāḥ*, p. 26.

[5] Ghazālī, *Nikāḥ*, p. 26.

[6] Bukhārī, *Ṣaḥīḥ*, Kitāb al-Nikāḥ, p. 19.

Q 4:21), which presumes more than just sexual intimacy from the two parties. Perhaps the Qur'ānic verse that best encapsulates this is:

> And amongst his signs is that he created for you spouses from among yourselves in order that you may live in tranquillity with them and he has put love and mercy between yourselves. (Q 30:21)[7]

The word *mawadda* in this context denotes conjugal love, and conjugal love itself is present because God places it between men and women. Despite the recognition of marriage as a personal commitment between a man and woman to a contractual relationship, the Qur'ān contains very little narrative about marriage. Various verses refer to different aspects of marriage and divorce such as whom one can and cannot marry, the duties and obligations upon the spouses, and the various kinds of separation should a marriage come to an end. The Qur'ān is affirming of marriage but there is no idealisation of marriage nor any exposition as to whether love or any other emotional connection between the two people is required at the point of the actual contract.

Considering the importance of marriage as a social institution and as a foundation for righteous societies, the Qur'ān does not go into any procedural details about marriage as a civil agreement between two people, whereas procedures relating to divorce (*ṭalāq*) are mentioned several times. The primary purpose of a marriage contract is the recognition and legitimisation of sexual intercourse between the two sexes. This contract, however solemn, is one that can be broken, and there are different ways of severing the contract. A survey of Qur'ānic verses shows an acceptance of divorce as a consequence of dissent or conflict between the married couple. Just as God places love between the two in marriage, God can also reconcile (*yuwaffiq*) the two in conflict, but only if they are willing:

> If you fear dissension between the two of them, then appoint an arbiter from his family and an arbiter from her family; if they wish to make amends, God will reconcile them. (Q 4:35)

The Qur'ān provides procedures for divorce including terms and conditions for the equitable release of a woman from the contract. It regards separation between husband and wife as a necessary consequence in certain irreparable circumstances and does not condemn separation outright.

[7] Qur'ān translations are taken mainly from Yusuf Ali, *The Holy Qur'ān*, Beltsville, MD: Amana Publications, 2003. I have modified translations slightly where it was appropriate to simplify the language while trying to remain faithful to the wording of the original Arabic.

Entering the marriage contract and ending the marriage contract can only be done through a particular form of verbal agreement or declaration. Elsewhere, I have published various aspects of the marriage contract including an analysis of the form and sense of the spoken words that bring about marriage. Here I will look at words that affect *and* end the marriage contract by looking at three Ḥanafī works that stand out as major contributions to the rich field of Ḥanafī jurisprudence, namely, *Fatāwā 'Alamgīrī*, known also as the *Fatāwā Hindīyya*, the *Hidāya*, and *Fatāwā Qāḍīkhān*. The *Hidāya* is a classic book of Islamic jurisprudence by Sheikh al-Islam Burhān al-Dīn 'Alī b. Abū Bakr al-Marghīnānī (d. 1197).[8] It is a commentary on the *Jami' al-Saghīr* and the *Mukhtaṣar* of Qudūrī and is considered a highly authoritative guide to *fiqh* amongst Muslims in Central Asia. The *Hidāya* was also adopted by the British government as the standard authority for its courts of civil justice. While many Ḥanafī works of jurisprudence bear the title '*fatāwā*', perhaps the most well-known are the *fatāwā* of the Transoxanian jurist Qāḍīkhān (d. 1196), known as *Fatāwā Qāḍīkhān*. The *Fatāwā 'Alamgīrī* is a collection of judicial opinions compiled under the rule of the Moghul emperor Aurangzīb 'Alamgīr during 1662–1672 CE. It covers six volumes and was put together by a group of legal scholars with the aim of achieving an authoritative body of Ḥanafī law.[9]

It is worth noting here that despite the use of the term *fatāwā* to describe two of the collections used here, both these books are predominantly works of *furū' al-fiqh*, to be part of the wider literary type of the *mabsūṭ*. Norman Calder is correct in claiming the following:

> The use of the term *fatāwā* in the titles of a lengthy sequence of works within the Ḥanafī tradition should not delude us into thinking that this type of literature is closer to the literary form of the fatwa, or the collection of fatwas. This is not the case. They are works of *furū' al-fiqh*, and the later works of the type – for example, the *Fatāwā Hindīyya* – have the literary characteristics of late *mabsūṭ*s (e.g., composition by juxtaposition of citations form earlier authorities) while lacking any noticeably 'practical' aspect.[10]

In *fiqh* works, contracts are defined as oral in nature: they come into being by being spoken rather than written. The word generally used for contracts is

[8] A new translation of the *Hidāya* by Imran Ahsan Khan Nyazee was published in 2006, by Amal Press. It is a translation of the original Arabic in two volumes.

[9] For a more detailed description of the *Fatāwā 'Alamgīrī*, see Mona Siddiqui, 'The Juristic Expressions of the Rules of Marriage as Presented in the Fatāwā 'Alamgīrī', unpublished Ph.D. thesis, Manchester University, 1992.

[10] Norman Calder, *Islamic Jurisprudence in the Classical Era*, ed. Colin Imber, Cambridge: Cambridge University Press, 2010, pp. 72–3.

ʿaqd but there is no theoretical discussion of the word contract in *fiqh* works. What we know from these works is that contracts were largely oral in formation so that what was spoken was fundamental in deciding whether a contract became valid (*ṣaḥīḥ*), defective (*fāsid*), or void (*bāṭil*). Thus the spoken word carried a primary significance in the making of a legally binding agreement. In this context the intention of the two parties to complete a contract is paramount. Without the intention to complete, the contract cannot be a bilateral agreement:

> The intention of a contract is completion whether it be a marriage contract or otherwise comprising the offer of one of two speakers followed by the acceptance of the other.[11]

The words of offer and acceptance where both or one are expressed in the past tense are the essential verbal elements for beginning and completing a contract:

> It takes place with offer and acceptance where both are expressed in the past or where one of them is expressed in the past and the other in the future like the imperative or the present.[12]

This agreement is not just a promise or intention, but is about the two parties entering into an agreement with consequences. This agreement assumes a priori the significance of performative utterances whereby to say something is to do something.[13] The utterance of the right words becomes synonymous with effecting a change of events. Performative sentences can be contractual or declaratory but what defines them, as Austin says, is that 'the issuing of the utterance is the performing of an action – it is not normally thought of as just saying something'.[14] Thus the person saying the words is also doing something at the same time. The contractual approach to marriage relies on the utterance of relatively simple formulae for any agreement to come into effect. Different tenses can be used including the imperative:

> And if the man should say "Marry yourself to me" and the woman accepts the contract, it is put into effect provided he did not intend future time by his words.[15]

[11] *Fath al-Qadīr* in Nizām Burhānpūr, *Fatāwā ʿAlamgīrī*, 3rd edition, vol. 3, Beirut, 1973, p. 270.
[12] Burhānpūr, *Fatāwā ʿAlamgīrī*, p. 270.
[13] John L. Austin, *How To Do Things with Words*, Oxford: Clarendon Press, 1965, pp. 6–7.
[14] Austin, *How To Do Things with Words*, pp. 6–7.
[15] Burhānpūr, *Fatāwā ʿAlamgīrī*, p. 270.

The intention to marry at any future time (*istiqāl*) cannot be the basis of a valid contract. Although a future tense may be used for a contract, a future sense renders it ineffective. This is discussed in the context of *muḍāf* and *mu'allaq* contracts. In Islamic law the concept of *muḍāf* is generally discussed in relation to divorce, but when connected to marriage it is a contract to which there are words added that imply future time:

> The *muḍāf* contract where a person should say, "I have married you to her tomorrow" is not valid.[16]

This utterance remains invalid because a future time is intended. A *mu'allaq* contract is one that is dependent on a condition which may or may not be in the future. In such a marriage if the condition has not yet been met and refers to an action or even in the future, the contract would be invalid. If the event has already passed, the contract is considered valid. It is perfection rather than intention of a deed that concerns the jurists. The example given:

> If a person whose daughter has been asked in marriage should falsely inform the applicant that he has already married her to such a one and say, "If I had not married her to him, I would have married her to your son." In such a case if the father of the son should thereupon accept in the presence of witnesses, and it should subsequently transpire that the daughter has not been married to anyone, the marriage would be valid.[17]

As the daughter has not actually been married to anyone else, the condition becomes irrelevant and the contract acquires validity because of the declaration in the past tense and the subsequent acceptance by the other party in the presence of witnesses. Although two parties have 'offered' and 'accepted', the daughter's presence or agreement to the declaration made by the father is not mentioned here.

Such declarations do not include issues of mental state or serious intention in the making of an offer or promise; what is important is to recognise that in the absence of any impediments, offer and acceptance would normally constitute a valid contract. Although other conditions such as *kafā'a* between the man and woman would normally be required as constituting the right conditions and circumstances for a valid contract, the verbal declaration is discussed as separate to the issue of right conditions. Ameer Ali distinguishes the verbal declaration from the 'conditions preceding and conditions

[16] Burhānpūr, *Fatāwā 'Alamgīrī*, p. 272.

[17] Burhānpūr, *Fatāwā 'Alamgīrī*, pp. 272–3.

ensuing', which he regards as essential to a valid contract.[18] This raises the question of the ambiguity inherent in the word contract. A contract is not simply a promise, an agreement or just a declaration hanging in the air – with both offer and acceptance, "a deal is closed" and consequences ensue.

Ḥanafī law also discusses the different terms by which marriage can come into effect as a valid contract: words that express clearly (*ṣarīḥ*) or obliquely (*kināya*) an offer of marriage. If a man uses expressions that are oblique in a contract then his intention (*nīyya*) to marry the girl must be present for the contract to be valid. But if the words used are plain or evident, then intention is irrelevant. This aspect of the marriage contract bears close analogies with the law of sale because words that are oblique are conceptually linked to transfer of ownership, sale, or purchase:

> And the contract takes place with the words of *nikāḥ*, marriage, gift, transfer of ownership and. But Shāfiʿī says, "No, it only takes place with the words *nikāḥ* and *tazwīj* because the word *tamlīk* does not bear the sense of marriage either literally or metaphorically." And it takes place with the word "sale".[19]

Thus, a marriage contracted by the use of words other than *nikāḥ* or *tazwīj* would be fully valid. Ḥanafī law recognises transfer of ownership (*tamlīk*) as the common principle in both marriage and slavery:

> It is reported from Abū Ḥanīfa that whatever word creates ownership of person if applied to the case of a female slave, creates ownership of *nikāḥ* when applied to a free woman.[20]

The *Hidāya* explains the opposing view from Shāfiʿī:

> Shāfiʿī is of opinion that marriage cannot be contracted except by the words *nikāḥ* and *tazwīj* because *tamlīk* does not have the true sense of marriage either in a literal or a figurative sense. *Tazwīj* means piecing together and *nikāḥ* means joining and there is no joining or coupling between the owner and the owned.[21]

The Ḥanafī position is that the concept of *tamlīk* allows the master to have sexual intercourse with his slave girl since he has complete ownership of her

[18] Ameer Ali, *Muḥammadan Law*, vol. 2, Calcutta: Thacker, Spink, 1917, p. 513.

[19] ʿAlī ibn Abī Bakr al-Marghīnānī, *al-Hidāya*, vol. 2, Maktabāt al-Tawfiqīyya, (n.d.), p. 26.

[20] For a fuller discussion of this aspect of the marriage contract see Mona Siddiqui, 'The Defective Marriage in Classical Ḥanafī Law: Issues of Form and Validity', in G. R. Hawting, J. A. Mojaddedi, and A. Samely, eds., *Studies in Islamic and Middle-Eastern Texts in Memory of Norman Calder*, Oxford: Oxford University Press, pp. 271–86.

[21] al-Marghīnānī, *al-Hidāya*, p. 159.

and the husband to have intercourse with his wife since he now has ownership of those parts of her that can be sexually enjoyed. Both slavery and marriage work on a similar principle in that they both legalise the right of intercourse over the person who is being possessed. In comparing marriage and slavery, Kecia Ali writes that for the pre-modern jurists, slavery affected how marriage and gender were thought about in that 'there was a vital relationship between enslavement and femaleness as legal disabilities, and between slave ownership and marriage as legal institutions'.[22]

This comparison in the *Hidāya* may be interpreted as implying a distinction that is to be made between partial and complete ownership. Complete ownership as in the case of a slave girl allows a man to own the person and, among other privileges, to have intercourse with her; he cannot however marry the slave girl until he gives her independence by setting her free first. By contrast, partial ownership is the relationship a man has with his wife in which he owns part of her with respect to the right to have sexual intercourse with her but that does not allow him to own her; she remains a free and independent being. Both relationships imply ownership and, irrespective of whether the ownership is partial or full, they both have legal constraints.

Words such as *tamlīk* convey ownership but the notion of having right of intercourse is only one principle of marriage. *Tamlīk* does not carry all the implications of a contract that has legal, religious, and sexual consequences. Moreover, it contains vestiges of a concept that has its roots in pre-Islamic society in which captivity was an important concept within marriage. Robertson Smith provides an interesting discussion on the issue of purchase in Arab marriages, stating that marriage by capture preceded marriage by contract. He explains that the subjection of Arab women to their husbands was regarded by the Arabs as 'virtual captivity' and, furthermore, the very words employed to express the relationship – the derivatives of *malaka* – imply that marriage originated in bondage.[23] The Ḥanafī incorporation and defence of words such as *tamlīk* and others implying sale or purchase to convey marriage shows an acceptance of the vocabulary that reflected the varying attitudes to marriage throughout history. However, Ali explains that this attitude was widespread across the ancient world:

> It is the particular way that Muslim thinkers frame the conceptual and legal relationship between marriage and slavery, hinging on the transfer of rights

[22] Kecia Ali, *Marriage and Slavery in Early Islam*, Cambridge, MA: Harvard University Press, 2010, p. 8.

[23] Robertson Smith, *Kinship and Marriage in Early Arabia*, Cambridge: Cambridge University Press, 1885, pp. 81–5.

> to licit sex that constitutes its unique formulation. Premodern Muslims were typical rather than unique in having both patriarchal marriage and slaveholding. The two existed throughout the ancient Near East and Mediterranean as well as in pre-Islamic Arabia. Male dominated marriage and patrilineal kinship predominated in Greek, Roman, biblical, rabbinic, Byzantine, Sassanian law and practice, though specific contours of these systems varied and shifted over time both within and across civilisations.[24]

While the *Hidāya* mentions several words by which marriage does not come into effect, the *Fatāwā Qāḍīkhān* goes into some detail to explain the effect of those words that imply temporary or permanent ownership:

> If a woman says to a man in the presence of witnesses. "I have donated myself to you" (*taṣaddaqa*) or "I have made a gift of myself to you by way of *nikāḥ*" and the man says, "I have accepted," this is a *nikāḥ*. And in the same way if the woman were to say, "I have made you the owner of my person" or if the man says, "Make me the owner of your person" and the woman were to say, "I have made you owner," this is a *nikāḥ*. And if the woman were to say, "I have sold to you my person for such an amount" and the man replied, "I have bought or I accepted," this would be a *nikāḥ*.[25]

Marriage is implied in language that transfers permanent ownership. While mutual rights to sexual intercourse become established through a valid contract, any offer of marriage that is premised on unlawful intercourse or notions of servility by a free woman do not constitute a proper contract:

> If a man asks a woman to commit unlawful intercourse (*zinā*) and she replies, "I have bestowed myself on you" and the man says, "I have accepted," there is no *nikāh*. This is the same as if the father of the woman were to say, "I have given her to you" to serve you and the man says, "I have accepted," there is no *nikāḥ*. And in the same way, if the woman were to say, "I have made a sacrifice of myself to you," there is no *nikāḥ* and this is correct.

WHEN IS A DIVORCE A DIVORCE?

In the same way that the Qur'ān does not mention any verbal formulae for entering a marriage contract, it is silent on any verbal formulae to end the marriage contract. While Islamic law recognises different ways in which a husband and wife can end the marriage contract, the *ṭalāq* separation,

24 Ali, *Marriage*, p. 11.

25 Fakhruddīn Hassan b. Mansūr al-Uzjandi al-Farghāni Qāḍī Khān, *Fatāwā al-Qāḍī-Khān*, vol. 1, ed. and trans. Mahomed Yusoof Khan Bahadur and Wilayat Hussain, New Delhi: Kitab Bhavan, 1994, pp. 1–2 of the main text.

commonly translated as divorce, is one separation between husband and wife which is instigated only – and normally orally – by the husband.[26] *Ṭalāq* can be both revocable (*raj'i*) or irrevocable/definite (*bā'in*). However, *ṭalāq* in itself does not always mean an immediate dissolution of the contract, but only an intention to dissolve the marriage contract. The English word divorce can be misleading in translating the Arabic *ṭalāq*. This is because divorce denotes the termination of matrimonial relations between husband and wife, while the Arabic *ṭalāq* is regarded fundamentally as a process of repudiation possibly leading to a final dissolution of the marriage contract.[27] The exception to this in Ḥanafī law may be when divorce is pronounced before the husband has consummated the marriage with his wife. Richard Bell is one of the first scholars to emphasise the gradual process of divorce:

> Divorce is a process beginning with the cessation of marital relations and ending with the actual divorce when the *'idda* has run its course. Divorce is not actually to take place until it has expired.[28]

The Qur'ān mentions *ṭalāq* in several verses as well as having a *sūra* with the title, *Sūrat al-Ṭalāq*. The approach to divorce is very much one of acceptance rather than condemnation of a marital breakdown, where the husband is advised to exercise this patriarchal privilege with caution and kindness. The Qur'ān also alludes to careful consideration of the possible consequences of a final divorce. However, one particular *ḥadīth*, while not appearing in all the six canonical collections and considered an incomplete transmission (*mursal*) by some, has been considered by Muslims to reflect God's own judgement of divorce, 'From that which is permitted, the most detestable to God is divorce.'[29]

In making his argument that the regulations in the Qur'ān on divorce are designed to restrict rather than encourage the practice that had prevailed amongst the Arabs prior to Islam, Bell writes that 'Muḥammad married a goodly number of women but he divorced none'. He says:

> According to Tradition, Muḥammad on some occasions withdrew from his wives without ultimately divorcing any of them. It may be noted that on the

[26] It should be said, however, that though divorce is the most usual translation of *ṭalāq*, it is not the exact equivalent of the Arabic.

[27] Note that *ṭalāq* here is translated as divorce when it is a first or second divorce, and also when it is a final divorce.

[28] Richard Bell, 'Muḥammad and Divorce in the Qur'ān', *Muslim World*, 29:1, pp. 55–62, Hartford Seminary, USA, published online, 3 April 2007.

[29] Abū Dawūd Sulaymān bin Ash'ath Sijistānī, *Sunan Abū Dawūd*, vol. 2, Lahore: Ihsān Publishers, 1987, p. 175.

> occasion of the scandal regarding Ayesha, when on the return from the expedition against the Bani Mustaliq she was left behind and brought into camp by Safwān, he adopted the same course with her. He treated her with distant politeness until she learning the reason, requested and was granted permission to withdraw to her parents' house, where she remained, until, her character having been cleared by special revelation, reconciliation was brought about.[30]

A separation by *ṭalāq* divorce is the prerogative of the husband only, and the Qur'ānic verses address the procedures for divorce to men. However, when divorce has been initiated by the husband, husband and wife both have rights over each other until the divorce is final (Q 2:228). The key elements are that a divorce is permissible twice, after which both husband and wife must stay together or separate (Q 2:229). If a husband divorces his wife a third time the divorce becomes irrevocable, which means that there is no possibility of a reunion and the two must separate; they cannot remarry until the woman has been married to another and divorced by him (Q 2:229–30). The Qur'ān does not say 'If a man divorces a woman three times.' It says, 'So if the husband divorces her [his wife], she is not permissible to him' (Q 2:230). The third time is inferred from the preceding verse, Q 2:229, which says that divorce may take place twice. A woman who is divorced must observe the *'idda* or waiting period of three months (three monthly periods), or the duration of her pregnancy if she happens to be pregnant at the time of her divorce. During this waiting period, a husband and wife can be reconciled by laying claim to each other, in which case no divorce would actually ever have taken place; only a preliminary proposal to divorce by the husband. A woman can also be divorced prior to the marriage being consummated and the husband can divorce her both revocably and irrevocably.

When looking at *fiqh* texts, it would seem that it was the rather ambiguous nature of these two verses that concerned the jurists. The Qur'ānic verses outline certain procedures, but as divorce is also realised through the spoken word and can be a 'staged' process, Muslim jurists looked at the possible complexities arising from both the form and oral content of divorce. The possibility of taking a wife back after having intimated a desire for divorce led to a variety of forms of divorce as well as variations on when exactly divorce becomes final. While allowing for only two divorces before divorce became irrevocable and binding abrogated a pre-Islamic practice when men could divorce and take back their wives many times, the problem of the right time and right number relating to divorce remained. While the right time was

[30] Bell, 'Muḥammad and Divorce', p. 56.

understood to mean a woman's time of purity, as opposed to her menstruation days, the right number was complicated by the possible revocability of divorce and a variety of interpretations arose from the apparently simple exhortation of "divorce is twice".[31]

The *Hidāya* explains:

> He said, "*Ṭalāq* divorce is of three types, proper, more appropriate and innovative. The more appropriate divorce is that a man divorces his wife with one divorce in a period of purity in which he has not had sexual intercourse with her. He then leaves her until she has completed her waiting period" *'idda*. The Companions (may God be pleased with them) preferred not to increase the number of repudiations from one until the waiting period had been completed. This was better according to them than the man who divorced his wife by pronouncing three divorces, one in every period of purity. This form is the farthest from remorse [for the man] and the least damaging for the woman.
>
> The proper divorce is that a woman with whom marriage has been consummated is divorced three times [i.e. with three repudiations] in three periods of purity. Mālik (God bless him) said that this is innovative and only a single repudiation is permitted. This is because the essence of divorce is its prohibition and permission [is granted] because of the need for separation; this can take place with one divorce.
>
> We rely on the *ḥadīth* of the prophet in a tradition from Ibn 'Umar (God be pleased with them both) that it is a *sunna* to wait for the period of purity and to divorce the woman with one divorce in each period. . . .
>
> The innovative divorce is that he divorce her three times with one statement or divorce her three times in a single period of purity. If he does this the divorce takes place but he was sinful. Shāfi'ī (God bless him) says that each form of divorce is permissible as it is discharged lawfully so that its legal effect is acquired. Legal effect does not meet with prohibition as opposed to a divorce pronounced during menstruation, for what is forbidden is the prolongation of the waiting period for the woman and not the divorce.[32]

While the innovative divorce is considered sinful, its legality is rarely disputed. In the case of a woman with whom marriage has been consummated, the command to divorce her in the period of purity is based on viewing this period as a time when sexual desire for the woman is renewed

[31] On the point of when *ṭalāq* is brought about, I disagree with Susan Spectorsky, who writes that 'If a man says "you are divorced" to his wife, she immediately begins her post divorce waiting period (*'idda*).' While the waiting period does start, one repudiation does not amount to divorce but rather to the beginnings of the divorce process. See Susan Ann Spectorsky, *Women in Classical Law: A Survey of the Sources*, Leiden: Brill, 2010, p. 145.

[32] al-Marghīnānī, *al-Hidāya*, pp. 213–14.

and can lead to sexual intercourse. This in turn means that any final divorce is further delayed. While the issue of valid timing and period of purity and impurity framed the larger debate on divorce, much of the discussion on divorce concentrated on the myriad combinations of verbal formulae. As the different forms of divorce made it possible for divorce to be either immediately binding, staged, and revocable, the combination of numbers and conditions that could lead to a revocable or irrevocable divorce multiplied. The possibility of different formulae to bring about the revocable and irrevocable divorce is far greater than the oral formulae that bring about marriage.

The *Hidāya* proceeds to explain the pronunciation of divorce:

> *Ṭalāq* is pronounced in two ways: direct expression (*ṣarīḥ*) and indirect expression (*kināya*). Direct expression includes a man's statement, 'You are divorced, you are a divorced woman and I have divorced you.' The revocable (*raj'i*) divorce takes place with these words. This is because these words are used for divorce and are not used for anything else. They are direct expressions and do not depend on intention.[33]

The *Hidāya* explains that express words do not depend on the presence of intention because these words are used for no other purpose than divorce. The *Fatāwā al-Qāḍīkhān* adds a further dimension that where divorce is not intended, divorce will still take place if the express words are spoken.

> And if there is an argument between the wife and her husband and she gets up to leave and the husband says, 'take three divorces with you' Sheikh Imam Abu Bakr Mohammed bin al- Fadhl, on whom be peace, says that if he intended divorce to take place then divorce takes place. If there was no intention whatsoever for divorce to take place, divorce still takes place because it is apparent [from the expression].[34]

Thus, direct expressions of divorce can bring about a divorce even in a situation where divorce may not be intended. Although intention (*nīyya*) is an important theological concept in Islam, which also has legal relevance, express statements of marriage or divorce do not require the presence of intention to make either a marriage or divorce valid. The Ḥanafī texts, however, do not as a principle explain how intention or its absence is known in the person pronouncing a divorce.[35] They do, however, look at

[33] al-Marghīnānī, *al-Hidāya*, p. 219.

[34] Qāḍī Khān, *Fatāwā al-Qāḍī-Khān*, vol. 2, p. 213.

[35] For more on intention in divorce, particularly in the Shāfi'ī law, see Erin Stiles, 'When is a Divorce a Divorce? Determining Intention in Zanzibar's Islamic Courts', *Ethnology*, 42:.4, 2003, pp. 273–88.

the issue of intention where pronouncements of divorce contain extra intensity on the part of the husband. They conclude that where the husband adds words that express irrevocability of the divorce, then the divorce should be understood as being irrevocable because that is clearly expressed in both words and intention by the husband. Shāfiʿī disagrees because inherent in divorce is the principle of retraction, and adding words that contravene this principle goes against the very intention of the law.[36]

LEGAL CAPACITY FOR DIVORCE

> Divorce pronounced by any husband is valid if he was sane and adult, and the divorce pronounced by a minor, an insane person and one who is sleeping is not valid. This is according to the words of the Prophet (peace be upon him) "Every divorce is valid except the divorce of the minor and the insane person . . . the person sleeping is devoid of choice."[37]

While these two factors are in accordance with the principles of legal competency for entering any contract, an interesting disagreement occurs between Shāfiʿī and Ḥanafī opinion on the divorce by coercion:

> The divorce of a person who is coerced is valid. Shāfiʿī (God bless him) disagrees. He says that coercion cannot be together with choice and it is through choice that acts are legally carried out. This is distinguished from the one who is for he has choice in speaking the words of divorce. According to us he has intended divorce to take place in this wife while he was in possession of his legal capacity.[38]

For the Ḥanafīs, coercion does not invalidate legal competency, while for Shāfiʿī, coercion removes the ability to make a voluntary decision that is an essential aspect of legal competency.

While sanity and majority are mentioned as prerequisites, freedom is not a requirement, as a slave can also pronounce a divorce:

> If a slave marries a woman with the permission of his master and then divorces her, the divorce takes effect. The divorce pronounced by his master [of the slave] against the woman does not take effect because ownership in

[36] al-Marghīnānī, *al-Hidāya*, p. 229.
[37] al-Marghīnānī, *al-Hidāya*, p. 217.
[38] al-Marghīnānī, *al-Hidāya*, p. 217.

> marriage is the right of the slave and its relinquishment belongs to him and not the master.[39]

Even though the slave's right to pronounce divorce is not dependent on his master's permission, he does need his master's permission to enter a marriage contract:

> The marriage of a male and female slave is not permitted without the permission of their masters. Mālik (God bless him) says it is permitted for the male slave because he possesses the right to divorce so he [should] possess right to marry. Our view is that based on the words of the Prophet (on whom be peace) "The slave who marries without the permission of his master is a fornicator."[40]

The *Hidāya* explains that as a married slave fetches a lower price than an unmarried slave, marriage become a defect for a slave and therefore he would need the permission of his master.

The *Fatāwā al-Qāḍīkhān* and, to a lesser extent, the *Hidāya* both contain multiple examples of verbal formulae whereby divorce comes into effect either revocably or irrevocably. The use of condition or oath in the statement is the most common way of expressing an intention to divorce (*ṭaʿlīq al-ṭalāq*). These statements can be related to time and analogy but, to be valid, the condition should be non-existent at the time of the pronouncement with the possibility of it being existent at some point in the future. If the condition mentioned in the statement is impossible then the pronouncement is invalid.

The juristic concern with exploring the valid nature of a pronouncement of divorce dominates in the absence of any real moral argument against divorce. Even if it is argued that divorce is accepted as a necessity and not approved of in the Qur'ān, it is still recognised as a legally valid end to a contract. Indeed, the Qur'ān, addressing itself to the husband, repeats in different ways the necessity of being decisive and not dithering about keeping a woman as a wife or letting her go in freedom.

> When you divorce women and they are about to complete the term of *ʿidda*, either retain them or let them go, but do not retain them to injure them or take undue advantage. If anyone does that he wrongs his own soul. (Q 2:231)

The following are examples of an ingenuity of legal casuistry, which allow for all kinds of different pronouncements of divorce to be considered valid or

39 al-Marghīnānī, *al-Hidāya*, p. 217. If the woman being divorced is a slave woman, then only two divorces will be necessary to divorce her irrevocably as opposed to three for a free woman.

40 al-Marghīnānī, *al-Hidāya*, p. 195.

invalid. Both the *Fatāwā al-Qāḍīkhān* and the *Hidāya* reflect this preoccupation by using multiple permutations on different possibilities. The *Hidāya* states:

> If he attributes divorce to the woman as whole or what is taken to be the whole, divorce takes effect because he has attributed it to the object of divorce and it is like saying, 'You are divorced.' If he says 'Your neck is divorced or your neck or your head is divorced or your soul or body or corpus or vagina or face.' The reason is that these words refer to the entire body.[41]
>
> The same applies if he divorces an inseparable part of her like saying 'One half of you is divorced.' The reason is that the inseparable part is the subject matter of all transactions like sale and others. In the same way it is the subject matter of divorce except that it cannot be separated in relation to divorce, and therefore the whole is confirmed by necessity.[42]
>
> And if he says 'You are divorced yesterday' and he has married her today then there is no effect. The reason is that he has based the divorce on a time already passed negating the [right of] ownership of the divorce. It is ineffectual as if he were to say 'You are divorced before I was created.'[43]
>
> If he says 'You are divorced before I marry you,' there is no effect. This is because he has based it on a negating time. It would be as if he were to say, 'I divorced you as a minor or as one sleeping.'[44]
>
> If he says, 'You are divorced upon my death' or 'upon your death', then there is no effect. This is because he has added the divorce to a situation which negates it, for his death negates his legal competence and her death negates the subject matter and the two are imperative [it is imperative that the two are present].

When there is a logical impossibility in the divorce statement in relation to time or condition, divorce does not take place. A *tashbīh* (similie) divorce is when the words of divorce are compared to an image that carries a sense of intensity, thus possibly making the divorce irrevocable:

> If he says, 'You are divorced with the most monstrous (*afhash*) divorce.' This is because he has used this expression for its effect and it is immediately irrevocable and becomes like his statement 'irrevocable'. It would be the same if he said the 'most wicked divorce' or the 'worst divorce' in the way we have mentioned.[45]

[41] al-Marghīnānī, *al-Hidāya*, p. 220.
[42] al-Marghīnānī, *al-Hidāya*, p. 220.
[43] al-Marghīnānī, *al-Hidāya*, p. 223.
[44] al-Marghīnānī, *al-Hidāya*, p. 223.
[45] al-Marghīnānī, *al-Hidāya*, p. 229.

> In the same way if he says 'like the mountain' for the analogy with the mountain is abound to be about excess.[46]

The *Fatāwā al-Qāḍīkhān* has a huge number of examples exploring oaths and conditions. Islamic law recognises as an oath 'a declaration by which a unilateral disposition is made dependent on the occurrence of a certain event, such as "If I do such and such a thing, or if such and such a thing happens, my wife is repudiated or my slave is manumitted."[47] This kind of divorce oath takes up considerable space in *fiqh* works and should be distinguished from oaths taken in the name of God such as 'By God, I will not enter this house'; such an oath is not judicially enforceable.[48] In his study of divorce in Mamlūk society, Yossef Rapoport writes that divorce oaths were very widespread, and by the Mamlūk period 'had become to be considered as the most solemn form of oath'.[49] The following are two examples relating to adultery and divorce:

> A man says to his wife, 'If I accuse you of adultery (*qaḍaftuka*) you are divorced.' Then he calls out to her, 'Oh daughter of an adulteress!' she is divorced. This is because in custom this is accusing the woman of adultery though in truth it is accusing the mother of adultery.[50]
>
> A man says, 'If I commit adultery (*zinā*), my wife is divorced' and two just people are witness to his admission of adultery, his wife is divorced but there is no *ḥadd* punishment for the man. If the two just people witness seeing the adultery his oath is not broken and his wife will not become divorced.[51] If four people witness the adultery, and only two of them are just, in that situation too the wife will not become divorced.[52]

This case highlights the anomalous situation arising from conditions in divorce in which the basis of the condition is a crime. In the first case, an accusation of adultery can bring about a divorce as simply being part of the divorce condition. In the second case admission of the crime after the oath has been made is enough to bring about a divorce in the marriage but, in the case of adultery, lacks the full criteria of evidence required to enforce the *ḥadd* penalty – four just witnesses to the actual adultery are required.

46 al-Marghīnānī, *al-Hidāya*, p. 230.

47 Schacht, *Introduction to Islamic Law*, p. 159.

48 See Norman Calder, '*Hinth*, *Birr*, *Tabarrur*, *Tahannuth*: An Inquiry into the Arabic Vocabulary of Oaths', *BSOAS*, 51, 1989, pp. 216–23.

49 Yossef Rapoport, *Marriage, Money and Divorce in Medieval Islamic Society*, Cambridge: Cambridge University Press, 2005, p. 90.

50 Qāḍī Khān, *Fatāwā al-Qāḍī-Khān*, p. 284.

51 This is because the legal requirement is that four righteous people should have witnessed the act of adultery.

52 Qāḍī Khān, *Fatāwā al-Qāḍī-Khān*, p. 290.

> A man says to his wife, 'If I separate from you then every woman with whose head I place my head on the pillow, she is divorced.' He separates from her and marries a woman and places his head with her head on the pillow, his [new]wife is not divorced because the divorce has not been linked with ownership or to the cause of ownership.[53]

It would appear that as the word marriage has not been used, that is, the man has not said, 'Every woman I marry will be divorced,' no words of ownership have been spoken and no divorce ensues. The jurists also look at the possible consequences of a pronouncement made by a minor who does not possess legal capacity:

> A minor boy says 'If I drink[54] then every woman I marry is divorced.' He then drinks while a minor and then marries as a youth. His father-in-law thinks that the divorce has become operative and the young man says in Persian, 'She is forbidden to me.' The jurists say that this is an admission from him about her being forbidden so she is forbidden [beginning now]. Others say she is not forbidden to him and this is correct for he did not mention the prohibition as a beginning but he only made an admission regarding the cause on which both he and the father-in-law agreed and that cause of the prohibition is void.[55]

As the condition in the statement was made while he was still a minor and therefore legally incapable, neither his statement nor the condition carry any legal consequences and his wife does not become divorced.

> If a man says 'Every woman I marry will be divorced whenever I speak to so and so.' He then marries a woman and speaks to so and so; the woman will be divorced. If he marries a second woman and speaks again [to so and so] his first wife becomes divorced for a second time with these words if she is observing her waiting period, and his second wife is not divorced.[56]

There are various explanations here. First, the oath is applicable only to the wife whose ownership he already has at the time of making the oath; second, the consequences of the oath have been met with her first divorce and, as divorce is a staged process, the first wife will be divorced continuously if her husband carries on speaking to "so and so", until she is no longer permissible to him. Ownership through marriage is a prerequisite to making divorce upon oath valid:

[53] Qāḍī Khān, *Fatāwā al-Qāḍī-Khān*, pp. 290–1.
[54] Drinking here implies drinking wine.
[55] Qāḍī Khān, *Fatāwā al-Qāḍī-Khān*, pp. 292–3.
[56] Qāḍī Khān, *Fatāwā al-Qāḍī-Khān*, p. 298.

> If he says to a stranger [strange woman], 'If you enter the house you are divorced,' then he marries her and she enters the house, she is not divorced. This is because the person taking the oath is not the owner nor has he associated it with ownership or its cause and it is necessary to do so with one of the two.[57]

Ownership as a result of marriage allows the man to have recourse to his wife during a revocable divorce as long as she is in her waiting period. This is based on Qur'ānic 2:23, 'Take them back on equitable terms.' Retraction during the waiting period implies continuing ownership of the woman but once the waiting period ends, there is no further possibility of retraction: taking the wife back. For retraction to take place, certain words must be spoken:

> Retraction takes place if he says, 'I have taken you back' or 'I have taken my wife back.' This makes retraction plain and there is no disagreement between the imams on this.[58]

While Shāfi'ī is of the opinion that a formal expression must be used to indicate a desire to return to the wife, Ḥanafī opinion allows other gestures and not only the spoken words.

> If he has intercourse with her, or kisses her, or touches her with desire or looks at her private parts with desire, then this is the position according to us (i.e. retraction has taken place).[59]

For the Ḥanafīs, a revocable divorce does not prohibit the possibility of sexual intercourse between the husband and wife. In their opinion, the whole purpose of a revocable divorce is that at some point desire is rekindled in the husband for his wife and the marriage continues. Commenting on the real purpose of the *'idda* period, Bell sums up:

> Thus outwardly the spouses are to continue living together as before in the hope that before the end of the waiting period some reconciliation may take place or as the Qur'ān expresses it, Allah may cause something to happen.[60]

DELEGATION (*TAFWĪD*) IN DIVORCE

Although divorce is initiated by the husband, its pronouncement can lie with the woman:

57 al-Marghīnānī, *al-Hidāya*, p. 243.
58 al-Marghīnānī, *al-Hidāya*, p. 253.
59 al-Marghīnānī, *al-Hidāya*, p. 253.
60 Bell, 'Muḥammad and Divorce', p. 62.

> If he says to his wife, "Choose" and he intends divorce by that or he says to her "Divorce yourself" she has the right to divorce herself as long as she is in that session. If she gets up [from this session] or occupies herself with some other work, the matter moves out of her hands. This is because on the consensus of the Companions (God be pleased with them all), the woman has the choice of divorce in that session for the passing of ownership of the act to her. The passing of ownerships demand a response within the session as in the case of sale. This is because the time of the session is considered a single time, except that the session is changed by departing from it or sometimes in occupation with something else.[61]

In order for the divorce to be effective to the woman, she must reply, 'I have chosen myself,' not simply, 'I have chosen.' If she replies, 'I have chosen myself with one divorce,' then one revocable divorce takes place.[62] It should be noted that in allowing the wife to 'choose herself' the husband transfers the right of pronouncing divorce to his wife and cannot take back his words because this kind of statement is like an oath:

> If he says to her 'Divorce yourself three times,' and she divorces herself once, then only one divorce takes place. Just as she owns the pronouncement of three, she owns the pronouncement of one by necessity.[63]

In the *Fatāwā al-Qāḍīkhān*, there are several examples of *tafwīd* where wording and syntax determine the outcome of a divorce pronouncement:

> If a man says to his wife, 'You are divorced once if you wish and you are divorced twice if you wish,' and she replies, 'I have indeed wished for once, I have indeed wished for twice,' if she has connected the two sentences she is divorced three times.[64]

There is a logic inferred from the grammar and syntax of these pronouncements that bear little or no relevance to the intention of the person making the pronouncement. This reflects the concern of the pre-modern jurists with form and content in the efficacy of the spoken word. Number is also an issue in the case of a divorce where the marriage has not been consummated:

> If a man divorces his wife three times before consummating his marriage with her, divorce will take place against her.[65]

[61] al-Marghīnānī, *al-Hidāya*, p. 235.
[62] al-Marghīnānī, *al-Hidāya*, p. 235.
[63] al-Marghīnānī, *al-Hidāya*, p. 240.
[64] Qāḍī Khān, *Fatāwā al-Qāḍī-Khān*, p. 301.
[65] al-Marghīnānī, *al-Hidāya*, p. 231.

> A man says to his wife, 'Divorce yourself if you wish.' The man then becomes completely insane and the woman divorces herself. Muḥammad on whom be peace, says, 'Everything in which the husband has power to revoke his words, becomes void by his insanity.'[66]

As insanity renders a person legally incompetent, the husband can no longer revoke his words and the woman is given freedom to divorce herself if she wishes. God's name can also be invoked in the divorce pronouncement:

> If he makes the divorce dependent on the wish of God, saying, 'You are divorced if it pleases God' or he says, 'God loves it' or 'God consents' or 'God decides' or 'God destines', the divorce does not take place. Also, if he says, 'You are divorced what God pleases' or he says 'You are divorced only if it pleases God,' or says, 'If it does not please God.'[67]

As no one can know what God wishes or what pleases God, the condition cannot be met and the divorce does not take place.

While most of these divorce formulae arise from the enormous range of possibilities pertaining to the Qur'ānic verse 'divorce is permissible twice', Ḥanafī legal texts also consider the specific issues of those words that, once spoken, can render a wife prohibited both temporarily or permanently to her husband. The main example of this is *ẓihār*, which applies only to the wife, is mentioned in the Qur'ān, and alludes to mother–son incest:

> Those who pronounce to their wives, 'Be as my mother's back,' they are not truly their mothers; their mothers are only those who gave them birth. They are surely saying dishonourable thing and a falsehood. (Q 58:2–3)

In the Qur'ān the oath of *ẓihār* was discouraged but still regulated. The implication of *ẓihār* is that the man has made his wife untouchable to him in the same way his mother is untouchable.

> If a man says to his wife, 'You are to me like the back of my mother,' she becomes prohibited to him. It is not permitted for him to have sexual intercourse with her, to touch her or to kiss her until her has paid expiation for his [oath of] *ẓihār*.[68]

[66] Qāḍī Khān, *Fatāwā al-Qāḍī-Khān*, p. 302.

[67] Qāḍī Khān, *Fatāwā al-Qāḍī-Khān*, p. 305.

[68] al-Marghīnānī, *al-Hidāya*, p. 269. *Ẓihār* should be seen in the same context as a performative utterance in that the very pronunciation of the words effects the relationship between two people. See also Bell, 'Muḥammad and Divorce', who explains that *ẓihār* was forbidden because 'relationships not founded in nature are not real relationships': p. 57.

In his excellent study of illicit relationships, Geert van Gelder considers *ẓ ihār* as a particularly abhorrent form of incest as it implies mother–son incest and explores the various meanings of *ẓihār*. For some lexicographers, *ẓihār* was a euphemism for the *pudendum*, for others it implied *coitus a tergo* as if this was the normal position for intercourse in pre-Islamic Arabia.[69] However, in the legal texts, allusion to any part of the mother's body likened to her back presumes the pronouncement of *ẓihār*:

> The same is if he says, 'Your head is like the back of my mother to me, or your private parts, or our face, or your neck or half of you or a third of you or your body.' The reason is that he expresses by that her whole body.

The *Hidāya* explains that while *ẓihār* amounted to divorce in pre-Islamic days, the consequence of *ẓihār* in Islamic law are that the pronouncement of *ẓihār* is an act of impiety, an extrajudicial oath, but no longer tantamount to divorce.[70] Nevertheless, it is still a grave declaration, thereby restricting mutual access between husband and wife until a penitence (*kaffāra*) has been made.

> The expiation [penitence] of *ẓihār* is the freeing of a slave. If a slave is not found, then fasting for two consecutive months. If he is able to do so, then the feeding of sixty poor people, according to the text before us.

Indeed, Sarakhsī places an obligation on the woman:

> The wife must not invite him to come near her until he has paid the penitence for she is forbidden to him until he pays the penitence.[71]

Sarakhsī goes into great detail about the various tensions between divorce and *ẓihār*, namely whether *ẓihār* always remains a separate category of prohibition. The issue is that where both *ẓihār* and divorce are declared on the woman, are they both binding or is *ẓihār* contained within divorce?

> And if he says 'If I marry you, you are divorced,' then he says if 'I marry you, you are like my mother's back to me,' then he marries her, both divorce and *ẓihār* become incumbent because each of these is dependent on marriage.[72]

[69] Geert Jan van Gelder, *Close Relationships: Incest and Inbreeding in Classical Arabic Literature*, London: I. B. Tauris, 2005, p. 118.

[70] al-Marghīnānī, *al-Hidāya*, p. 269. See also Muḥammad ibn Aḥmad Sarakhsī, *Kitāb al-Mabsūṭ*, vol. 5, Beirut: Dār al-Maʿrifa, 1993, p. 223.

[71] Sarakhsī, *Mabsūṭ*, p. 230.

[72] Sarakhsī, *Mabsūṭ*, p. 230.

Despite the Ḥanafī emphasis on form in legal casuistry, which allowed for such possibilities, van Gelder is right in his assessment:

> It is difficult to say how often the formula was actually uttered in Islamic times, but it is striking how frequently *ẓihār* is discussed by the jurists. The efforts of jurists are probably prompted above all by the mentioning of *ẓihār* in the Qur'ān and less by its occurrence in actual cases, which if found at all, must have been overwhelmingly outnumbered by the divorce formula.[73]

However, making a wife unlawful to himself can be expressed by the husband in many ways:

> A man says to his wife, 'You are prohibited to me,' and according to him, prohibited means divorce except that he did not intend divorce, the wife becomes divorced. This is because if divorce is what he means then he intended divorce. If he says to his wife, 'You are with me in prohibition (*fi-l ḥarām*), it would be as if he said, 'You are prohibited to me,' and the wife shall become prohibited to him.[74]
>
> When a man says to his wife, 'By Allah, I will not come near you,' or he says, 'By Allah I will not come near you for four months,' he is one who has made an oath of *'ilā*, according to the words of the Exalted, 'For those who take an oath of abstention from their wives, waiting for four months is ordained.' If he has intercourse with her within four months, he has broken his oath and becomes liable for penance because penance is obligatory when an oath is broken and the oath of *'ilā* will be removed as an oath is removed by the breaking of the vow. If he does not come near her until four months have passed, she is divorced from him irrevocably.[75]

In the case of *li'ān*, separation requires that both the husband and wife say the required words and that the *qāḍī* separate them subsequent to them testifying:

> The description of *li'ān* is that the *qāḍī* begins with the husband and he testifies four times saying each time, 'I testify by God that I am from those who tell the truth in my accusing her of *zinā*.' He says on the fifth time, 'May God's curse be upon him if he is among the liars in accusing her of *zinā*.' In all these statements he points to her. Then the wife testifies four times saying each time, 'I testify by God that he is one of the liars in the accusation made against me with respect to *zinā*.' In the fifth testimony she says, 'The wrath of God be on her if he is truthful with respect to the accusation against me about *zinā*.[76]

[73] van Gelder, *Close Relationships*, p. 119.
[74] Qāḍī Khān, *Fatāwā al-Qāḍī-Khān*, p. 331.
[75] al-Marghīnānī, *al-Hidāya*, p. 259.
[76] al-Marghīnānī, *al-Hidāya*, p. 276.

According to Abū Ḥanīfa, the exact wording should be 'In what I have accused you of *zinā*,' so as to remove any uncertainty as to who is being accused. The peculiar aspect of *li'ān* is that though the husband and wife both make an oral accusation to each other, separation occurs only when the *qāḍī* separates them with his pronouncement.

There are a few cases in which a wife can demand separation from the *qāḍī*. The husband's impotence is used as the most common example:

> If the husband is impotent, the *qāḍī* is to grant him a year. If he is able to have intercourse with her in that time [then that is good], and if not the *qāḍī* is to separate the two if the woman requests this. This is how it has been reported from 'Umar, 'Ali and Ibn Mas'ūd. This is because her right to intercourse is established but it is possible that the inability is due to a temporary illness or due to a more a more fundamental illness; it is important to have a period of time to know about this. We have decided on a year as this period consists of the four seasons. When this time passes and he has not had intercourse with her, it becomes obvious that his inability is due to a more fundamental illness and retention of the marriage comes to an end with this knowledge. It becomes imperative to act in accordance with what is good. If he refuses, the *qāḍī* acts as his representative and separates the two of them. The woman must demand separation because separation is her right and this separation is tantamount to an irrevocable divorce. This is because the action of the *qāḍī* is attributed to the husband as if the husband has divorced her himself.[77]

The divorce has to be an irrevocable divorce, otherwise the wife will be kept waiting if the husband decides to retract the divorce; this would be unjust on her. Furthermore, if the two experienced any seclusion (*khalwa*), the wife would be entitled to her full *mahr*[78] even if the husband is impotent. If the husband and wife disagree as to whether he is able to have intercourse with her, then if the woman is a non-virgin the husband is to be believed along with an oath from him.[79]

CONCLUSION

The above examples of formulaic utterances reveal how important the spoken word could be in Islamic classical law for establishing and ending a marriage contract. While a valid contract of marriage could be established with very

77 al-Marghīnānī, *al-Hidāya*, p. 279. The word for impotent is *'innīn*.
78 *Mahr* is the dower given or owed to the woman at the time of marriage. It may be given in full or in part.
79 al-Marghīnānī, *al-Hidāya*, p. 279.

few words, *ṭalāq* was a lengthier process that involved various considerations relating to the time, manner, and number of declarations made. The multiple ways of declaring a divorce are subject to intense scrutiny by the jurists because *ṭalāq* is only *possibly* a verbal dissolution of a contract. As dissolution of the marriage necessitates the recognition of mutual rights and obligations between husband and wife, it is imperative to know when is divorce really a divorce. The matter is further complicated as Ḥanafī law condemns the triple divorce in one sitting, but still recognises it as legally valid resulting from the Qur'ānic principle that "divorce is permissible twice" but that divorce pronounced three times would make the divorce binding. In most situations it is not until the third declaration of divorce that divorce becomes final with the husband having no recourse to taking back his wife. These divorce formulae present the principle of private autonomy whereby private individuals possess the power to effect, within certain limits, changes to their legal relations.

One could expect a certain level of emotive language in discussions on marriage and divorce but law does not deal overtly with sentiments but with rights and consequences. Ḥanafī law looks at marriage through a particular contractual lens. In this contract, marriage is essentially arranged between the parents or guardians of the bride and groom, and notions of romantic love or desire as an emotion between two people prior to marriage do not feature. In the *ṭalāq* divorce, however, intention to separate lies with the husband with no dependence on any elders or parents. In both situations the legal discourse is a pre-modern discourse where the main concerns for the jurists are the mutual rights and obligations in a valid contract rather than the complexities of a marriage of choice or love relationship. In fact, there is nothing in the debates that show how frequent divorce was and how often separation could be initiated by the wife as well as the husband. Islamic law is concerned with the oral statements and diverse formulae, which could lead to the first stages of divorce and, eventually, a final divorce. *Ṭalāq* was a patriarchal and unilateral privilege but the jurists try to put balances and checks on this right, namely, by ensuring that the wife's financial rights are observed. The spoken word carried enormous weight in divorce pronouncements and it was important to ensure which verbal formulae constituted divorce as the consequences affected people and property. However, this discussion does not shed light on the reaction of women to divorce and how they negotiated the challenges faced by the husband's intended or unintended divorce pronouncements. Although legal texts do not provide or illustrate any quantitative data, I will conclude with Rapoport's findings on the frequency of divorce in medieval Islam. It seems paradoxical that in a patriarchal society, *ṭalāq* was a unilateral and seemingly easy way of ending the very unit that patriarchy is supposed to uphold. Rapoport writes that contrary to modern assumptions based on an ideological framework of the past, divorce was common in medieval Middle East societies:

> If the family was indeed the central building block of pre-modern Muslim society, and an institution that was to be protected from the penetrating eyes of the public gaze, then we should expect the incidence of divorce to be as low as possible. Indeed, if the ideal family of medieval Muslim societies was the patriarchal household, frequent divorce would surely have resulted in the creation of familial institutions that were less than ideal, as many more women would have had to make a living on their own. Moreover, if medieval Muslim societies looked upon the unattached young female as threat to morality, and if marriage was so highly prized for both men and women, we would expect to find divorce being used only as a last resort. This was clearly not the case for much of the history of the Islamic Middle East.[80]

If this is true then it is odd that over the course of time, in some parts of the Muslim world, divorce became such a taboo subject. However, today divorce perhaps does not carry the same stigma it did only one generation ago in popular Muslim piety. It is increasingly viewed as a pragmatic, albeit undesirable, ending of a marriage, permitted in the Qur'ān. In my view it is precisely because the Qur'ān recognises the possibility of divorce in every marriage that it does not stigmatise divorce but provides the skeletal framework for dissolving the contract.

[80] Rapoport, *Marriage*, p. 4.

2

Between Person and Property: Slavery in Qudūrī's *Mukhtaṣar*

> Slavery and freedom are intimately connected, that contrary to our atomistic prejudices it is indeed reasonable that those who most denied freedom, as well as to those to whom it was most denied, were the very persons most alive to it. Once we understand the essence and the dynamics of slavery, we immediately realize that there is nothing in the least anomalous about the fact that an Aristotle or a Jefferson owned slaves. Our embarrassment springs from our ignorance of the true nature of slavery.
>
> (Orlando Patterson)

The analysis of divine law in the Islamic context took place primarily in the literary genre known as *furūʿ al-fiqh* (branches of jurisprudence). Works of *furūʿ* can be classified in two categories, *mukhtaṣar*s or epitomes of the law and *mabsūṭ*s or expansums.[1] When writing my Ph.D. thesis on the *Fatāwā ʿAlamgīrī*, I was directed to the *Mukhtaṣar* of Aḥmad b. Muḥammad al-Qudūrī (d. 428/1037) as a text containing a succinct exposition of the Ḥanafī laws of marriage. I found the text to be very concise and clear in elucidating the major issues around marriage as a contract. The style was one of offering the rules rather than discussing points of disagreement. Yet I did not return to the *Mukhtaṣar* after the initial analysis of marriage laws. In his later work on form and content of *furūʿ* texts, my supervisor, the late Norman Calder, describes this particular *mukhtaṣar* (also called *matn* or text) as 'the finest of the Ḥanafī *mukhtaṣar*s' which was 'for centuries a teaching tool, a point of

[1] See Norman Calder, *Islamic Jurisprudence in the Classical Era*, Cambridge: Cambridge University Press, 2010, p. 22. The book is a collection of Calder's writings on Islamic law, carefully edited after his death by his colleague at Manchester University, Dr Colin Imber.

reference and a focus of commentary, due to its reliability as an expression of the basic norms of the Ḥanafī tradition'.[2]

Qudūrī's *Mukhtaṣar* presents Ḥanafī law through a select and concise summary of arguments under the loosely organised headings to be found in the foundational texts of *furū'*. In his analysis of the *mukhtaṣar* style, Calder states that the norms discussed in the *mukhtaṣar* form have already been weighed and established in larger works. The *mukhtaṣar* style does not allow for the elaboration of contentious norms, which are normally the domain of the *mabsūṭ* genre where details and arguments are multiplied. In the *mukhtaṣar*, what we find is more of a manual of basic beliefs and statements aimed at providing in 'epitome form' essential guidance to the reader on a wide number of issues.[3] The excellence and popularity of Qudūrī's *Mukhtaṣar* meant that for centuries it was taught in religious schools across the Islamic world as a foundational text for Ḥanafī law and acquired the reputation of being a '*fiqh* classic'. It continues to be taught as a foundational text in the Indo-Pakistan subcontinent. However, in his introduction to Qudūrī's *Mukhtaṣar*, Tahir Kiani writes:

> Over the centuries, few books could compete or even co-exist with the *Mukhtaṣar* in success and dominance but in modern times, the introduction of more up to date authorship in Ḥanafī *fiqh*, being relatively easier to read and providing legal references has caused the *Mukhtaṣar* to be overshadowed to some extent and these works have undermined its supremacy. Sadly, it is not surprising to find among modern day 'scholars' those who have never come across the *Mukhtaṣar al-Qudūrī*.[4]

In this chapter I wish to examine miscellaneous issues pertaining to slavery as covered in Qudūrī's *Mukhtaṣar* and the elaboration of certain points discussed in Sarakhsī's *Mabsūṭ*, which is the most influential of all the Ḥanafī *mabsūṭ*s. Sarakhsī's *Mabsūṭ* is a commentary on the *Kāfi* of al-Ḥākim al-Marwazī and not Qudūrī's *Mukhtaṣar* but, as an extraordinarily rich presentation of *furū'*, it is interesting to compare how longer treatises on *furū'* deal with argument and evidence in contrast to the shorter *mukhtaṣar*. This chapter does not aim to exhaust the legal and historical issues around slavery. The primary focus is to show how jurists dealt with the tension inherent in the position of slaves who possessed natural rights as human

[2] Calder, *Islamic Jurisprudence*, p. 23.

[3] Calder, *Islamic Jurisprudence*, p. 23.

[4] Aḥmad ibn Muḥammad Qudūrī, *The Mukhtaṣar al Qudūrī*, trans. Tahir Mahmood Kiani, London: Ta-Ha Publishers Ltd, 2010, p. xxxiii. It is this particular text that will be used for this chapter. The translations are my own.

beings but who were nevertheless denied rights by being property of their masters.

In recent years there has been a steady growth in slavery studies where the focus has been on a comparative assessment of slavery in different societies throughout history. In this context, much has been written on slavery as a social and historical institution in the pre-Islamic Arab world as well as slavery after the advent of Islam. Historians generally acknowledge that the institution of slavery existed in all the ancient civilisations of Asia, Africa, Europe, and pre-Columbian America as well as being accepted by major world religions including Judaism, Christianity, and Islam. Owning slaves was a societal and ubiquitous feature of the ancient world, and the Qur'ān sees the division between free and slave as divinely ordained. There has also been much discussion that although the Qur'ān did not ban slavery, it improved the situation for slaves in many areas. Like the Hebrew Bible and the New Testament, the Qur'ān recognises slavery as part of the surrounding culture of the Near East, and mentions slavery in various contexts. These can be broadly divided into the freeing of slaves and sexual relations with slaves. There are multiple references to slaves, slave concubinage, women slaves who have their masters' children, and the freeing of slaves as a form of expiation for wrong-doing. The Qur'ān regulates slave ownership and the rights of the slave on the basis that while there is an inherent social and legal inequality between master and slave, their relationship demands that each recognises and observes their responsibilities to one another. Slaves are mentioned in at least twenty-nine verses of the Qur'ān, usually with reference to their legal status. The most common word for slave in classical Arabic is *'abd*, the root meaning of which is associated with labour in Semitic languages.[5] The Qur'ān uses the word *'abd* to mean worshipper. The vocabulary referring to slaves in the Qur'ān however is complex:

> There is strong evidence to suggest that the Qur'ān regards slaves and slavery differently from both classical and modern texts. First, the vocabulary is distinct. Several words for slave in classical Arabic (such as *mukātab*, *raqīq*, *qinn*, *khādim*, *qayna*, *umm walad* and *mudabbar*) are not found in the Qur'ān while others (*jāriya*, *ghulām*, *fatā*) occur but do not refer to slaves. Likewise, *'abd* (along with its plurals *'ibād* and *'abīd*) is used over a 100 times to mean servant or worshipper in the Qur'ān; in each occasion when it is used to refer to male slaves, a linguistic marker is appended, contrasting *'abd*

[5] Arthur Jeffrey, *The Foreign Vocabulary of the Qur'ān*, Baroda: Oriental Institute, 1938, pp. 209–10. In the Qur'ān, *'abd* means worshipper.

> to a free person (*al-hurr* in Q 2:178) or a female slave (*ama*, pl. *ima* in Q 24:32) or qualifying it with the term possessed (*'abd mamlūk* in Q 16:75).[6]

The slave is mentioned in various contexts in the Qur'ān, often in exhortations to show kindness to the slave:

> Do good to parents, kinsfolk, orphans, those in need, neighbours who are of kin and neighbours who are strangers, the fellow traveller and the wayfarer and the slave whom your right hands possess. (Q 4:36)

> Do not marry idolatresses until they believe. A believing slave woman is better than an idolatress even though she may please you. And do not give your women in marriage to idolators until they believe. A believing slave is certainly better than an idolator even if he pleases you. (Q 2:221)

> Never should a believer kill another believer, except by mistake. If anyone kills a believer by mistake he must free one Muslim slave and pay compensation to the victim's relatives unless they charitably forgo it. If the victim belonged to a people at war with you but is a believer then the compensation is only to free a believing slave. If the victim belonged to a people with whom you have a treaty, then compensation should be handed over to his relatives and a believing slave set free. (Q 4:92)

Islamic legal texts do not enter any discussion about inequality between slave and free in any systematic way. This inequality is recognised in the rulings on slaves and their rights rather than explained in any philosophical way. Nevertheless, it is notable that recognition of this inequality was against knowledge that human beings were naturally free. By this I mean that human beings were born as free creatures notwithstanding the social conditions of slavery and the potential consequences of being captured.[7] This is why:

6 Jonathan E. Brockopp, 'Slaves and Slavery', in Jane McAuliffe, ed., *Encyclopaedia of the Qur'an*, vol. 5, Leiden: Brill, 2006, pp. 56–60.

7 This debate has also been viewed in the context of natural law and natural rights pointing to a particular tension relating to human freedom and divine revelation. In his recent work, Anver Emon has argued against those Islamicists who claim there is no natural law tradition in Islam. He writes, 'Respected Islamicists like Patricia Crone and the late George Makdisi have stated in no uncertain terms that there is no natural law tradition in Islam. Presumably what they mean by this claim is that there is no "orthodox tradition" whereby pre-modern Muslims (e.g., ca. ninth–sixteenth century CE) allowed human beings to speak on behalf of the divine without recourse to scripture. But lawyers and judges often face de novo situations where no positivist legislation, scripture or legal text necessarily provides insight, guidance or precedent for judicial decision. As such, a judge having to decide a case must utilize a degree of discretion in determining the rule of law.' See Anver M. Emon, 'Natural Law and Natural Rights in Islamic Law', *Journal of Law and Religion*, 20:2, 2004–5, pp. 351–95.

> Slavery could only arise from two circumstances: (1) being born to slave parents or (2) being captured in war. The latter was soon restricted to infidels captured in *jihād*.[8]

In his major camparative work, Orlando Patterson argues that though legally the Muslim was not allowed to enslave other Muslims, many ways were found to get round this injunction:

> As a cultural mode of representation, however, the image of the slave as the captured enemy and internalized outsider in a state of social death was firmly fixed in Islamic thought. The most frequent expression for female slave in the Qur'ān is 'that which your right hand possesses.'[9]

While slave ownership was recognised social and legal practice, the presumption of freedom as a natural state for human beings took precedence. One evidence of this is on the rules regarding foundlings (*laqīt*) or unclaimed children, who could not be adopted as slaves; they were legally free, and no presumption of slavery could be imputed to a foundling. Even if lineage with a slave is established, the foundling is still considered free.[10] In theory, slavery originates only through birth or the captivity of a non-Muslim who is not protected by any safe treaty and falls into the hands of Muslims. Yet, even a cursory glance at the Islamic law on slaves shows that slaves have rights as persons and under law even if they are not considered legally competent owing to the absence of freedom. In his entry under slavery, Juynboll wrote of slaves as beings virtually stripped of their humanity:

> Theoretically slaves have no legal rights whatsoever; according to Mohammedan law they are merely things, the property of their owner. The latter can alienate them as he likes, by sale, gift, dowry, or in other ways. In the eyes of the law they are incapable of making any enactment, can therefore neither alienate, nor undertake responsibilities, nor make wills, and therefore cannot be guardians or testamentary executors; what they earn belongs to their master. Neither can a slave appear as witness in a court of Justice. He can however, at the order of his master make contracts concerning properties and accept liabilities.[11]

8 Bernard Lewis, *Race and Slavery in the Middle-East*, Oxford: Oxford University Press, 1990, p. 6.

9 Orlando Patterson, *Slavery and Social Death: A Comparative Study*, Cambridge, MA: Harvard University Press, 1982, p. 41.

10 Qudūrī, *Mukhtaṣar*, p. 346.

11 T. W. Juynboll, 'Islam and Slavery in General', *Encyclopaedia of Islam*, vol. 1, Leiden: Brill, 1913, p. 17.

Various accounts of slavery in the ancient world use the word 'chattel' to describe the status of the slave. Norman Cantor estimated that 'roughly one quarter of any major society in antiquity were human chattel – someone's property'.[12] But in a more recent historical survey of slave abolition in the Islamic world, William Gervase Clarence-Smith acknowledges that while slaves endured restricted legal rights, 'slaves were allocated a bewildering variety of social roles, from emirs to outcasts. Rulers relied on military and administrative slaves to such a degree that they sometimes seized power.'[13]

In most texts of *furū'*, issues pertaining to slavery are scattered under the different topics and headings. Slaves are referred to as *'abd* or *mamlūk* and female slaves as *ama* or *jāriya*. There are usually separate sections for the slave who contracts to buy his freedom, the *mukātab*, and various forms of slave freedom. In Qudūrī's *Mukhtaṣar* there are separate chapters for the setting free of slaves (*'itāq*), setting free of slaves on the death of a master (*tadbīr*), and the slave who runs away from his master (*ibāq*). Slavery therefore becomes part of the legal discussions on a wide variety of issues, and slaves are seen as contributors to society even though they have restricted legal capacity. One of the earliest references to slaves in the *Mukhtaṣar* is on the issue of Friday prayers:

> The *jum'a* prayer is not obligatory for a traveller, a woman, a sick person, a minor, a slave or a blind person. If they attend and pray with the people, it suffices them for the obligatory prayer of the time. It is permitted for the slave, the traveller and the sick person to lead *jumu'* prayer as *imām*.

However the slave, traveller, or an ill person can lead the Friday prayer as an *imām*.[14] It is in the *Mabsūṭ* where we find a *ḥadīth* supporting this right and the explanation for the slave's exemption from Friday prayers:

> According to Jabīr, God be pleased with him, the messenger of God said, '*jum'a* prayers are incumbent upon whosoever believes in God and the Last Day, except for a traveller, a slave, a minor, a woman and a sick person.'
>
> The slave is busy in the service of his master and the master will find it hard with the slave abandoning his service, attending *jum'a* prayers and waiting for the *imām*.[15]

While freedom is not essential to lead *jum'a* prayers, a free person must attend *juma'* prayers except for those in the above categories.

[12] Norman F. Cantor, *Antiquity: From the Birth of Sumerian Civilisation to the Fall of the Roman Empire*, Harper Perennial, 2003, p. 225.

[13] William Gervase Clarence-Smith, *Islam and the Abolition of Slavery*, Oxford: Oxford University Press, 2006, p. 2.

[14] Qudūrī, *Mukhtaṣar*, p. 64.

[15] Muḥammad ibn Aḥmad Sarakhsī, *Kitāb al-Mabsūṭ*, book 2, Beirut: Dār al-Ma'rifa, 1993, p. 22.

Regarding the prayers of slave women, their *'awra*[16] is similar to that of a man and not that of free women:

> The nakedness of a man is what is below the navel to the knee and the knee is nakedness but the navel is not.
>
> All of the body of a free woman is nakedness except her face and her two hands.
>
> What is nakedness in a man is nakedness in a slave woman including her stomach and her back. Anything else of her body is not nakedness.[17]

The association of the slave woman's body with a free man concerning prayer distinguishes between slavery and freedom rather than alluding to any difference between the body of a free woman and slave woman. The slave woman's *'awra* remains greater than a free man's *'awra* in that she is required to cover slightly more, but she must not be seen to be emulating a free woman in her dress for prayer. This is explained in some detail in other Ḥanafī texts:

> Muḥammad said, 'Abū Ḥanīfa informed us from Hammād that Ibrāhīm said concerning slave women, "They pray without a head-cover or a veil, even if they reach a hundred years and have children by their owner."'
>
> Muḥammad said, 'Abū Ḥanīfa informed us from Hammād from Ibrāhīm that 'Umar b. Khattāb used to beat slave women if they covered their heads saying, "Do not look similar to free woman."'[18]

The slave woman must keep the appearance of a slave woman even if she is old or becomes an *umm walad*; there must be no confusion between her and a free woman. The issue of veiling therefore becomes a marker of distinction between slavery and freedom.[19]

SLAVES AND SALE

In contracts of sale, the *khiyār al-'ayb* or option of defect gives a buyer a choice. The buyer may take the item with its defect at full payment or reject the item. This option extends also to the purchase of slaves:[20]

16 *'Awra* can mean the genitals or nakedness, and in law refers to the parts of the body that should be kept covered by both men and women.

17 Qudūrī, *Mukhtaṣar*, p. 31.

18 Abū Ḥanīfa Nu'mān ibn Muḥammad, *Kitāb al-Āthār of Imām Abū Ḥanīfah*, ed. Muḥammad ibn al-Haşan ash-Shaybāni, London: Turath Publishing, 2006, p. 126.

19 The *umm walad* is a slave woman who gives birth to her master's child and becomes free on his death. Her child is born free.

20 Note that those slaves who are in contract to purchase their freedom from their masters, the *mukātab* and the *mudabbar* such as cannot be sold.

> Everything which requires a decrease in the price according to the practice of traders, is a defect. Running away, wetness on the bed and theft are defects in the minor until he attains majority. Once he attains majority that is no longer a defect unless he returns to his former habits after reaching majority.
>
> Halitosis and bad smell are defects in the female woman but not defects in the male slave unless they are due to illness. Fornication and having an illegitimate child are defects in the slave girl but not in the male slave.[21]

Bodily odours are not considered defects in the male slave, as presumably such smells are more commonly associated with the male slave and in themselves do not directly affect the quality of physical labour and service that a male slave is expected to provide. However, if the slave is ill and it is the illness that causes odours, his illness is considered a defect. This is in contrast to the female slave, who would be judged on the quality of her physical appearance as one of her functions would be to provide sexual service to her master. Thus bodily smells in a female slave constitute a defect. The distinction between male and female morality applies also to the slave, where illicit sexual practice in the female slave is considered a defect but not in the male slave.

While such a distinction recognises the 'human' aspect of slave ownership, slaves are subject to the same rules of buying and selling that would apply to other commodities. Thus when defects are found in a commodity after purchase, the buyer can demand compensation by a decrease in price. With slaves, a defect can be compensated for even when the slave dies:

> Whoever buys a slave and sets him free or the slave dies while he is with him, then the buyer becomes aware of a defect he can recover the loss [caused by the defect].[22]

However, this would not apply if immunity from defects was stipulated by the seller at the time of the purchase:

> Whoever buys a slave and the seller makes a condition of immunity from [being responsible for] every defect, the buyer cannot return the slave for any defect even if the seller did not mention all the defects nor count them.[23]

Ma'dhūn slaves are slaves who have been given authority by their masters to carry out certain types of transactions. They can exercise restricted rights as given to them by their owner:

[21] Qudūrī, *Mukhtaṣar*, p. 167.
[22] Qudūrī, *Mukhtaṣar*, p. 168.
[23] Qudūrī, *Mukhtaṣar*, p. 169.

> If a master authorises his slave with a general permission [authority] his transaction in all trades is permitted and he is allowed to buy, sell make a pledge and take a pledge.[24]

In carrying out these transactions, the slave is acting under authority from the master and not as one legally competent in his own right. Thus:

> He may not marry, nor marry off his [master's] slaves. He cannot contract his own freedom nor give a slave his freedom against wealth.[25]

However, Marmon writes that the *ma'dhūn* slave often enjoyed ties to his master that made him a far more trusted agent than someone outside the family. She writes that "it was not uncommon for a young slave to be taken quite literally as a 'substitute son like the Biblical Joseph in the house of Potiphar by a childless master'".

MARRIAGE, CONCUBINAGE, AND SEXUAL RELATIONS WITH SLAVES

Marriage between slaves and marriage between free men and female slaves are recognised as valid in Islamic law. But it is worth reflecting in a little detail on an aspect of master–slave relationship, which has generally been accepted as sanctioned by the Qur'ān. According to Schacht, men in pre-Islamic Arabia could take their women slaves as sexual partners and this practice was permitted after the advent of Islam.[26] In fact, as Orlando Patterson states:

> It is extremely unusual to find a slaveholding society in which freemen, especially masters, were prohibited from – or in practice refrained from – cohabiting with female slaves with the inevitable result of producing children by these women.[27]

Islamic law allows for free men to have sexual relationships with their women slaves within the understanding that a man may have sexual relations with two categories of women: his wives and his slave women, whom he could take as concubines. This did not mean that all slave women were concubines, but all concubines were slave women with whom the master enjoyed sexual relations. While free women could also own slaves, they did not enjoy any

[24] Qudūrī, *Mukhtaṣar*, p. 363.

[25] Qudūrī, *Mukhtaṣar*, p. 364.

[26] Joseph Schacht, *The Origins of Muḥammadan Jurisprudence*, Oxford: Clarendon Press, 1967, p. 264.

[27] Patterson, *Slavery*, p. 229.

similar rights over their male slaves. Numerous Qur'ānic verses refer to legitimate sexual relations with wives and slave women who are referred to as those women whom 'their right hands possess' (*mā malakat aymānuhum*): In one Qur'ānic verse success is for those who, amongst other virtues:

> Guard their modesty except with their wives or whom their right hands possess, for in their case, there is no blame on them. (Q 23:6)[28]

Elsewhere, the Qur'ān places these two categories of women as permissible to the Prophet:

> O Prophet, we have made lawful to you your wives to whom you have paid their dowers and those whom your right hands possess. (Q 33:50)

In the section concerning prohibited women:

> Prohibited to you are women already married except those whom your right hands possess. God has ordained all this for you. Except for these, all other women are lawful to you provided you seek them in marriage with gifts from your property, desiring chastity not fornication. (Q 4:24)

While Islamic legal texts base their discussions on permitting sexual relations with slave women, there are several Muslim scholars who dispute the meaning of the phrase 'those whom their right hands possess' to refer to a slave woman in this context. In his *tafsīr*, Muhammad Asad writes of Q 4:24:

> The term *muḥṣanah* signifies literally a 'woman who is fortified [against unchastity]' and carries three meanings; a married woman, a chaste woman and a free woman. According to almost all the authorities, *al-muḥṣanāt* denotes in the above context, 'married women'. As for the expression *mā malakat aymānukum* (those whom your right hands possess), ie those whom you rightfully possess, it is often taken to mean female slaves captured in a war in God's cause. The commentators who hold this meaning explain that such slave girls can be taken in marriage irrespective of whether they have husbands in their countries of origin or not. However, quite apart from the fundamental differences of opinion, even amongst the Companions of the Prophet regarding the legality of such a marriage, some of the most outstanding commentators hold the view that *mā malakat aymānukum* denotes here 'women whom you rightfully possess through wedlock'. Rāzī in particular points out that the reference to 'all married women' (*al-muḥṣanāt min an-nisā*) coming as it does after the enumeration of prohibited

[28] Similarly Q 70:30.

> degrees of relationship, is meant to stress the prohibition of sexual relations with any woman other than one's lawful wife.

Asad maintains that in Q 23:6 the same error has been made by commentators:

> Most of the commentators assume unquestioningly that this relates to female slaves and that the particle *aw* (meaning 'or') denotes a permissible alternative. This conventional wisdom is, in my opinion, inadmissible inasmuch as it is based on the assumption that sexual intercourse with one's female slave is permitted without marriage: an assumption which is contradicted by the Qur'ān itself (see 4:3, 24, 25 and 24:32). Nor is this the only objection to the above mentioned interpretation. Since the Qur'ān applies the word 'believers' to men and women alike and since the terms '*azwāj*' spouses, too, denotes both the male and female partners in marriage, there is no reason for attributing to the phrase *mā malakat aymānuhum*, the meaning of 'their female slaves'; and since it is out of the question that female and male slaves could have been referred to here, it is obvious that this phrase does not refer to slaves at all but has the same meaning as in Q4:24 ie those whom they rightfully possess in wedlock; with the significant difference that in the present context this expression relates to both husbands and wives who 'rightfully possess' one another through virtue of marriage. On the basis of this interpretation, the particle *aw* which precedes this clause, does not denote an alternative 'or' but is, rather in the nature of an explanatory amplification, more or less analogous to the phrase, 'in other words' or 'that is' thus giving the whole sentence the meaning – save with their spouses ie those whom they rightfully possess (through wedlock).[29]

In recent years, this debate has been reflected in works on gender and Islam. The following is one of the few Qur'ānic verses that refer to marriage with slave women as an alternative to marriage with free women:

> If any of you have not the means to wed free believing women, they may wed believing girls from among those whom your right hands possess ... Wed them with the leave of their owners and give them their dowers according to what is reasonable ... this is for those of you who fear sin but it is better for you that you practice self-restraint. (Q 4:25)

Yūsuf Ali explains that the girls referred to here are not slaves meaning personal property. The phrase 'what your right hands possess' refer to the 'captives' taken in *jihād*, and all captives in a war belong to the whole

[29] These two quotes are from an online *tafsīr* of Muhammad Asad at http://www.archive.org/details/TafsirUlAsad.

community. Amira Al-Azhary Sonbol argues that this explanation makes more sense than the usual explanation for 'what your right hands possess' meaning slave women who could be married off by their masters. She argues boldly on the basis that the Qur'ān prohibits *zinā*:

> The rules against *zinā* are very strict in the Qur'ān and nowhere is permission given for men to have sexual intercourse with women outside marriage, be they slaves or not. If anything, the Qur'ān (S4:25) admonishes men to take slave women as wives and not as concubines. Perhaps because the Qur'ān does not forbid concubinage in so many words, it was considered permissible by later *fuqahā'* given the expansion of Islam, the taking of hostages, the lucrative commerce in slaves and the concubinage habits of pre-Islamic society, which continued in the Islamic period.[30]

Al-Azhary Sonbol adds in relation to Q 4:24:

> It is true that Q4:24 includes 'those whom your right hands possess' who [were] maybe already married in the category of women who can legitimately be taken as wives. But Q4:24 discussed legitimacy for marriage and is clearly against lust.[31]

Despite such dissenting voices, it is generally accepted that Islamic law permits a master to have sexual relations with his female slaves who then become his concubines. This is evident in rulings related to sexual intercourse and what is or is not permissible between a master and his female slave. However, sexual relations with a wife and sexual relations with a slave woman had to be kept distinct. The wife enjoyed a legal contract based on mutual rights and obligations between her and her husband; she was not simply a sexual partner. The concubine with whom the master enjoyed sexual relations was in every respect still a slave girl until she became an *umm walad*.[32] An example of differing rights in the *Mukhtaṣar*:

> A man may practice coitus interruptus (*'azl*) with his slave woman without her permission but he may not practice *'azl* with his wife except with her permission.[33]

[30] Amira Al-Azhary Sonbol, 'Rethinking Women and Islam', in Yvonne H. Haddad and John Esposito, eds., *Daughters of Abraham: Feminist Thought in Judaism, Christianity and Islam*, Gainesville: Florida University Press, 2001, p. 136. This issue was brought to my attention in a recent article by Aysha Hidayatuulah: 'Māriyya the Copt: Gender, Sex and Heritage in the Legacy of Muhammad's *umm walad*', *Islam and Christian–Muslim Relations*, 21: 3, July 2010, pp. 221–43.

[31] Al-Azhary Sonbol, 'Rethinking Women', p. 126.

[32] An *umm walad* is a slave woman who has a child with her master.

[33] Qudūrī, *Mukhtaṣar*, p. 692.

Schacht states that practising *'azl* was a means of avoiding possible paternity issues regarding the child of a slave girl.[34] However, seeking the wife's permission is simply a reflection of acknowledging her status and right as a free woman in matters important in marital relations.

Marriage contracts in legal texts are mostly defined and discussed as a civil contract between two parties.[35] One of the principal considerations in the marriage contract of free persons is *kafā'a*, or equality between the man and woman. Freedom or *hurrīya* is one of the conditions to be met when considering suitability between the two and, although elaborated in great detail in most *furū'* texts, the issue of freedom is absent in Qudūrī's *Mukhtaṣar*:

> *Kafā'a* is taken into account with respect to lineage, and religion and wealth and that is that he possesses the *mahr* and the maintenance and it is also taken into account with respect to skills.[36]

Freedom is a condition for being *mukallaf* or legally competent, but it is absent in the analysis of *kafā'a*. In the *Mabsūṭ*, the requirement of freedom is explained in detail:

> The male slave is not equal to the woman who is born free and in the same way, the one who is set free is not equal to the one who is born free. The one whose father has been set free is not equal to the woman whose father and grandfather were free. This is because slavery carries the marks of unbelief and in slavery there is lowliness.[37]

While most of the rulings in marriage are about the rights of free agents, slaves can also marry, and the legal texts reflect on these rights in some detail. In fact, slaves enjoy many of the rights in marriage similar to a free person. However, as they do not possess full legal capacity owing to the absence of freedom and are thus not *mukallaf*, marriage of slaves is only allowed with the permission of the master:

> The marriage of a slave or a slave woman is not permitted except with the permission of their master.[38]

34 Joseph Schacht, 'Umm al-Walad', in *Encyclopaedia of Islam*, 1st edition, Leiden: Brill, 1934, p. 1014.

35 For a fuller survey of the analogy between slavery and marriage, the language used for a husband's control of his wife, and a master's power over his female slave see Kecia Ali, *Marriage and Slavery in Early Islam*, Cambridge, MA: Harvard University Press, 2010.

36 Qudūrī, *Mukhtaṣar*, p. 383.

37 Sarakhsī, *Mabsūṭ*, pp. 24–5.

38 Qudūrī, *Mukhtaṣar*, p. 389.

The permission is essential to the validity of the contract:

> The marriage of the slave and the slave woman without the permission of their masters is suspended. If the master permits it is permitted [valid] and if he rejects it is void.[39]

However, marriage and subsequent freedom allows a slave woman to exercise her right of option or *khiyār*:

> If a slave woman has been married off by her master and then she is manumitted, she has the option [to stay in the marriage] whether her husband was a free person or a slave and likewise in the case of a *mukātaba*.[40]

In exercising this option on freedom, the slave woman's position becomes analogous to the minor girl or boy who can exercise their *khiyār al-bulūgh* or option of puberty. This option gives a minor who has been married off by their guardian the right to have the marriage annulled by the *qāḍī* on reaching puberty. The slave woman enjoys this right on obtaining her freedom.[41] The *Mabsūṭ* explains this right on the following basis:

> If she wishes she can stay with him or she can leave him, according to what has been related from Aisha when she freed Barira, the Prophet said to her, 'you now own your body so choose'.[42]

In acquiring freedom, the slave woman is considered *mukallaf* and in charge of her own person and is therefore obliged to exercise her own will. However, marriage without permission from her master cancels this option as the slave woman has exercised her own will when she was not *mukallaf* and acted without the legal consent of the master. The marriage becomes binding and is not considered defective or void *ab initio* even though her master did not give her permission to marry.

The master can also give away his slave woman in marriage:

> When a master marries away his slave woman, he is not liable to lodge her in a house for the husband but she is to serve her master. It is said to the

39 Qudūrī, *Mukhtaṣar*, p. 390.

40 Qudūrī, *Mukhtaṣar*, p. 393. The *mukātab* slave is one who has acquired their freedom against future payments to their master, mostly by instalments.

41 For more on options in marriage see Mona Siddiqui, 'The Concept of *Wilāya* in Hanafi Law', *Yearbook of Islamic and Middle-Eastern Law*, 5, 1998–9, Kluwer Law International 2000, pp. 171–185.

42 Sarakhsī, *Mabsūṭ*, pp. 98–9. The *Mabsūṭ* gives details of Shāfiʿī's *ikhtilāf* on this matter. On the marriage rights of slaves, the Ḥanafīs are often in disagreement with the Shāfiʿīs and the Mālikīs, as can be seen from the discussions in the *Mabsūṭ*.

> husband, 'whenever you can seize an opportunity with her, have sexual intercourse with her'.[43]

Although permission to marry must be sought from the master, the master cannot divorce on behalf of the slave husband:

> When a slave marries with the permission of his master and divorces, his divorce takes effect. A divorce pronounced by his master against his wife does not take effect.[44]

The absence of legal capacity is elaborated in the *Mabsūṭ* on the issue of witnesses. Generally speaking, Ḥanafī law requires that the marriage contract is concluded in the presence of two witnesses: two men, or one man and two women. Witnesses also need to fulfil certain criteria if their witnessing is to be considered legally valid:

> Marriage between two Muslims is not permitted by the witness of two slaves or two unbelievers or two minors or two insane people or women with whom there is no man according to us. If there are two free male Muslims with the couple the marriage is permitted as the condition has been met. If the two minors have reached maturity and the two slaves have been freed and the two unbelievers have become Muslims then they bear witnesses in front of the judge their testimony is permitted. This is because the conditions for giving the testimony have been fulfilled.[45]

Slavery therefore can be seen as a temporary or accidental state of being, allowing for a freed slave to exercise the same rights as a free person. With the emphasis on various means of emancipation, slavery, however socially lowly for the individual, does not need to be a permanent status.

The relationship between masters and slaves is complex in the area of marriage allowing for a variety of marriage contracts to take place between master and slave (not his own) and between slaves. A free man may marry a slave woman whom he does not own:

> It is permitted to marry a slave woman whether she is a Muslim or a woman of the People of the Book [*kitābi*].[46]

A free man may not take a slave woman as his wife if he is already married to a free woman:

[43] Qudūrī, *Mukhtaṣar*, p. 389.
[44] Qudūrī, *Mukhtaṣar*, p. 410.
[45] Sarakhsī, *Mabsūṭ*, vols. 5–6, p. 35.
[46] Qudūrī, *Mukhtaṣar*, p. 393. Only the Ḥanafī school permits marriage with Jews and Christians.

> It is not permitted for him to marry a slave woman as well as (being married to) a free woman but he is permitted to marry a free woman.[47]

The rationale for this is the possible indignity suffered by the free wife if the husband wishes to take a slave as his wife as well. However, he can marry a free woman even though he is married to a slave woman. In such a case, the husband can travel with whichever wife he wants and they both have equal rights to his time during travel. However, when not in travel, the allocation of time spent with the wives reflects the inequality of their legal status and not their status as wives who share equal demands on the husband's time:

> If one of the two women is free and the other is a slave woman, the free woman is entitled to two thirds of his time and the slave woman is entitled to one third.[48]

Marriage to a slave woman is considered marrying one woman: her status as a person is equivalent to that of a free woman.

> The free man is permitted to marry four free women and slave women and he is not permitted to marry more than that.[49]

Although marriage is restricted to four women, there is no restriction on the number of slave women with whom a man can have sexual relationships. The option of taking more than one wife is also allowed to the slave but, in the absence of freedom, he is restricted to two wives. The permission given to the male slave to take two wives reflects the tension between exercising a man's right to more than one wife and his restricted legal status as a male slave:

> The slave cannot marry more than two wives.[50]

It is in the *Mabsūṭ* where we find a distinct difference between the Mālikīs and the Ḥanafīs on this point. The Mālikīs allow the male slave to marry without his master's permission on the basis that if the male slave possesses the right to divorce, he also possesses the right to contract himself in marriage. The Mālikī view is that on the issue of marriage, the male slave shares similar rights to a free person:

> The slave cannot marry more than two but Mālik says that he can marry up to four since the condition of being a slave does not affect the right to marriage.

47 Qudūrī, *Mukhtaṣar*, p. 393.
48 Qudūrī, *Mukhtaṣar*, p. 400.
49 Qudūrī, *Mukhtaṣar*, p. 393.
50 Qudūrī, *Mukhtaṣar*, p. 393.

> According to us it has been related from ‘Umar who said, ‘The slave cannot marry more than twice since the condition of slavery has the effect of halving what was calculated in essence for him like flogging for the *ḥadd*, the number of divorce repudiations and the duration of the *‘idda*.’[51]

The issue of numbers appears when Qudūrī mentions the irrevocable divorce of a slave woman later on:

> The divorce of a slave woman is two repudiations and her *‘idda* is two menstrual cycles whether her husband is a free man or a slave. The divorce of a free woman is three repudiations whether her husband is a free man or a slave.[52]

It is the legal status of the woman and not the man that determines the number of pronouncements in a divorce case. A tradition from Shāfi‘ī that is rejected as weak by the Ḥanafīs argues that the number of repudiations depends on the status of the man. Shāfi‘ī bases this view on the tradition ‘Divorce depends on the status of men while *‘idda* depends on the status of women.’[53] Despite this variability on numbers between a free woman and a slave woman, in certain aspects of marriage the divorced wife and the husband must *conform* to the same practices and restrictions as free persons:

> If the divorce is pronounced three times for the free woman or twice for the slave woman she is not permitted to the husband until she marries a husband other than him in a valid marriage and he consummates with her and then he divorces her or dies [leaving her as a widow].[54]

‘ITĀQ: MANUMISSION OR SETTING FREE

It is in the area of setting free or manumission of slaves where the language of slave ownership is most present. As Jonathan Brockopp says in his work on early Mālikī law:

> By far the most common reference to slaves is the phrase, ‘that which your right/their right hands own,’ found in fifteen places. This phrase, often used to refer to female concubines, also serves as a general term for slaves.[55]

51 Sarakhsī, *Mabsūṭ*, p. 124.
52 Qudūrī, *Mukhtaṣar*, p. 419. If the slave woman no longer menstruates, her *‘idda* is for a month and a half: p. 453.
53 *al-Hidāya*, trans. p. 566.
54 Qudūrī, *Mukhtaṣar*, p. 427.
55 Jonathan E. Brockopp, *Early Mālikī Law: Ibn ‘Abdal Ḥakam and his Major Compendium of Jurisprudence*, Leiden: Brill, 2000, p. 129.

Although the Qur'ān accepts slaves as part of the social structure of society, freeing a slave or manumission was either an act of piety or an act of penance. The *Mukhtaṣar* does not enter into the legal or philosophical debate of what it meant to manumit or set free a slave, but manumission was an intrinsic part of the process of slavery. Yet it did pose a conceptual dilemma. After all, if everything the slave is and enjoys belongs to the master, then by definition it is not possible for the slave to buy back his freedom from his own resources as he does not own anything in his own right.[56]

Nevertheless, setting free a slave is seen almost as a life-giving act for the slave. There are different ways of freeing the slave or for the slave to buy his freedom if the master consents to it. When a man frees a slave or when a woman frees a slave, clientage (*walā'*) of that freed slave belongs to the man or woman who has freed the slave. This relationship is a personal one of clientship and includes the master becoming an heir of his former slave.[57] When a master manumits the slave, the spoken words of the master are fundamental in assessing when a slave actually becomes free:

> The adult, sane, free person's setting free takes place in his property. If he says 'You are free,' or 'You are set free,' or 'You are emancipated' or 'freed' or 'I have freed you' or 'I have freed you,' then the slave is free, whether or not the master intended freedom.
>
> Likewise when the master says, 'Your head is free' or 'Your neck is free' or 'Your body is free' or if he says to his female slave, 'Your vagina is free.'[58]

In relation to the last phrase, referring specifically to the sexual organ of a female slave emphasises the point that the primary role for a female slave was that of a sex object or a potential mother of free children (*al-istifrāsh wa-talab al-walad*).[59] Similar to certain express statements that result in divorce, these phrases are express declarations that result in the manumission of slaves; the master's intention does not affect the legal consequence of the slave's freedom. Where expressions only imply manumission in an indirect manner, the master's intention is important for the slave to become free:

> If the master says, 'I have no ownership over you.' And he intended freedom by these words, [the slave] is set free. If he did not intend freedom of the slave, [the slave] is not freed. This is the case with all indirect expressions of freedom.[60]

56 Patterson, *Slavery*, p. 210.
57 Qudūrī, *Mukhtaṣar*, p. 497.
58 Qudūrī, *Mukhtaṣar*, pp. 475–6.
59 Shaun E. Marmon, *ed., Slavery in the Islamic Middle-East*, Princeton, NJ: Markus Wiener Publishers, 1999, p. 4.
60 Qudūrī, *Mukhtaṣar*, p. 476.

It is the actual setting free of the slave rather than the motivation behind the manumission that matters:

> Whoever sets his slave free for the face of God or for Satan or for an idol, [the slave] is set free.
>
> The setting free [of a slave] by a coerced or intoxicated person is valid.[61]

The *Mabsūṭ* emphasises this point:

> If it is said, 'I have freed you for the face of God,' then some people say, the manumission does not take place unless the person freeing intends the face of God but we do not say this. So that if he says, 'I have freed you for the face of God or Satan,' the manumission takes effect.[62]

A point of disagreement occurs between Abū Ḥanīfa and his two companions on whether a slave can be partially free:

> When a master sets a part of his slave free, that part is set free and he works for the rest of his value for his master according to Abū Ḥanifa. They [Abū Yūsuf and Muḥammad] say he is completely free.[63]

If the slave is viewed as property, his worth can be estimated in parts; if he is viewed fundamentally as a person, he remains indivisible. However, on the issue of a pregnant female slave, the slave woman and the foetus inside her are considered two separate beings to be freed together or individually:

> When a person manumits a pregnant slave woman, she is set free and her foetus is also freed. If he manumits the foetus specifically, the foetus is freed and the mother is not set free.[64]

This is not the case when the slave woman is bearing the child of her master and acquires the status of *umm walad*:

> The child of the slave woman from her master is born free, and the child of her husband is the property of her master. The child of the free woman from a slave is born free.[65]

The word *walad* refers to a child, be it male or female. Bearing the child of a master (*istīlād*) leads to particular consequences for the mother and the child:

[61] Qudūrī, *Mukhtaṣar*, p. 479.
[62] Sarakhsī, *Mabsūṭ*, vol. 7–8, p. 62.
[63] Qudūrī, *Mukhtaṣar*, p. 477.
[64] Qudūrī, *Mukhtaṣar*, p. 480.
[65] Qudūrī, *Mukhtaṣar*, p. 480.

> When a slave woman gives birth to a child from her master, she becomes the mother of his child (*umm-walad*). It is not permitted for the master to sell her nor to transfer her in ownership. He is permitted to have sexual intercourse with her, to make use of her services, to hire her out or to marry her away.[66]

Giving birth to a child from her master privileges the slave woman's child in that the child is born free and the mother can no longer be sold off to another owner. However, the slave woman remains a slave woman and does not acquire any legal rights by virtue of giving birth to her master's child. This includes not having the rights of maternal custody over her free child. But where Islamic law differs from pre-Islamic custom is that the children of the *umm walad* are born free. The children are born free with all the rights this confers on them in the wider kinship of the family, even if there was at times a level of prejudice against the free child of a concubine.[67] The rights would amount to being a legitimate heir of the father and the enjoyment of all legal and social rights equal to that of the father's other children by his wives. The *umm walad* only becomes free when her master dies.

> When the master dies, she is set free from all the property. If her master had a debt, she does not have to work for the creditors.[68]

However, for lineage to be established from the master, the master must acknowledge the child as his own:

> The lineage of her child is established only when the master acknowledges it. If she bears a child after that [the acknowledgement of the first one], lineage is established from the master without his acknowledgement. If he denies lineage, it is denied by his words.[69]

An interesting hypothetical case, typical of legal logic and strategy, is raised regarding dual claim to a slave's child:

66 Qudūrī, *Mukhtaṣar*, p. 482.

67 Shaun E. Marmon, 'Concubinage, Islamic', in Joseph R. Strayer, ed., *Dictionary of the Middle-Ages*, vol. 3, New York: Scribner, 1983, p. 528. Marmon states that this freedom is the fundamental difference between Islamic law and most Western slaveholding societies. Roman law 'set down the harsh principle that the child of a slave mother followed her into slavery (*partus ventrum sequitur*) regardless of the father's status – a principle upheld by subsequent slaveholding societies in the West including those in the New World': p. 528. See also example in Schacht, *Encyclopaedia of Islam*, p. 18, 'The best known case is probably that of the poet 'Antara; he was originally a slave, his mother being an Abyssinian slave; it was only later in life that his father gave him his freedom as a reward for his bravery.'

68 Qudūrī, *Mukhtaṣar*, p. 483. Qudūrī has placed this in the section on *istīlād* and not in *umm walad*. She is free from all debts and can not be sold to pay off debts.

69 Qudūrī, *Mukhtaṣar*, p. 483.

> If the slave woman is shared between two masters and she bears a child and one of the two masters claims the child, lineage is established from him; she becomes his *umm walad.* The master is liable for half her compensatory dower (*'uqr*) and half her value but he is not liable for any value of her child. If both of the masters claim the child together, lineage is established from both of them and she becomes the *umm walad* to both of them. Each of the two is liable for half her compensatory dower, they are even with each other in their wealth. The son inherits from each of them the full inheritance of a son and both of them inherit the equivalent inheritance of one father [they divide between them the inheritance of one father is the son dies].[70]

It is inherent in the structural logic of arguments in *furū'* that the issue of dual lineage illustrates how rights and liabilities are shared. The slave woman and her son are both at an advantage over the disputed lineage since the slave woman, who is now an *umm walad*, can no longer be transferred to another master and her son inherits a full inheritance from each master. There is no onus on the slave woman to identify or specify paternity to either of the two masters.

The status of the *umm walad* is an interesting legal phenomenon. It transfers the slave woman's status from a permitted but informal relationship of concubinage with her master into a legally sanctioned framework giving her and her child certain rights. This has been pointed out by Shaun Marmon, who writes of the inaccuracy of imposing the Western sense of concubinage onto the status of the *umm walad*:

> Concubinage denotes a type of informal but semi-permanent sexual relationship between a man and a woman that is by definition outside of the established laws of marriage and inheritance. Such a relationship, depending on the specific cultural context, may or may not be socially acceptable but is always legally inconsequential, for the children produced in concubinage are necessarily illegitimate ... Islamic concubinage was a clearly defined legal institution that served a vitally important social function: the production of free, legitimate offspring; furthermore, it was part of the greater institution of slavery.[71]

THE *MUKĀTAB* SLAVE

Slaves can buy their freedom from their masters as a way of ending their servile status. This is also applicable to slaves who are still minors if they understand the concept of buying and selling:

[70] Qudūrī, *Mukhtaṣar*, p. 485.
[71] See Marmon, 'Concubinage', pp. 527–9.

> When a master makes his slave or his slave woman a *mukātab* on the payment of property which he makes a condition on them and the slave accepts that contract, the slave becomes a *mukātab*.[72]

The concept of *mukātab* is primarily contractual, entailing regular payments by the slave to the master in exchange for freedom when payments are complete. For the duration of the contract, however, the slave is still owned by the master albeit exercising greater autonomy:

> When the contract for the slave to purchase his freedom is valid, the *mukātab* slave goes out from the possession of his master but does not leave his ownership. He is permitted to buy, sell and travel but he is not permitted to marry unless his master gives him permission. He may not give anything as a gift or as charity except if it is something small.[73]

By virtue of working towards full freedom, the slave acquires certain rights, especially the right to enter into transactions, but as a person he still remains in his master's ownership; he is neither completely free nor in complete bondage. However:

> If the master has sexual intercourse with his slave woman who is a *mukātaba*, the *'uqr* or compensatory dower is binding on him. If he harms her or her child, he is responsible for the crime and if he destroys her property, he owes her damages.[74]

The implication here is that a slave woman as a *mukātaba* is considered a free woman with respect to any crimes against her, and any harm to her person or her property must be compensated for. In terms of child custody, a slave woman has no right to custody of her child, but after being set free the slave woman and the *umm walad* both acquire the same rights as a free woman over the custody of their child.[75]

There is some dispute as to whether an owner can set free a part of his slave:

> When a master sets free some part of his slave, he is set free in that part. He works for the rest of his value for the master according to Abū Ḥanīfa. The two companions say that the slave is set completely free.[76]

The *mukātab* slave must pay all the instalments to his master to purchase his freedom and it is only when the final payment has been paid that the slave

[72] Qudūrī, *Mukhtaṣar*, p. 485.
[73] Qudūrī, *Mukhtaṣar*, p. 488.
[74] Qudūrī, *Mukhtaṣar*, p. 489.
[75] Qudūrī, *Mukhtaṣar*, p. 471.
[76] Qudūrī, *Mukhtaṣar*, p. 477.

is fully free. Qudūrī goes into detail over the possible annulment of a contract. There is a responsibility on the master to give the slave a real opportunity to earn his freedom, so that the slave who might have difficulty in paying his instalments should not be considered insolvent until all possibilities for payment have been exhausted. If he does have to return to the status of being a slave with the contract to purchase his freedom annulled by the judge, all his earnings now belong to his master. The jurists declare their desire to give a slave, time to maintain his payments with Abū Yūsuf stating that only when two successive instalments have been missed should a slave be considered insolvent by the judge.[77] Moreover, the death of a master does not cancel this contract:

> If the master of a *mukātab* slave dies, the contract for the slave to purchase his freedom is not rescinded.[78]

Shaun Marmon writes that amongst all the dependents of a free man, the slaves were the most dependent as they were a kinless people:

> If the master chose to manumit the slave, he cemented this dependency forever by making the slave his fictional kinsman – a kinsman whose burden of obligation however, was in some ways more profound than that of any blood kinsman.[79]

TADBĪR – A SLAVE'S FREEDOM ON THE MASTER'S DEATH

Tadbīr is another way of setting free a slave contingent on the master's death; the slave in such an agreement is known as a *mudabbar*:

> If the master says to his slave, 'When I die you will be free,' or 'You are free when I pass away' or 'You are a *mudabbar*' or 'I have made a *mudabbar* of you' the slave becomes a *mudabbar*. Selling him and giving him away as a gift is not permitted but the master has the right to use his services and hire him out.[80]

If the slave is a woman, he can continue to exercise his rights:

> If she is a slave woman he has the right to have sexual intercourse with her and the right to marry her off to someone.[81]

[77] Qudūrī, *Mukhtaṣar*, p. 490.
[78] Qudūrī, *Mukhtaṣar*, p. 493.
[79] Marmon, *Slavery*, p. 19.
[80] Qudūrī, *Mukhtaṣar*, p. 481.
[81] Qudūrī, *Mukhtaṣar*, p. 481.

Furthermore, the status of *tadbīr* applies also to the child:

> The child of the woman who is to be set free on her master's death is also set free on the master's death.[82]

A master can also enter into a *mukātab* contract with the *umm walad*, who will in any case be freed upon his death:

> It is permitted for a master to give his *umm walad* a contract to purchase her freedom. Then if he dies, the property of the contract is waived from her.[83]

A slave can benefit from various freedom contracts at the same time:

> If he decides that his slave woman who is a *mukātaba* is to be set free after his death, the act of setting her free after his death is valid and she has a choice. If she wants she can continue with her contract to buy her freedom, or if she wants she can become incapacitated and be one who is free after her master's death.[84]

SLAVES AND *ẒIHĀR*

In the Qur'ān there is a specific reference to *ẓihār*, a pre-Islamic formula of repudiation by the husband. In using this word, a man likened his wife to the back of his mother, thereby implying that she is as untouchable to him as his mother, i.e. no longer a sexual partner. The Qur'ān refers to this practice in the context of a woman complaining to the Prophet about her husband:

> God has heard the words of the woman who disputed with you about her husband and complained to God. God hears the arguments between both sides among you for he sees and hears all. Those of you who say regarding their wives, 'You are to me as my mother's back,' they are not their mothers; their mothers are only those who gave them birth. What they are saying is truly dishonourable and false, but God is pardoning and forgiving . . . Those who say regarding their wives, 'You are to me as my mother's back,' and then retract what they have said, must free a slave before the two touch one another. (Q 58: 2–3)

Ṭabarī explains this as a form of divorce in the *jāhilīyya* period. During this time, pronouncing such words had the effect of making the wife prohibited to

[82] Qudūrī, *Mukhtaṣar*, p. 482.
[83] Qudūrī, *Mukhtaṣar*, p. 493.
[84] Qudūrī, *Mukhtaṣar*, p. 494. I have translated this as 'incapacitated' in the context of financially incapacitated, or no longer able to buy her freedom.

the husband forever with no possibility of return.[85] Sarakhsī also begins his discussion on *ẓihār* as a form of divorce in the *jāhilīyya* period but says that it amounts to a temporary prohibition of relations between the husband and wife.[86] In the Qur'ān the emphasis is on the dishonourable and impious nature of such a declaration, which implies that the wife is as untouchable to him as his own mother. Making this declaration necessitates a punishment for the husband. Although *ẓihār* does not amount to a divorce proper, the husband must show penitence and make an expiation or *kaffāra* before he can resume physical marital relations with this wife. In the Qur'ān the expiation amounts to either feeding sixty needy people, fasting for two months, or freeing a slave before the husband can resume sexual contact with his wife. In law, the freeing of a slave needed qualifying and this is developed in the *Mukhtaṣar*:

> When a husband says to his wife ' You are to me like my mother's back,' she becomes prohibited to him. It is not permissible for him to have sexual intercourse with her, nor to touch her or kiss her until he has atoned for the ẓihār.[87]

If the husband resumes sexual intercourse before atoning or paying a penance, he should seek forgiveness but he does not incur any extra liability:

> If he says, 'You are to me like the stomach of my mother or like her thigh or like her vagina' then this is *ẓihār*.

A husband is responsible for the expiation of each declaration of *ẓihār*:

> If he declares *ẓihār* against his wife twice or three times either in one sitting or in different sittings, he is liable for the expiation of each *ẓihār*.

Although *ẓihār* is most commonly associated with a comparison with the husband's mother, the effects would be the same if he compared his wife to another female relative who would be amongst those who are sexually prohibited to him in the category of *maḥārīm* such as his sister or his paternal aunt. *Ẓihār* can only be made against one's wife:

[85] Muḥammad ibn Jarīr Ṭabarī, *Jāmi' al-Bayān 'an Ta'wil āy al-Qur'ān*, Beirut: Dār al Kutub, 1995, pp. 10–11.

[86] Sarakhsī, *Mabsūṭ*, vol. 6, p. 224.

[87] Qudūrī, *Mukhtaṣar*, p. 439. Common translations for *ẓihār* are 'incestuous comparison' or 'injurious assimilation'. However, I will keep the word *ẓihār* in the translated text. Schacht includes *ẓihār* in the 'irrational elements' of Islamic law which he says are 'partly of religious–Islamic and partly of pre-Islamic and magical origins': Schacht, *Introduction to Islamic Law*, pp. 202–3.

> *Ẓihār* only occurs with one's wife so that if he pronounces *ẓihār* against his slave woman, he has not committed a *ẓihār*.

Although no mention is made in the *Mukhtaṣar*, the *Mabsūṭ* debates whether a wife can also make a declaration of *ẓihār* and, if so, whether she would be liable for paying the *kaffāra*.[88]

While the freeing of a slave is a commendable act, not all slaves will fulfil the criteria for expiation:

> It is permitted to free a Muslim or non-Muslim slave, male or female, minor or major. But a blind slave does not suffice, nor one both of whose hands or feet are cut off. It is permitted to free a deaf slave and one whose one hand and one foot are amputated on opposite sides. But it is not permitted to free a slave whose thumbs are amputated nor is it permitted to free an insane slave who does not understand.[89]

The slave who is freed as an expiation for *ẓihār* must be a slave who is fit and healthy for work and who is sane and aware of his freedom. If the extent of amputation or disability diminishes the use of a slave, freeing such a slave does not suffice for the purpose of expiation. Similarly, freeing a slave who is under some form of contract to buy their freedom such as the *umm walad*, *mudabbar*, or the *mukātab* would not be permitted as an act of expiation as these slaves would eventually become free anyway.[90] Furthermore, freeing only half a slave before resuming sexual relations with his wife is not permitted:

> If he frees a half of his slave as his expiation then has sexual intercourse with the one against whom he had declared *ẓihār*, then frees the rest of his slave, it is not permitted according to Abū Ḥanīfa.[91]

A slave can also make a declaration of *ẓihār* in his capacity as a husband. However, his only option for expiation is to fast for two consecutive months as he does not own a slave nor would have the means to feed sixty needy people:

> If a slave declares *ẓihār*, he can only seek expiation through fasting. If the master frees a slave on his behalf or feeds [needy people] it is not enough [for expiating the slave].[92]

88 Sarakhsī, *Mabsūṭ*, p. 227.
89 Qudūrī, *Mukhtaṣar*, pp. 441–2.
90 Qudūrī, *Mukhtaṣar*, p. 442.
91 Qudūrī, *Mukhtaṣar*, p. 443.
92 Qudūrī, *Mukhtaṣar*, p. 442.

Sarakhsī adds to this point that a master may not prohibit a slave from fasting in that this is a right of the slave's wife.[93]

The slave can also be set free as expiation for the breach of an oath:

> The expiation for the breach of an oath is to set free a slave, the slave who is sufficient for expiation of *ẓihār* is sufficient for this. If he wants he may clothe ten poor people, each one of them with one or more garments and the minimum is that in which prayer is valid. If he wants he can feed ten poor people like the feeding in expiation for *ẓihār*. If he is unable to do any one of these three things he can fast for three consecutive days.[94]

MISCELLAENEOUS CRIMES AND TESTIMONY

The most important kind of evidence is the testimony of witnesses (*shahāda*). However, certain categories of people may not provide testimony:

> Testimony is not accepted from the blind, slaves, the one convicted of punishment for *qadhf* even if he repents nor the testimony of the father for his child or the child for his father nor the testimony of the child for his parents or grandparents.[95]

In Islamic law *ḥadd* (pl. *ḥudūd*) are the punishments for those crimes that fall in the category of crimes against religion.[96] The prescribed punishment is reduced for these crimes when the perpetrator is a slave:

> The *ḥadd* punishment for wine and drunkenness is eighty lashes for the free person, dispersed across his body just as we mentioned in the case of unlawful sexual intercourse. If he is a slave, his *ḥadd* punishment is forty lashes.

The rules for *qadhf* are complex. What is important is that the person falsely accused of unlawful intercourse must be free, sane, adult, Muslim, and one who has abstained from the act of unlawful sexual intercourse.

> It is not permitted for the slave to demand the *ḥadd* punishment for his master for false accusation of unlawful sexual intercourse against his own free mother.

[93] Sarakhsī, *Mabsūṭ*, p. 234.

[94] Qudūrī, *Mukhtaṣar*, p. 583.

[95] Qudūrī, *Mukhtaṣar*, p. 629. *Qadhf* in Islamic law refers to the false or unsubstantiated accusation of unlawful intercourse against another man or woman. The punishment for making this accusation is eighty floggings for the free man and forty for the slave.

[96] See Schacht, *Introduction to Islamic Law*, for a good summary of this topic, pp. 175–80.

The master cannot be punished on account of his slave. However:

> Whoever makes a false accusation of unlawful sexual intercourse against a slave woman or a slave or an unbeliever or makes a false accusation against a Muslim of an act other than unlawful sexual intercourse, and says, 'O wicked one,' or 'O unbeliever,' or O bad person,' is to receive the discretionary punishment. If he says, 'O donkey,' or 'O pig' he is not to receive a discretionary punishment.[97]

The reason why punishment is due here is that *qadhf* remains a crime whoever the accused may be. If the accused does not fall in the category of being *iḥṣan*, namely, that they are not free, the prescribed punishment is reduced to a discretionary punishment. In accusing the Muslim of some form of sexual misconduct but not fornication, and adding names that impute dishonour, the accuser must still receive a punishment. Just calling names that are insulting but not dishonourable, however, does not demand that the accuser be punished.

Basing their rulings on various Qur'ānic verses the Sunnī schools of law differ as to when *qiṣāṣ* or retaliation become due:

> O you who believe, the law of retaliation is prescribed for you in the matter of the murdered: the free man for the free man and the slave for the slave and the female for the female. But if the culprit is pardoned by his aggrieved brother, this shall be adhered to fairly and the culprit shall pay what is due in a good way. (Q 2:178–9)

Slaves carry a price and a value as they fall between persons and property on many issues of crime under Islamic law. When a slave is killed by mistake, a financial compensation must be made:

> When a man kills a slave by mistake he is liable for his value which must not exceed ten thousand dirhems. If his value was ten thousand dirhems or more, judgment is given against him for ten thousand dirhems minus ten. As for the slave woman when her value exceeds the amount of *diya* (compensatory payment), five thousand less ten is incumbent.[98]

Killing or wounding a person will only entail the retaliation of capital punishment if the killing was intentional. Where homicide or bodily harm

[97] Qudūrī, *Mukhtaṣar*, p. 550. The maximum number of lashes for discretionary punishment is thirty-nine and the minimum number of lashes is three. In Ḥanafī law, if a person is subjected to *ḥadd* or *ta'zīr* by an *imām* and he dies as result of it, then there is no liability for such a death as the *imām* undertook the act according to the law.

[98] Qudūrī, *Mukhtaṣar*, p. 527.

was committed accidentally, there is a liability for financial compensation or blood price.[99] As the most salient aspect of Islamic law of homicide or bodily harm is the principle of private prosecution, the claims of the victim or of his next of kin are regarded as claims of men and not as claims of God. In seeking retaliation, the notion of equivalence is taken into account, meaning that a person may not be sentenced to death for killing a person of lower monetary value or one who has a lower blood price. While the *Mukhtaṣar* does not enter into any details of *ikhtilāf* on this matter between the schools, it reflects the particular Ḥanafī view that it is the permanent protection of life and not the value of the blood price that is the basis of the required equivalence. Thus, a free man can be killed in retaliation for intentionally killing a slave:

> The free man is killed in retaliation for a free man, a free man for a slave, a slave for a free man, a slave for a slave, a Muslim for a *dhimmī* [a non-Muslim living under Muslim rule]. A Muslim is not killed for killing a *musta'min* (someone under temporary protection) and a man is killed in retaliation for a woman, an adult for a minor and a healthy person for blind person or one who is chronically ill.[100]

However, if the slave belongs to the master, the master is not liable since the slave is his own property:

> A man is not killed for killing his son, his own slave nor for his *mudabbar* slave, his *mukātab* slave nor for his son's slave.[101]

An offence caused by the slave makes the master liable for compensation of some kind:

> When a slave commits an offence by mistake, it is said to his master, 'Either you hand him over for that offence or you ransom him.'[102]

If the master hands him over to the person seeking redress for the offence, the latter acquires ownership for the slave and the compensation for the offence is called the *arsh*:

> When a slave who is a *mudabbar* [due to be freed on the death of his master] or an *umm walad* [mother of her master's child] commits an offence, the master is

99 *Khata'* means accidentally here and *diya* or *arsh* refers to financial compensation. See Rudolph Peters, *Crime and Punishment in Islamic Law*, Cambridge: Cambridge University Press, 2005, pp. 43–7.

100 Qudūrī, *Mukhtaṣar*, p. 505.

101 Qudūrī, *Mukhtaṣar*, p. 505.

102 Qudūrī, *Mukhtaṣar*, p. 524.

liable for what is less – the value of the slave or the compensation for the offence.[103]

CONCLUSION

In comparing the different attitudes to slavery, Brockopp writes:

> Christians may have emphasised the equality of slaves as believers, Judaism the reduction of penalties for adultery with slaves, and Romans the prohibition of slave prostitution, but only the Qur'ān combines these three elements, perhaps providing the most progressive legislation on slavery in its time.[104]

The *Mukhtaṣar* allows us to see all three issues, albeit in a concise manner at times, to acquire some understanding of the slave's legal position. Where I have quoted the *Mabsūṭ*, the point has often been extricated only alongside much detail and elaboration of argument in the text. The combined reading of the two on this issue provides a legal analysis of the slave's status in Ḥanafī law from which it is possible to get a glimpse of other sociological matters relating to slavery and the legal tension in considering slaves as fully human but legally deficient. Legal texts like the *Mukhtaṣar*, however, do not cover historical surveys nor anecdotal tales of the subject matter, nor is there any emotional language ascribed to the various relationships in question.

In Islamic law, slaves, like all human beings, carried value as legal persons. That they were possessions owned by their masters determined their legal status and social and domestic roles, but it did not deny them certain rights. They were not merely 'things'. Female slaves were not just domestic slaves but could also become concubines, creating a different kind of dynamic between master and his slave girl, especially if the slave girl gave birth to her master's child and thereby ensured an improved status for herself as well as freedom for her offspring. Freeing a slave, male or female, and allowing, even encouraging, slaves to buy their freedom meant that although servitude was accepted as serving a domestic as well as a societal purpose, there was greater moral value attached to ending the unequal relationship between master and slave. Thus, there were various ways in which the slave could earn his freedom as well as ways in which the master could grant conditional freedom; either way, the slave then became a citizen who could enjoy full legal rights.

The fundamental basis of slavery is that slaves could not be *mukallaf* or legally competent as they lacked the criterion of freedom. But this legal

103 Qudūrī, *Mukhtaṣar*, p. 525.
104 Brockopp, *Early Mālikī Law*, p. 138.

deficiency which determined their social and personal status disqualified the slaves from certain rights; absence of freedom did not however deny them fundamental human rights such as the right to marry, albeit with the desired permission from their masters, or the right to have children. The tension lay in acceptance of slavery as part of the social order and the realisation that servitude was not the natural order. Thus a child born to a slave woman by her master was born free, allowing for a rupture in the slave status and influencing a future generation. In the Ḥanafī school the slave's life carried an intrinsic value so that the wilful murder of a slave could carry a corporal punishment though their status as possessions of their master, but excused the master from any severe penalty for killing his own slave. It cannot be denied that slaves must have been subject to the callous cruelty and capriciousness of their masters. Stories and anecdotes of courtly attitudes between caliphs and their slave girls reflects the low regard in which slaves, and especially slave girls, were held.[105] However, the Qur'ānic exhortation to be good to 'those whom your right hands possess' (Q 4:40) places slaves in the same category as the weak, strangers, and orphans, as ones who deserve protection, dignity, even affection, and not contempt from the very people who exercised social and legal power over them.

[105] For example, see Abū 'Uthmān 'Amr b. Baḥr al-Jāḥiẓ, *The Epistle on Singing Girls*, ed. and trans. Alfred F. L. Beeston, Warminster: Aris & Philips Ltd, 1980. Jāḥiẓ writes, 'Mu'āwaiyah used from time to time to have a slave girl brought to him and stripped off her clothes in the presence of his courtiers, and he would then place his rod on her sexual organ and say, "This would have been enjoyment of sexual intercourse if it could have found enjoyment." Then he would say to Ṣa'ṣa'ah b. Ṣuḥān, "Take her for one of your sons, since she is not permissible for Yazīd after what I have done to her": p. 20.

3

Pig, Purity, and Permission in Mālikī Slaughter

It is impossible for persons of culture to keep the Dietary Laws.

C. G. Montefiore[1]

Several years ago a retired academic and Church minister at Glasgow University stood next to me in line for a morning coffee in the University's canteen. It was around 8.30 a.m. and the canteen was busy serving breakfast. We were both familiar faces at that time of the morning, but on this occasion he came up to me with his breakfast on his tray and said with a smile, 'Mona, I could never convert to being a Muslim, I would miss my bacon butties too much.' This gentleman, like many people in the West, was aware that Muslims generally observed the scriptural prohibition on eating pig meat but could not quite understand why. Indeed, he found it faintly amusing that worship of God could be reduced to a particular focus on dietary prohibitions, especially in relation to such succulent animals like the pig. But even after a brief conversation in which I tried to explain the issue of slaughter requirements in general and not just the prohibition on pig meat, he found it difficult to understand from his Christian perspective how dietary laws could continue to have any spiritual or indeed meaningful relevance in today's society. In man's relationship with God, surely there other more important ethical issues to be observed than the meat that one ate? It begged the larger question as to whether Muslims think of the transcendent and connect with the sacred primarily through the observance of certain rituals and obedience to certain laws.

[1] Albert Montefiore Hyamson, *The Jewish Quarterly Review*, 9:2, January 1897. This quote is taken from the author's own reply to a critical article by Claude Goldsmid Montefiore. Hyamson vigorously defends the traditional interpretations of the biblical dietary laws.

Recently, an American Muslim colleague of mine, observing that I was scrutinising the fish and vegetarian dishes in a restaurant menu, asked me why I did not want to order a meat dish. In my response to him that I only ever ate meat that I knew to be *ḥalāl*,[2] he looked puzzled and said, 'Why are you making this an unnecessary problem for yourself? Just say "Bismillah" over the food and eat it.'

Such conversations can be common for Muslims living in non-Islamic countries. Abstention from pork and eating meat that has undergone ritual slaughter – technically *dhabīḥa*, termed *ḥalāl* in popular usage – is a devotional feature in the lives of many Muslims. The word *ḥalāl* technically refers to things and persons that are not forbidden to the believer and lies at the other end of the spectrum from *ḥarām*, meaning forbidden or prohibited. While awareness of diverse dietary laws and preferences is more commonplace now, nevertheless, telling people that as a Muslim I prefer to eat only *ḥalāl* meat is usually met with a sympathetic but confused nod. Trying to explain that *ḥalāl* is essentially about the clinical and spiritual processes of slaughtering is lost on most who see meat in its visually sanitised and neatly packaged appearance and don't quite understand how meat consumption for many is based on a larger and prior ritual process. Even today in many parts of the Western world, despite the numerous Islamic food stores that are frequented mainly for their *ḥalāl* butcheries, the concept of any kind of restriction on dietary laws seems anomalous to many. The confusion is exacerbated when non-Muslims see many Muslims eating non-*dhabīḥa* meat and base this view on the verse 'The meat slaughtered by the *ahl al-kitāb* [those who were given a book, most commonly referring to Jews and Christians] is permissible.'

While many people are familiar with Jewish concept of *kosher* within the body of orthodox dietary laws known as *kashrut*, as well as the Jewish and Muslim scriptural prohibition on pig meat, they are often confused by the term *ḥalāl*. The concept of *ḥalāl* covers all manner of acts lawful and permissible in God's eyes. In those Western countries where there are significant Muslim minorities, the word has over the years been used as shorthand to refer to a particular type of meat slaughter. This is in accordance with the Qur'ānic prescription, which necessitates the pouring out of blood from the animal. The technical term for is this type of slaughter is *dhaka* and the issues around slaughter are discussed largely in the *Kitāb al-dhabā'iḥ*.

[2] While *ḥalāl* means permissible in Islamic law, its popular usage amongst Muslims is a shorthand to refer primarily to meat that has been slaughtered according to ritual prescription.

The act of slaughter in Arabic, *dhakā*, *tadhkiya* (from the root *dh-k-w* which occurs once in Q 5:3), includes a number of ways of slaughtering an animal. There is no obligation to eat meat, but meat is one of the blessings from God. The observation to eat from God's bounty is an ethical imperative and assumed under a general principle of observing moderation in life, 'Eat and drink but avoid excess' (Q 7:31). The necessity of bodily sustenance reminds the believers of their dependence on God, and the emphasis in the Qur'ān is on the awareness of food being part of God's bounties and available for the believer among all of God's other blessings. God's desire is not to make things difficult for the believer, and the Qur'ān in its most literal reading prohibits only four things. It was up to the jurists to explain the prohibition and deduce the details of permitted and prohibited food.[3] The rules are elaborated in *fiqh* literature, but a close reading of these texts displays fluidity rather than stringency in adherence to the various aspects of ritual slaughter.

In classical Sunnī Islam, interaction with the *ahl al-kitāb* (Christians and Jews) can be seen from a variety of theological, sociological, and political perspectives. The Qur'ānic verses on the scriptures, ethics, and beliefs of the people to whom God had previously sent revelation are open to a wide range of interpretations. One area that highlights many of the tensions between the emerging Muslim community defining itself through God's laws and the other communities who have also received divine revelation is in the area of dietary laws. The phrase 'dietary laws' presupposes extensive prohibitions in the Qur'ān as to what can and can't be eaten, often in parallel or comparison with Jewish dietary restrictions, which are far greater. This is not to say that Muslim legal scholars do not discuss at some length what can and can't be eaten but Qur'ānic prescriptions alone are very few. Furthermore, the rules around slaughter in the Qur'ān are not detailed, and thus defining what constitutes lawful slaughter becomes a complex issue especially when considering whether the meat of animals slaughtered by other religious communities can be eaten by Muslims.

The Qur'ān has broadly four themes on animal slaughter. The first can be incorporated within the general encouragement to eat from God's blessings, where animal meat is one of God's blessings. Here, there is encouragement

[3] In what is considered one of the earliest *ḥadīth* collection, the *Muṣannaf* of Abū Bakr 'Abdarrazzāq b. Hammām al-Ṣan'ānī, there is a saying attributed to 'Ikrima, 'Eat whatever God has created except for three things: carrion, blood, and the flesh of the pig.' This saying is sandwiched between two different questions on the permissibility of eating dog in the *Bāb al-kalb* of the *Muṣannaf*, pp. 528, 8739. This is the online edition of the *Muṣannaf* found at Maktabh.org.

if not an obligation on the believers to eat rather than to create restrictions for themselves:

> O people, eat of what is on earth lawful and good. (Q 2:168)

> O you who believe, eat of the good things which we have provided for you and give thanks to Allāh if it is him you worship. (Q 2:172)

> Eat what Allāh has provided for you and do not follow the footsteps of Satan for he is indeed your enemy. (Q 6:142)

> But do not utter lies with your own tongues saying 'This is lawful and this is forbidden' to fabricate lies against God. For those who fabricate lies against God will never prosper. (Q 16:116)

The second is the actual prohibition on four things where different forms of the word *ḥarām* have been used specifically. In this category of verses, the issue of necessity overrides the prohibition:

> He has only forbidden you (*ḥarrama*) carrion[4] and blood and the flesh of swine and that which has been slaughtered to any other than Allāh. But if one is driven by necessity, neither craving nor transgressing, there is no sin, for God is most giving and most merciful. (Q 2:173)

> Forbidden to you are carrion, blood and the flesh of swine and that which has been slaughtered to another than Allāh. You are forbidden the flesh of strangled animals (*munkhaniqa*), those beaten to death (*maqqūdha*), those killed by a fall (*mutaraddiya*) and those gored to death (*nāṭiḥa*) or devoured by wild beasts (*ma akala l-sabuʿu*) except what you have slaughtered yourselves. (Q 5:3)

> Say, I do not find in what has been revealed to me any food forbidden to be eaten by one who wishes to eat it, except if it is carrion, or blood spilt forth, or the flesh of swine. For that is indeed foul or what is impious immolated to a name other than Allāh. But if a person is forced by necessity, through neither disobedience nor transgressing due limits, your Lord is most forgiving and most merciful. (Q 6:145)

The third is in relation to the slaughter of animals carried out by the 'People of the Book' which is framed within the larger discourse of relations with the 'People of the Book'.

[4] Carrion refers specifically to animals that die by themselves or are dead without undergoing any slaughter.

> The food of those to whom the Book was given is lawful for you and your food for them. And so are the virtuous women of the believers and the virtuous women of those who received the scripture before you. (Q 5:5)

Finally, there is animal slaughter where God's name has not been pronounced, and this particular issue has generated much controversy among the jurists:

> Do not eat of that on which God's name has not been pronounced for that would be wickedness. But the devils inspire their allies to dispute with you and if you were to obey them you would be among the idol worshippers [those who associate]. (Q 6:121)

Fiqh texts divide the issue of food into animal slaughtering (*dhabā'iḥ*), animal hunting (*ṣayd*), and foods and beverages as linked but separate discourses. While most legal manuals contain chapters on slaughter and hunting, not all contain a section on foods and drinks. The emphasis in these chapters is primarily on methods of animal slaughter and the consumption of those foods and drinks about which there is doubt. The rules on animals around which there is doubt are complex, and it is not my intention here to go into the different categories.[5] What I am concerned with is the issue of slaughter and the strictness of the legal debates in what makes an animal lawfully *dhabīḥa*. It is, however, worth giving an overview of the main issues relating to animal consumption that Ibn Rushd provides in the opening to the *Kitāb al-dhabā'iḥ*.

> Animals for which slaughtering is a condition for their consumption are divided into two types; animals that are permissible only with slaughter and animals which are permissible without slaughter. In this the jurists are agreed about some and disagree about others. They agreed that the animal which is to be slaughtered [for eating] is the land animal with blood which is not prohibited nor that for which there is no hope because of a blow, goring, a fall, an attack by a predator or disease. And the sea animal is not in need of slaughter. They disagreed about the permissibility of eating an animal which does not have blood like the locust and others like it, whether or not they need slaughter. And the animal that bleeds which lives partly in water and partly on land like the turtle and others like it. They disagreed about the effect of slaughter on the categories which have been forbidden for consumption in the Qur'ān with the intention of making permissible the use of their skins and the removal of impurity from them.[6]

5 For an idea of the complexity of arguments relating to certain land and sea animals, see Michael Cook, 'Early Islamic Dietary Law', *Jerusalem Studies in Arabic and Islam*, 7, 1986, pp. 217–77.

6 Muḥammad ibn Aḥmad Ibn Rushd, *Bidāyat al-Mujtahid wa-Nihāyat al-Muqtasid*, vol. 1, Beirut, 1992, p. 539.

Within the two broad categories of land and sea animals, there are lots of other categories of animals which do not neatly fall into warm-blooded land animals and simple sea animals. Juristic speculation on these animals is detailed. As for animals that are forbidden for consumption, the discussion focuses on the possible use of their skin.[7]

In the *Kitāb al-dhakā*, Ibn Rushd discusses the correct manner and the correct tools for slaughtering an animal as well the various categories of people whose food is permissible, namely, Jews and Christians. Ibn Rushd explains that there are two types of slaughtering for land animals. The first is *naḥr*, which is the slaughter of a camel by cutting the jugular vein at the base of the neck, and the second is *dhabḥ*, which is slaughter of most cattle by cutting the throat.[8] While there is some disagreement as to which parts of the throat need to be cut, for example, jugular, gullet, and pharynx – the primary motive for slaughter is to cause the blood to flow from the animal, preferably in one single, uninterrupted movement:

> An animal whose blood has been caused to flow and on which the name of Allah has been pronounced, may be eaten.[9]

The flow of blood must be caused from a suitable instrument:

> The learned are agreed that anything which allows the blood to flow and the jugular veins (*awdāj*) to be cut, is permitted whether it is made from iron, rock, a reed or wood.[10]

A disagreement, however, arises as to whether slaughter is permissible with three other things: teeth, claws, and bones. Ibn Rushd attributes this disagreement to a tradition from Rafiʿ ibn Khadij, who said:

> 'O Messenger of God, We will meet with the enemy tomorrow and we do not have knives. Shall we slaughter with a cane?' The Prophet said to him, 'Whatever causes the blood to flow and has the name of Allāh pronounced on it as long as it is not a tooth or a claw and I will tell you about them, the tooth is bone and as for the claw, it is the knife of the Ethiopians.'[11]

Ibn Rushd explains that as the tooth and claw are still sharp enough to cause blood to flow, jurists were divided as to whether the Prophet's words

[7] For example, it is only the flesh of pigs that is forbidden, not necessarily the pig's skin or fat.
[8] Ibn Rushd, *Bidāyat*, p. 545. Cutting the throat includes cutting the windpipe. *Naḥr* applies to horses and cows also.
[9] Ibn Rushd, *Bidāyat*, p. 545.
[10] Ibn Rushd, *Bidāyat*, p. 548.
[11] Ibn Rushd, *Bidāyat*, p. 548.

implied mere disapproval or complete prohibition. In what is considered probably the earliest legal handbook, the *Muwaṭṭa'* of Mālik ibn Anas,[12] essentially a collection of reports about the Prophet, there are a small number of sayings about animal slaughtering:

> Yaḥyā related to me from Mālik that Abdullāh ibn 'Abbās used to day, 'You can eat whatever has had its jugular vein cut.'
>
> Yaḥyā related to me from Mālik, from Yaḥyā bin Sa'īd that Sa'id bin al-Musayyab said, 'As long as whatever you use for slaughtering can cut, there is no harm in using it, if you are forced by necessity.'[13]

The emphasis lies in the sharpness of the instrument coupled with the necessity of blood flow from the animal. However, where an animal is dying, slaughter can be carried out with a stone if necessary:

> Yaḥyā related to me from Mālik from Nāfi' from a man from the *ansār* from Mu'ādh bin Sa'd or Sa'd bin Mu'ādh that a a slave girl of Ka'b bin Mālik was herding some cattle at Sal'. One of the sheep was afflicted so she went to it and slaughtered it with a stone. The Messenger of God was asked and he said, 'There is no harm in it so eat it.'[14]

Regarding the prohibition on blood, there is disagreement as to whether prohibition applies only to blood which flows out of the animal to be slaughtered or whether it also applies to the blood that does not flow out. Ibn Rushd explains however that blood in small or large quantities is prohibited.[15]

CONDITIONS OF SLAUGHTERING

Ibn Rushd mentions the three issues regarding these conditions: the stipulation of the *tasmiya*; 'I begin with the name of Allāh'; the importance of turning the animal towards the *qibla*; and the condition of intention. While Q 6:121 commands believers not to eat meat that has been slaughtered without the

[12] For a detailed account of form and style of Mālik's Muwaṭṭa' see Norman Calder, *Studies in Early Muslim Jurisprudence*, Oxford: Clarendon Press, 1993. Calder analyses the various formulaic utterances *haddatha-ni Yahya 'an Mālik, haddatha-ni 'an Mālik, qālā Mālik* and *su'ila Mālik 'an*, and also the distribution and structure of the material in the book and concludes that the *Muwaṭṭa'* belongs to the period after 250: p. 36.

[13] Mālik ibn Anas, *al-Muwaṭṭa'*, Cairo: Dār al-Ḥadīth, 1999, p. 390.

[14] Ibn Anas, *al-Muwaṭṭa*, p. 390. The slight variation on this *ḥadīth* is found in Muslim's *Ṣaḥīḥ*, where the girl breaks the stone first, and thereby presumably creates the desired sharper edge. This particular *ḥadīth* is no. 5502 in Muslim, Muḥammad ibn Ismā'īl Bukhārī, *Ṣaḥīḥ al-Bukhārī: The Translation of the Meanings of Ṣaḥīḥ al-Bukhāri, Kitāb al-nikāḥ*, vol. 7, Saudi Arabia: Maktaba Darrussalām, 1997, p. 72.

[15] Ibn Rushd, *Bidāyat*, p. 573.

pronunciation of God's name, it would seem that at least one Prophetic *ḥadīth* does not consider this wickedness if someone has forgotten to say the *tasmiya*:

> Ibn ʿAbbās said, 'Whoever forgets, there is no harm in it ... the one who forgets is not to be called wicked.'[16]

However, the jurists disagreed on its obligation:

> They disagreed about the *ḥukm* of *tasmiya* over the slaughtered animal and there are three opinions. One said, it is an absolute obligation, one said it is an obligation when remembered and dropped when forgotten and one said it is a strong *sunna*.
>
> The reason for their disagreement is based on the apparent meaning of the Book on this and a tradition. In the Book it is said in the words of the Almighty, 'Do not eat that on which the name of God has not been pronounced for that is indeed a wickedness.' The *sunna* opposing this verse has been related from Mālik, from Hishām, from his father who said, 'When the messenger of God was asked, 'O Messenger of God, the people from the desert (Bedouin) bring us their meat and we do not know whether or not they have mentioned Allāh's name over it.' The messenger of Allāh said, 'Say the name of Allāh over it and eat it.' Mālik stated that the verse abrogates the tradition and explained that the *ḥadīth* belonged to the first period of Islam. Shāfiʿī did not agree for it is apparent from this *ḥadīth* that it was Medinese and the verse about mentioning the name of Allāh is Meccan.[17]

> And if it is not known if the People of the Book have mentioned the name of Allāh over the slaughtered animal, the majority say it may be eaten which is also related from ʿAlī and I do not remember a disagreement about it at the moment. It is possible to say that the principle is that their slaughtered animals should not be eaten except those which conform to the conditions of Islam. And if it is said that the *tasmiya* is a condition of slaughtering it is important that their slaughter should not be eaten because of doubt. And if it is known that they have slaughtered for their feasts and their churches there are some of the learned who consider [eating this animal]repugnant and this is Mālik's opinion. Some consider it permissible and this is the opinion of the *aṣḥāb*. Some prohibited it and this is Shāfiʿī's opinion.[18]

The difference of opinion arises out of a fundamental problem emerging from three separate Qur'ānic verses, 'The food of those who were given the book is lawful for you' (Q 5:5), 'Forbidden to you is that which has been

[16] Muslim, *Ṣaḥīḥ*, p. 265.
[17] Ibn Rushd, *Bidāyat*, pp. 550–1.
[18] Ibn Rushd, *Bidāyat*, p. 553.

immolated to any other than Allah'(Q 5:3), and 'Do not eat of that on which God's name has not been pronounced'(Q 6:121). Those jurists who were cautious to the point of prohibition about the slaughter of the People of the Book, considered the dedication of slaughter by the *ahl al-kitāb* to their places of worship similar to 'dedicated to any other than Allah'. However, in the *Mudawwana* of Saḥnūn (d. 854), the debate is raised from a different angle:

> If a woman slaughters [an animal] when it is not necessary [for her to do so] can the animal be eaten according to Mālik? He said "Yes, it can be eaten." He asked Mālik about the woman who slaughters under necessity when there is a Christian man; should she order him to slaughter the animal for her? He said, "No, she should slaughter." I said, "Is the slaughter of the women of the *ahl al-kitāb* and their youths permissible?" He said, "I have not heard anything on this from Mālik but if the slaughter of their men is permissible, there is no harm in eating of the slaughter of their women and youth if they are capable of slaughtering." Did he allow eating what they slaughtered for their feasts and places of worship? He said, Mālik said, "I think it is repugnant but I do not prohibit it" and Mālik explained it he thought it really very repugnant without prohibiting it.[19]

Ibn Rushd writes that Shāfiʿī reconciles the two positions by stating that the *tasmiya* should be a recommendation:

> Those who made remembrance a condition in the obligation arrived at this based upon the words of the Prophet, "[Liability] has been lifted from my community for what they do by mistake, forgetfulness and that which they have been compelled to do."

In the *Mudawwana* we have a firm affirmation of the *tasmiya* according to Mālik and the significance of the actual words that are spoken:

> [Saḥnūn] I said [to Ibn al-Qāsim], 'How did Mālik perform the *tasmiya* over the animal [to be] slaughtered?' He said, 'In the name of Allāh and Allāh is

[19] Saḥnūn Ibn Saʿīd, *al-Mudawwana al-Kubra l-il-Imām Mālik*, vol. 2, Beirut, 1999, p. 641. Mālik's dislike of the slaughtered meat of the Jews and Christians is mentioned again on p. 642 of the *Mudawwana* but, again, he does not forbid it or consider it unlawful. The *Mudawwana* is one of the two major canonical texts of the Māliki legal tradition in North Africa and Andalusia. Again, see Calder, *Studies*, ch. 1, p. 17, in which Calder accepts with some caveats the ascription of the *Mudawwana* to Saḥnūn. He places the *Mudawwana* after the *Muwaṭṭa'* (p. 21). However, Calder argues that 'Saḥnūn did not author the texts. It could not have reached its present form in a single authorial or even redactional process. One such reason is the incorporation of *qultu* and *qālā Saḥnūn* formulae in one text. This is not decisive and I would prefer to rely on the extensive evidence of interpolation gloss, and so on, as indicative of a redactional process requiring more than one redactor and more than one generation.'

> great.' I said, 'Did Mālik consider it *makrūh* to mention over the slaughtered animal "May Allāh's blessings be upon the Messenger of Allāh" after the *tasmiya* or to say "Muḥammad is the messenger of Allāh" after the *tasmiya*?' He said, 'I never heard Mālik say anything on this matter and that issue is mentioned here only as 'in the name of Allāh'.[20]

Qurṭubī, a thirteenth-century Mālikī exegete, discusses in some length Q 6:121, taking into consideration earlier juristic opinions and disagreements. He states that the learned have concluded that the *tasmiya* is not obligatory (*wājib*) based on the above *ḥadīth* from Mālik. Qurṭubī enters the debate of mentioning God's name from another angle:

> You can eat that from which blood has poured forth and over which the name of Allah has been mentioned. What is intended by the name of Allāh is with the heart, for mentioning [remembering] is the opposite of forgetting, and the place of forgetting is the heart and the place for mentioning is the heart. It is related from Bara min 'Azib 'The name of Allāh is on the heart of every believer whether he recites it or does not recite it i.e. Allāh.' We say mentioning is done with the heart and with the tongue and the Arabs used to perform the *tasmiya* over the idols and statues with the tongue and Allāh forbade mentioning him with tongues.[21]

In the *tafsīr* of the Shāfiʿī jurist Ibn Kathīr there is a long explanation of the various perspectives on the obligation of the *tasmiya*. Ibn Kathīr also leans towards making the *tasmiya* a recommended practice, and explains that the issue of wickedness in the absence of the *tasmiya* relates only to an animal slaughtered in the name of a being other than God. This includes those animals sacrificed at altars by idol worshippers or by the Magians.[22]

These arguments show that as far as the jurists were concerned with the 'mechanics' of slaughter, the primary purpose of lawful slaughter is the removal of blood from the animal. Thus any animal from which blood has poured out at the point of slaughter is permissible for consumption by Muslims. The jurists disagree over the *tasmiya* for both the Muslim and the non-Muslim and the necessity of facing the animal in the direction of the *qibla* because opinion is divided as to whether slaughter entails worship. What this means in effect is that the jurists are debating whether the process of slaughter is an act of worship or *taʿabbud*. The word *taʿabbud* has no exact equivalent in English, but denotes both the sense of slave (of God) and, in a theological context,

[20] Saḥnūn, *Mudawwana*, p. 641.

[21] Muḥammad ibn Aḥmad al-Qurṭubī, *al-Jāmiʿ al-Aḥkām al-Qur'ān*, Cairo: Dār al-Hadīth, 1996, pp. 76–8.

[22] Ismāʿīl ibn 'Umar Ibn Kathīr, *Tafsīr Qur'ān al-'Aẓīm*, vol. 2, Cairo: Dār al-Hadīth, 1994, p. 161.

worshipper (of God). It would appear that the jurists were leaning more towards the view that slaughter as a procedure may not be strictly speaking an act of worship even if it required some ritual observance. There is no agreement on the issue of mentioning the *tasmiya* whether by the Muslim or the non-Muslim who is slaughtering the animal. The presence of doubt regarding the meat slaughtered by the People of the Book allows the possibility of abstention from consuming this meat but this does not seem to be a strongly held view. What the jurists were keen to make clear is that an animal slaughtered to any other than Allāh is not permissible. This is a separate issue to a slaughter, which is carried out in the Christian and Jewish places of worship. Even then, Qurṭubī elaborates Q 5:5 'The food of those to whom the Book was given is lawful for you' in the following way:

> This refers to the Jews and the Christians. If the Christians say at their slaughter 'In the name of the Messiah' and the Jews say, 'In the name of 'Uzayr,' that is because they slaughter to God. And 'Aṭā' said, 'Eat the slaughter of the Christian if he has said "In the name of the Messiah" for Almighty and Exalted God has permitted their slaughter and he knew what they said.'[23]

On the issue of turning the animal to face the *qibla*, Ibn Rushd is fairly brief, stating that there is silence on this issue. He adds that one could adopt the *qiyās mursal*, 'an analogy which does not rely on a specific rule' and argue that slaughtering is a form of worship and the *qibla* is a venerated direction so the animal should face this direction. However, Ibn Rushd himself remains unconvinced by this approach, calling it weak:

> Not every worship has the condition of this direction stipulated except for prayer, and the analogy of slaughter with prayer is remote, in the same way as taking the [direction of] *qibla* for the dead.[24]

In the *Mudawwana*, the debate is brief:

> [Saḥnūn] I said [to Ibn Qāsim], 'Did Mālik say that the slaughtered animal should face the direction of the *qibla*?' He said, 'Mālik said, "Yes, the slaughtered animal should face the direction of the *qibla*."'[25]

However, later on Mālik also allows the animal that has not been slaughtered facing the *qibla* to be eaten. The issue of whether or not slaughter is a form of worship also impacts on stipulation of intention or *nīyya*. While Ibn Rushd confirms that the Mālikīs regard intention as obligatory, he points out that

[23] Qurṭubī, *Jāmi*, p. 78.
[24] Ibn Rushd, *Bidāyat*, p. 551.
[25] Saḥnūn, *Mudawwana*, p. 640.

there is a difference of opinion amongst those who see this act as a rational act (*faʿl maʿqūl*) only, which requires the taking of life and does not require the presence of intention.[26] The issue of intention is taken up later in the discussion about the permissibility of eating the meat of an animal slaughtered by a non-Muslim but when the authority to slaughter has been given by a Muslim. Ibn Rushd states that the argument is between those who say that Islam is a condition for the validity of intention, so the intention of a *kitābī* is not valid, and those who abide by Q 5:5, "The food of those who were given the Book was given, is lawful to you and your food for them."[27] In this case, the intention of a *kitābī* becomes irrelevant in the process of slaughter.

What can be seen from the discussion so far is that ritual slaughter does not appear to be an act of worship. Neither the direction of the *qibla* nor the mention of the *tasmiya* over the animal to be slaughtered is obligatory for the meat to be lawful for consumption. For exegetes such as Qurṭubī, meat slaughtered by the People of the Book is permitted for the Muslim even if they slaughter to other names, as long as the other name is not the name of another god. Qurṭubī does not go into the details of what is meant by the Christians slaughtering to the Messiah or the Jews to ʿUzayr[28] by stating quite simply that God knew how they slaughtered. Only if the slaughter is carried out in the name of another god would that animal be unlawful as that would be tantamount to idolatory.

THOSE WHO CAN PERFORM SLAUGHTER

Ibn Rushd begins by explaining that the jurists are agreed on the five qualifications needed in performing animal slaughter: Islam, being male, age of puberty, sanity, and one who observes regular prayers.[29] Those who are prohibited from slaughter are the polytheists (*mushrikūn*) who worship idols.[30] Then there is the category of persons about whom there is disagreement; and even though this

[26] Ibn Rushd, *Bidāyat*, p. 551.

[27] Ibn Rushd, *Bidāyat*, p. 552.

[28] The Qur'ān contains differing discussions of Jews and Christians, seeing them at times as believers and at others as polytheists. Perhaps the most significant verse that indicates that Jews and Christians can be defined as polytheists is Q 9:30–3, 'The Jews believe that ʿUzayr is the son of God, the Christians believe that the *masīḥ* is the son of God and both consider their sages and monks as lords besides Allāh.' ʿUzayr is generally identified with Ezra but as Bernard Heller writes 'such a belief among the Jews that Ezra was the son of God, can hardly be imagined'. For further exploration of legends and commentaries on ʿUzayr, see *Encyclopaedia of Islam*, 1st edition, vol. 4, Leiden: Brill, 1934, p. 1062.

[29] Ibn Rushd, *Bidāyat*, p. 552.

[30] This is with reference to Q 5:3: 'and that which has been immolated to another than God'.

category can be divided into subcategories, there are ten that are well known. These are the People of the Book, the Magians, the Ṣābi'ūn,[31] a woman, a minor, an insane person, a person who is drunk, one who does not pray, a thief, and one who usurps the property of others.[32] While Ibn Rushd is explicit that according to the Qur'ān the food of the People of the Book is permitted, he states that the jurists disagree on the details:

> They are agreed that if they are not Christians from the Banū Taghlib, nor apostates and slaughtered [the animals] for themselves and it was known that they had recited the name of Allāh over their slaughtered animals and the slaughtered animal was one not prohibited to them in the Torah and they had not prohibited it for themselves, it is permitted, except for the fat.
>
> They disagreed in what is the opposite of these conditions. That is when they slaughter for a Muslim with his permission, or when they are Christians from the Banū Taghlib, or apostates, or when it is not known if they have recited the name of Allāh or are ignorant to the purpose of their slaughter, or when it is known that they have recited the name of another than Allāh in what they slaughter for their churches/synagogues and their feasts. Or if the animal slaughtered is one that is prohibited to them in the Torah as in the words of the Almighty 'everything with claws', or if it is one they have prohibited to themselves like the slaughtered animals that according to the Jews have a defect in their creation. In the same way they also disagree about fats.[33]

The Christian Arabs, and more specifically those from the Banū Taghlib, remain outside the category of the People of the Book. The issue of the apostate (*murtadd*) is interesting as the disagreement is based on whether the apostate should be included in the category of the People of the Book:

> As for the apostate, the majority are agreed that their slaughter should not be eaten. But Isḥāq says their slaughter is permitted and Thawrī says it is disapproved. The reason for their disagreement is whether the apostate should not be included within the meaning of the People of the Book. Thus, should he not be given the protection of the People of the Book?[34]

[31] Although the Ṣābi'ūn (also written Sabian) are mentioned favourably in the Qur'ān in three places (2:62, 5:69, and 22:17), Muslim commentators had very little information about them. Some stated that the Ṣābi'ūn believed in the *zabūr* but there are a wide variety of views about their status. For a detailed discussion see Jane McAuliffe, 'Exegetical identification of the Ṣābi'ūn', *Muslim World*, 72, 1982, pp. 95–106.

[32] Ibn Rushd, *Bidāyat*, p. 552.

[33] Ibn Rushd, *Bidāyat*, p. 552.

[34] Ibn Rushd, *Bidāyat*, p. 553.

In the *Muwaṭṭa*', there is one tradition on the issue of meat slaughtered by Christian Arabs:

> Yaḥyā related to me from Mālik from Thawr ibn Zayd al-Dhīlī that 'Abdullāh ibn 'Abbās was asked about the animals slaughtered by the Christian Arabs. He said, 'There is no harm in them' and he recited this verse, 'Who takes them as friends, is from them.'[35]

On the issue of valid slaughter, Michael Cook writes:

> There seems to be no evidence on the Sunnī side that the status of Christian and Jewish meat had ever been in doubt in Sunnī circles, although Imāmi sources claim otherwise. In sharp contrast to the Sunnī view is that normally found amongst the Shi'ites: the meat of all infidels is forbidden without distinction. This is the view predominant among the Imāmis. The Imāmi interpretation of the relevant Qur'ānic texts is accordingly the reverse of the Sunnī view. The permissive reference to the food of 'those to whom the Book was brought' in Qur'ān 5:7 is explained away: 'food' (*ṭa'am*) in this verse covers only grain and the like, to the exclusion of meat.[36]

From the discussion here, clearly the Sunnī jurists were divided over the issue of the People of the Book and also over the other categories of unbelievers. Cook also states earlier on that there are 'two classes of infidels' by separating the Jews and the Christians as one class whose meat is permitted for the Muslim from the Magians whose meat is not permitted.[37] But the *Bidāyat* is not unequivocal about this distinction:

> As for the Magians, the majority of jurists are of the opinion that their slaughter is not permissible because they are polytheists. A group permitted their slaughter based upon the saying of the Prophet (God's peace and blessing be upon him),'Establish with them the practices of the People of the Book.'[38]

What the Mālikī jurists seem to be suspicious of is the possibility of the animal being slaughtered to an idol or another god, but this would not apply to the People of the Book or any other group of people who were to be considered in the same category.

35 Mālik, *Muwaṭṭa*, p. 390.

36 Michael Cook, 'Magian Cheese: An Archaic Problem in Islamic Law', *Bulletin of the School of Oriental and African Studies*, 47:3, 1984, pp. 449–67. The Qur'ānic verse is actually 5:5, not 5:7 as Cook states.

37 Cook, 'Magian Cheese', p. 451.

38 Ibn Rushd, *Bidāyat*, p. 555.

The issue of fat derived from slaughter by the People of the Book raises the same issues of permissibility and prohibition. Ibn Rushd however attempts to draw a conclusion to this debate by raising the issue of abrogation and stating:

> The truth is what was prohibited for them or what they prohibited for themselves became at the time of the *sharī'a* of Islam, void as Islam abrogated all the laws. It is necessary not to comply with their belief on this nor should it be a condition that their beliefs on the permissibility of their slaughtered animals be the beliefs of the Muslims nor that of their *sharī'a*. For if it is a condition then it would not be permissible at all to eat their slaughtered animals.
>
> Their belief in their *sharī'a* is abrogated and their belief in our *sharī'a* is not valid for them. This is a *ḥukm* which God Almighty has specified for them. Their slaughter, and God knows best, is permitted to us without qualification, if not, the *ḥukm* of the verse permitting this is lifted completely.[39]

Ibn Rushd is of the opinion that if the slaughtered animals of the People of the Book are permissible to Muslims, then the fat of these animals should also be permissible. The exception to this is the fat of the pig. He continues:

> As for the Sabians, the disagreement about them is whether or not they belong to the People of the Book. As for the woman and the minor, the majority are of the opinion that their slaughter is permitted and not disapproved. This is according to Mālik. Ibn al-Mus'āb disapproved of them. The reason for their disagreement is the deficiency in the woman and the minor.[40]
>
> As for the insane or the intoxicated person, Mālik did not permit their slaughter but Shāfi'ī allowed it. The reason for their disagreement is on the condition of intention in slaughter. Those who made intention a condition for slaughter disallowed it as the intention of the [formed by the] insane person and the intoxicated person is not valid, especially the fool.[41]

In her work on purity rules, Janina Safran examines how purity and pollution conventions are found in dietary laws that create 'classifications within societies and delineate boundaries between insiders and outsiders'. Her argument focuses on Mālikī texts and the discussion is principally about whether

39 Ibn Rushd, *Bidāyat*, p. 555.

40 Ibn Rushd, *Bidāyat*, p. 555. Deficiency here implies legal deficiency though there is no explanation as to why a woman would be considered legally deficient for the purpose of carrying out slaughter.

41 Ibn Rushd, *Bidāyat*, p. 555. The word used here is *multikh* – a fool/ass.

the Christian is impure (*najas*) and polluting.[42] She posits two main arguments. First, 'Mālikī jurists treated the Christian as a serious threat to ritual purity.'[43] Second, Safran states that purity systems in Sunnī Islam were permeable and accommodate 'not only conversion, but also the contact, interaction and even intimacy with people of the Book sanctioned by the Qur'ān and *sunna*'.[44] The impurity of the unbeliever is a complex issue in Islamic law because of the various typologies of unbelief. As Hava Lazarus-Yafeh states:

> In Islam this meant from the beginning the impurity of the idol-worshipper himself (*innamā al-mushrikūna nadjas* – those who attribute a partner are impure). In early Muslim stories the *Mushrik* (idolator) appears as the only unclean person who defiles by touching or through his seat . . . Among the idolators some Muslim sages counted also those hypocrites (*munāfiqūn*), who in the early days of Islam in Al-Madīna, hesitated to join Muḥammad, without however being genuine idolators. Sometimes even the 'People of the Book' e.g. Jews and Christians, were included in this category, but it was emphasized that their impurity was spiritual. Some even ridiculed the idea that unbelievers were physically impure (if this were true, the mere fact of their conversion to Islam would not cleanse their body).[45]

In the juridical discussion around meat slaughter, the Christian is not viewed as *najas* and indeed the jurists have to reconcile, at times reluctantly, the permission given in Q 5:5 with their various concerns over whether the meat may not have been lawfully slaughtered. The Prophetic *ḥadīth* that allowed the unknown meat brought to the Muslims to be eaten if the *tasmiya* is pronounced gives even more flexibility to the issue of meat consumption. Such is the leniency within Mālikī law that one might wonder how ritual slaughter in the form of *dhabīḥa* survived as a defining practice of Islamic piety amongst Muslim communities.

PIG AND BLOOD

If juridical discussions reflect social practice to some extent, it would seem that the Mālikīs were relatively liberal with their views regarding the slaughtered

42 Janina M. Safran, 'Rules of Purity and Confessional Boundaries: Mālikī Debates about the Pollution of the Christian', *History of Religions*, 42:3, 2003, pp. 197–212. The discussion is based on Q 9:28, 'Believers know that the *mushrikūn* are *najas*. Let them not approach the sacred Mosque after this year has ended.'

43 Safran, 'Rules of Purity', p. 199.

44 Safran, 'Rules of Purity', p. 201.

45 Hava Lazarus-Yafeh, 'Some Differences between Judaism and Islam as Two Religions of Law', *Religion*, 14, 1984, pp. 175–91.

animals of all non-Muslim communities. Even their understanding of apostates stretched to those who could have once been under Muslim protection. The Qur'ānic directives, while specific against the consumption of blood, pig meat, carrion, and idolatorous slaughter, are still too general. There is an underlying emphasis in the Qur'ān to eat of God's bounty and for the believer not to impose any kind of dietary restrictions according to will. Those animals that could not be consumed if found gored, killed, or strangled, and so on, as in Q 6:145, have been explained by Qurṭubī as a later Medinan prohibition. The Meccan portion of this verse, 'Say I do not find in what has been revealed to me any food forbidden to be eaten except' show that at that time in Mecca the law only forbade the four things mentioned in the Qur'ān; wine (*khamr*) too was a later and gradual Medinan prohibition.[46] The only animal meat that is prohibited is the meat of the pig, which Q 6:145 terms *rijs* (unclean). But even in those verses where prohibition is explicit, people can if forced by necessity to eat what has been prohibited, at least until other food has been found. Qur'ānic verses make clear that apart from pig meat, the prohibited meat is that which has been immolated to a being other than God. While pig meat is rarely mentioned in the Qur'ān and discussed very little in *fiqh* texts, there has been some scholarly attempt to understand the reason behind the prohibition during Muḥammad's prophecy.

As is well documented, the ban on eating pig has a longer pre-Islamic history. The fifth-century historian Sozomenus wrote of Judaising Arabs in the Arabian peninsula in his *Church History* (*Historia Ecclesiastica*). He describes the Saracens thus:

> This is the tribe which took its origin and had its name from Ishmael, the son of Abraham; and the ancients called them Ishmaelites after their progenitor. As their mother Hagar was a slave, they afterwards, to conceal the opprobrium of their origin, assumed the name of Saracens, as if they were descended from Sara, the wife of Abraham. Such being their origin, they practice circumcision like the Jews, refrain from the use of pork, and observe many other Jewish rites and customs.[47]

Rodinson's arguments are well known within the larger framework of Muḥammad's relationship with the Jews of Medina and 'biblical borrowings' which links the Islamic ban to the prior Jewish ban. Rodinson argues that

[46] Qurṭubī, *Jāmi'*, p. 115. For a fuller analysis of wine drinking and intoxication in Mālikī law see Chapter 4, 'Drinking and drunkenness in Ibn Rushd'.

[47] S. Sozomenus, *The Ecclesiastical History of Salaminius Hermias Sozomenus*, Book VI, Chapter XXXVIII, online version eng.orthodoxonline.org/early_church_fathers/volume25/ECF00014.htm.

it was Muḥammad's attempts to win over the Jews in Medina that led to the adoption of various Jewish laws, especially the avoidance of blood and pork. When the Jews rejected Muḥammad's brand of monotheism, some laws changed – for example, Ramadan replaced the Jewish Day of Atonement and the *qibla* (direction of prayer) was changed from Jerusalem to Mecca. Muslims, however, continued to regard the dietary prohibitions as part of their religious and cultural identity.[48]

The taboo around pig meat has fascinated anthropologists and cultural ecologists for many years. For them, and indeed for us, the question is not that there is a scriptural prohibition on eating pig, but the history of the evolution of this prohibition across cultures. The pig taboo has no monocausal explanation and its curious place in agricultural and cultural history has been observed by many over the centuries. Herodotus wrote in Book II of his history of the Middle East:

> The pig is regarded among them as an unclean animal, so much so that if a man in passing accidentally touches a pig, he instantly hurries to the river, and plunges in with all his clothes. Hence, too the swineherds notwithstanding that they are often of pure Egyptian blood, are forbidden to enter any of the temples which are open to all other Egyptians.[49]

Robertson Smith claimed that pigs were forbidden to pre-Islamic Semites though he mentions only the Jews and the Syrians.[50] Mary Douglas looked at the concept of religious taboos from various angles, concluding that taboos establish a separate, supernatural world and that dietary taboos are concrete expressions of an orderly and 'holy' world.[51] Her thesis, however, that Judaic and Islamic rules are heavily concerned with pollution and cleanliness in all areas of human behaviour places the two religions on an equal footing, but there are real differences between the biblical and Qur'ānic worlds, which say something distinct about their respective attitudes to purity and the prevalence of cultural purity laws in the Near East. It is clear from this discussion that Muslim jurists allowed pig bristles to be used even though pig meat was banned. This raises the question regarding the essential nature of certain animals that can be distinct from their possible use. Purity laws and dietary

48 Maxime Rodinson, *Mohammed*, New York: Pantheon Books, 1974, pp. 187–8.

49 Manuel Komroff, ed., *The History of Herodotus*, Book II, New York: Tudor Pub. Co., 1956, found in Richard A. Lobban, Jr., 'Pigs and their Prohibition', *International Journal of Middle East Studies*, 26, 1994, pp. 57–75. Marvin Harris, *Cows, Pigs, Wars and Witches: The Riddles of Culture*, New York: Random House, 1974.

50 Robertson Smith, *The Religion of the Semites*, New York: Meridian, 1957, p. 218.

51 Mary Douglas, *Purity and Danger: An Analysis of the Concepts of Pollution and Taboo*, London: Routledge & Kegan Paul, 1996, p. 54.

laws are kept largely distinct in Islam though pig and blood blur the boundaries. Generally speaking, however, principal sources of defilement are more limited in Islam than in Jewish *halacha*. It would be correct to say that in Islam the place of purity laws in religious doctrine is secondary, appearing predominantly in laws relating to prayer or marriage, As Lazarus-Yafeh writes:

> The Islamic laws of purity and impurity are founded on the everyday life of the common man, and they are not derived from a special source such as the Temple cult or the Priesthood from which purity extended over the whole of Israel. The Temple in Jerusalem and the Ka'ba in Mecca have little in common and Islam knows of neither priests nor sacrifices.[52]

The interest in cultural and religious ambivalence towards the pig continues in the modern world and is echoed in an article by Merrill Bennett, whose last essay before he died was called 'Aspects of the Pig'. In it Bennett writes:

> The attitude of the English speaking peoples toward the pig seems to be accurately expressed in the old adage, 'The hog is never good save when he is in the dish.' The mature pig stands alone among the world's larger domestic animals as unloved when adult and alive but well regarded when dead and cooked. Living horses, cattle, water buffalo, yaks, camels, llamas, alpacas, reindeer, sheep, goats, dogs or elephants are rarely the objects of a distaste comparable to this antipathy to live adult pigs.
>
> Such pigs are commonly characterized as filthy, gluttonous, ill-tempered, and obstinate. They are spoken of with disgust as scavengers and garbage eaters, as wallowers in their own stinking ordure, as grubbers for corn in the droppings of cattle. In their usual confinement they smell bad. They are not affectionate to people or to each other. Sometimes a pig will even eat its own young. Pigs were the animals into which Circe transformed Ulysses' companions, with intent to abase. Victor Hugo wrote, 'Upon the first goblet he read this inscription: monkey wine; upon the second, lion wine; upon the third, sheep wine; upon the fourth, swine wine. These four inscriptions expressed the four descending orders of drunkenness.[53]

The scriptural prohibition on eating pig meat, however, has intrigued scholars from various disciplines. As Richard Lobban writes in his discussion of the Near Eastern setting of this taboo, the prohibition on eating pig meat is common to both the Judaic and Islamic traditions, with pig meat often being used as a grave religious insult:

[52] Lazarus-Yafeh, 'Differences', p. 179.

[53] Merrill K. Bennett, "Aspects of the Pig", *Agricultural History*, 44: 2, 1970, pp. 223–36.

> In India the meat of swine has been thrown on mosque steps and has provoked major inter communal rioting. Even as one flies to the Middle-East in modern, high technology European airlines, the companies commonly inform all passengers that the meals contain no pork. In Spain, the ritual public slaughter of pigs, the *matanza* ritual has come to symbolize the resistance of Christians to the Muslim occupation. Yet the debate about the origins of this modern taboo is unresolved and still continues.[54]

Many theories have been put forward as to why the pig was banned and why it came to symbolise the ultimate unclean animal in Islam. These range from ecological, mythological, and scientific concerns between clean and unclean meat to the simple defence by the faithful that this is a divine command. Marvin Harris argued that pig prohibition was a response to an ecological crisis caused by the growth of population in the region. The ecological goals of the Middle East could only be reached with proper domestic animal farming and, for that reason, pig prohibition became part of Islam.[55] One of the most controversial studies of recent times, largely refuting Harris's work, has been the work of Diener and Robkin, who put forward the hypothesis that pigs were big grain consumers and that pork prohibition was a pragmatic attempt by Muḥammad to prevent surplus grain being fed to the animals rather than being passed to the state. This was a way of providing adequate grain for all:

> Grain reserves were not only important to maintain the Muslim community but politically necessary. Grain had to be requisitioned from peasants. Again pig prohibition served a useful purpose.[56]

Despite the theories and arguments put forward by scholars from various disciplines, nothing more conclusive can be established, and the debate remains unresolved. Muslims usually observe the ban without question, viewing it essentially as obedience to a divine command.

The ban on pig meat is not the only prohibition common to Islam and Judaism. One of the main objectives of lawfully slaughtered meat is the draining of blood from the living animal. While blood is prohibited, there is no Qur'ānic explanation analogous to the Jewish prohibition on animal blood. In looking at Jewish dietary laws, Jacob Milgrom writes that the human race after Adam was vegetarian but that God 'reluctantly accommodates to its carnivorous

54 Lobban, 'Pigs'.

55 Harris, *The Riddles of Culture*.

56 Paul Diener and Eugene Robkin, 'Ecology, Evolution and the Search for Cultural Origins: The Question of Islamic Pig Prohibition', *Current Anthropology*, 19:3, 1978, pp. 493–540, p. 503. This article has comments and responses from several anthropologists and ecologists.

proclivities by allowing the slaughtering and eating [of] animals under restrictive conditions. Human beings in general are allowed to eat all kinds of meat provided the blood, the repository of life, has been drained from it.'[57] Milgrom argues that the blood prohibition is one ritual that is the very basis of ethics:

> Every creature that lives shall be yours to eat; I give them all to you as I did the green plants. You must not however, eat flesh with its life blood. For your life blood too I will require a reckoning. Whoever sheds the blood of man, for that man shall his blood be shed. For in the image of God was man created. (Gen. 9:3–6)

God's command is that human blood must not be shed and animal blood must not be ingested. Milgrom argues that this Noachide law was imposed on all humans and lies above the Ten Commandments – the Decalogue – which was intended solely for Israel.[58]

Contemporary debates regarding the stunning of an animal prior to it being slaughtered have evoked a mixed response. In many European countries animal rights advocates have protested strongly against ritual slaughter without stunning because they claim it causes unnecessary suffering for the animal. The result is that some European countries have enacted their views in law. But many Jewish organisations have argued against this stance on the basis that the rights of religious minorities in the modern nation state must be upheld and asked on this particular issue, 'can nations provide realistic alternatives for avoiding such suffering that are compatible with current religious mandates about animal slaughter?'[59]

Muslim opinion, however, remains divided about stunning the animal. While local and national conversations continue as to the rights and wrongs of stunning, there have also been formal pronouncements. In 1935 the Mufti of Delhi stated that it is permissible as long as the animal does not die in the process. In 1982, a similar view was expressed by the rector of al-Azhar University in Cairo. Any kind of machine or process that would kill the animal before it was slaughtered remains prohibited, but if an animal becomes

57 Jacob Milgrom, 'Ethics and Ritual: The Foundations of the Biblical Dietary Laws', in Edwin B. Firmage, ed., *Religion and Law: Biblical, Jewish and Islamic Perspectives*, Winona Lake, IN: Eisenbrauns, 1989, pp. 159–91.

58 Milgrom, 'Ethics', pp. 160–1.

59 Pablo Lerner and Alfredo Mordechai Rabello, 'The Prohibition of Ritual Slaughtering (Kosher, Shechita and *ḥalāl*) and Freedom of Religion for Minorities', *Journal of Law and Religion*, 22:1, 2006–7, pp. 1–62. The article provides an overview of European legislations and regulations around *kosher* and *ḥalāl* meat and the controversial issue of what is considered 'humane' slaughtering.

unconscious through stunning, it is technically still alive and slaughter can be carried out.[60]

Finally, perhaps there is also an issue of the use of certain kinds of language in the modern age. While *kosher* and *ḥalāl* are known as religious terms in most European societies, they evoke a language of the past, a tie to tradition in a way that has become unfamiliar in the West. This may be seen as one of the issues alluded to by Nikki Keddie, who wrote that the 'Western world, however, has undergone centuries of evolution away from traditional medieval patterns, so that we no longer find men expressing themselves according to medieval norms and presuppositions, while the Islamic world has been suddenly thrust from a medieval to a modern situation'.[61]

CONCLUSION

Returning to my own *ḥalāl* meat quandary, I should admit that despite the relatively relaxed views around what constitutes lawful *dhakā*, I remain tied to my upbringing, cultural preference, and a certain conservatism around the meat I consume. This may simply be a matter of custom and taste. The consumption of meat slaughtered in a certain way and dedicated to God has become a defining aspect of a religious community that sees in *dhakā* a reflection of a particular kind of devotion and obedience to God's desired commands. Even though the classical Mālikī juridical texts are an example of how relaxed interpretation of God's commands could be, Muslim slaughter became and remains an important feature of Muslim community life – and now, in the modern period, Muslim identity. Yet obedience to God can be understood in multiple ways in Islam – the law is one feature of humankind's developing relationship with God. If obligation comes from the law, so does choice. The jurists interpreted the Qur'ānic and Prophetic sayings in the context of logic and practicality as well as trying to remain true to an ideal of what constitutes lawful slaughter and interpretation of divine will. On the issue of pig prohibition, it may be that despite all the historical speculation and reasoning behind the ban, there is no other reason to continue with this prohibition other than simple obedience to the Qur'ānic command. In Islamic law, dietary prohibitions become one of the many categories of discussion around the understanding of divine will. The laws on slaughter are subject to the same formal structures of discussion, the same hermeneutical tools applied to a juridical understanding of prayer, marriage, or fasting. They

60 Lerner and Rabello, 'Prohibition', p. 11.

61 Nikki Keddie, 'Symbol and Sincerity in Islam', *Studia Islamica*, 19, 1963, pp. 27–63, p. 29.

are emblems of faith for those who see in law an expression of piety and active participation in leading an observant life. As for emerging identities and communal boundaries, one can read Q 22:34, 'For every nation we have appointed a ritual' (*mansik*) in different ways. Either the issue of ritual slaughter ties Muslims to other religious communities, especially the People of the Book, or it becomes a fundamental prescription in separating Muslims from the communities around them. The jurists themselves saw logic in both perspectives, and their discussions reflect this very tension. Written law remained flexible to the tools of human reasoning and its discursive style cautioned against finality, rigidity, and restrictive expression.

4

Drinking and Drunkenness in Ibn Rushd

Several years ago, a distinguished professor of Islamic Studies from North Africa said to me as he drank a glass of wine, 'Mona, you should have one. Enjoy one glass, God will not smite you over one glass.' His tone was affectionate and sincere, and although I didn't drink any wine then nor since, his words have stayed with me. I was brought up in a religious and cultural environment where alcohol never featured as any part of daily personal, ritual, or communal life. Yet I soon learnt that my own complete abstinence was simply one way of reflecting an understanding of the divine message; for many other Muslims, abstinence was not part of this understanding. It was not until I began to look at *fiqh* texts that I understood the contrast between traditional piety and complex legality when analysing the ambiguities inherent in conceptualising prohibited acts in Islam; wine drinking is one of them.[1] In this chapter I wish to focus on the issue of wine drinking as a conceptual intoxicant as discussed by the Andalusian jurist and philosopher Ibn Rushd in one of his most celebrated legal works, *Bidāyat al-Mujtahid wa-Nihāyat al-Muqtasid.* While most legal schools developed the view that drinking wine was a crime and liable to punishment, there lay an ambivalence surrounding wine consumption and intoxication. It seems that the Qur'ān condemns wine drinking in certain inappropriate contexts, only leading one to argue that its condemnation of wine consumption is neither uniform nor absolute.

The writings of Goldziher and Wensinck amongst others have demonstrated that in the social context of the Arabian peninsula there were many

[1] This chapter was first published as an invited contribution to a festschrift for Colin Imber. The full reference is Andreas Christmann and Robert Gleave, eds., *Studies in Islamic Law: A Festschrift for Colin Imber, Journal of Semitic Studies*, 23, Oxford: Oxford University Press, 2007, pp. 281–95. Oxford University Press and the *Journal of Semitic Studies* have kindly given me permission to republish the article. However, in this chapter, there is considerable additional material including new references and new biographical material.

incongruities between doctrine and practice on the question of wine drinking. During the pre-Islamic period known as the *jāhilīyya*, wine drinking was glorified both in society and by the pre-Islamic poets. While stating that wine was not prohibited in the early part of the Prophetic mission, Wensinck writes:

> In the days of Moḥammed the people of Mecca and Medina used to indulge in drinking wine as often as an occasion offered itself, so that drunkenness often became a cause of scandal, and of indulgence in a second vice, gambling, which together with wine, incurred Moḥammed's condemnation.[2]

However, Goldziher writes of the pre-Islamic Arabs, including their poets:

> But it was asking too much that Arabs should confine themselves to drinking soft date juice, give up wine altogether, and even consider wine drinking as sin and dishonour. Arabs found nothing less to their taste than asceticism, and sang of their national heroes as 'givers of wine'.[3]

He adds that while the prohibition of wine remains a distinctive mark of the Muslim world:

> The praise of wine remained one of the favourite topics also of Muslim poets (cf. The wine songs by Ibn al-Muʿtazz, Abu Nuwās etc.) and at the court of the Caliphs, wine was drunk at revelling parties as if no prohibition existed at all. Even the common people could not always and everywhere refrain from their national drink, date wine of several kinds; the caliph 'Umar b.ʿAbd al-ʿAzīz deemed it necessary to promulgate a special edict in order to abolish this custom.[4]

Despite this prohibition, several notables of Islamic civilisation did drink, including Ibn Sīnā:

> Readers both Muslim and non-Muslim are sometimes surprised to learn that Ibn Sīnā resorted to wine. Al-Sijistāni tells us that Ibn Sīnā justified his drinking on the ground that he was a Ḥanafite – as though Ḥanafite latitudinariaism extended to the permission of intoxicants. But even in explaining the material requirements of logical rigor, Ibn Sīnā stuck to his rejection of moral rigorism, pointedly choosing as an illustration of loose reasoning the

[2] A. J. Wensinck, 'Khamr', *Encyclopaedia of Islam*, 2nd edition, ed. P. J. Bearman, T. Bianquis, C. E. Bosworth, E. van Donzel, and W. P. Heinrichs et al., Leiden: Brill, 1960–2005, pp. 894–97. Owing to popular demand for this entry, it has been reprinted as an article with the title 'Wine in Islam', *The Muslim World*, 18:4, 1928, pp. 365–73.

[3] Ignaz Goldziher, *Muslim Studies*, ed. S. M. Stern, London: Allen & Unwin, 1967, vol. 1, p. 29.

[4] Wensinck, 'Khamr', p. 896.

> proposition 'Wine intoxicates' and arguing 'one should take into account whether potentially or actually, and whether a little or large amount'.[5]

In the legal works the jurists attempt to distinguish the various concepts associated with wine as an intoxicant and the problem of defining intoxication in the believer. What we find in the *Bidāyat* is one of the most sophisticated analyses of this tension.

Ibn Rushd (d. 1198), famous in the medieval West under the name of Averroes, belonged to an extremely important Spanish family, his grandfather being a distinguished Mālikī jurist and *imām* and also occupying the prestigious post of *imām* of the Great Mosque of Cordoba. Ibn Rushd himself is well known as a philosopher, physician, and jurist. Brought up and practising for the most part within the Mālikī *madhhab*, he was eventually appointed the chief *qāḍī* of Cordoba by the Almohad caliph. He also wrote extensively on medicine and philosophy, but in his legal works he wanted to offer the caliph the diversity of opinions arrived at by the great *mujtahid*s of the past.

The *Bidāyat al-Mujtahid wa-Nihāyat al-Muqtasid* (The beginning for the one who exercises independent reasoning and the end for the one who exercises moderation) is a monumental work on *ikhtilāf* within the Sunnī schools and the Ẓāhirī school, which took the author almost twenty years to write; he completed it in July 1188 CE. Although Ibn Rushd mentions in the *Bidāyat* his intention to write a book on Mālikī *furū*', the school of law in al-Andalus, he does not appear to show preference for a specific school of law or give the Mālikī school any privileged status. R. Brunschvig who wrote extensively on Ibn Rushd says that not only is the *Bidāyat* striking in its absence of a clear-cut inclination to one school but also for its clarity of exposition and concern with logic and rationality.[6] As a *qāḍī* working for the Almohads, Ibn Rushd displays the eclecticism derived from his exercise of *ijtihād*, but he wrote knowing that he was under the patronage of the Almohad caliph. Maribel Fierro writes that it is not clear whether Ibn Rushd wrote his work before or after having been named *qāḍī* of Seville but that the position of *qāḍī* stimulated him to write the book.[7] She states:

> It is not surprising that a philosopher like Ibn Rushd should decide to write a legal work, contrary to what some scholars have felt. For Ibn Rushd,

[5] Lenn Goodman, *Avicenna*, Ithaca, NY: Cornell University Press, 2006, p. 43.

[6] R. Brunschvig, 'Averroès juriste', *Études d'orientalisme dédiées à la mémoire de Lévi-Provençal*, Vol 1, Paris, 1962, pp. 35–68.

[7] Maribel Fierro, 'The Legal Policies of the Almohad Caliphs and Ibn Rushd's *Bidāyat al-Mujtahid*', *Journal of Islamic Studies*, 10:3, 1999, pp. 226–48. Fierro also points out in this article that Ibn Rushd was accused of plagiarism.

religions are obligatory because they can lead everyone to knowledge by a common path, whereas philosophy is open only to a small number of persons. Religion is basically law, and political power is crucial in ensuring its application. To attack religion is to attack social life.[8]

In the 'Book of Foods and Beverages' the *Bidāyat* begins its discussion of intoxicating drinks: 'As for *khamr*, they agreed about its prohibition whether it is in small quantities or large quantities; I mean that which is derived from the juice of grapes.'[9] The word used here is *khamr*, the most common word for wine in the Qur'ān. The Qur'ān mentions *khamr* on five separate occasions in the following verses:

> They ask thee concerning wine and gambling. Say in them is great sin and some profit for men; but the sin is greater than the profit.
>
> O ye who believe! Wine and gambling [games of chance] and sacrificing to stones and [divination] by arrows are a disgrace, the works of Satan. So stay away from it so that you may flourish. Satan wants to cause enmity and hatred between you with wine and gambling and hinder you from the remembrance of God and prayer. Will you not then abstain?
>
> Now with him came two young men. One of them said, 'I see myself in a dream, pressing wine.' The other said, 'I see myself carrying bread on my head.'
>
> O my two companions of the prison. As to one of you he will pour out the wine for his Lord to drink.
>
> Here is the description of the Garden which the righteous are promised. In it are rivers of unstaling water; rivers of milk of which the taste never changes; rivers of wine, a joy to those who drink and rivers of honey pure and clear.[10]

8 Fierro, 'The Legal Policies', pp. 242–23. Fierro's work looks at the desire by the Almohad caliphs to impose discontinuity in the legal field in the same way that they did in coins, epigraphy, and art. The old scholarly elites were replaced by party members whose training involved the study of the writings of the *mahdī* Ibn Tūmart (d. 1130). The Almohad criticism against Mālikī Islam was that it did not follow the primary sources of the Qur'ān and *ḥadīth* and that there was a need to return to these. No comprehensive study of Almohad jurisprudence exists so far except for Ibn Rushd's *Bidāyat* written under Almohad patronage that Fierro claims should be considered the response to a certain stage in the evolution of Almohadism (p. 243).

9 Muḥammad ibn Aḥmad Ibn Rushd, *Bidāyat al-Mujtahid wa-Nihāyat al-Muqtasid*, vol. 1, Beirut, 1992, p. 578. In 1994, the Centre for Muslim Contribution to Civilization produced an English translation in two volumes by Imran Ahsan Khan Nyazee from Michigan and reviewed by Muhammed Abdul Rauf from Cairo, under the title of *The Distinguished Jurist's Primer*.

10 Qur'ānic quotes are taken mainly from the translation by Yusuf Ali, *The Holy Qur'ān*, Beltsville, MD: Amana Publications, 2003. I have modified translations slightly where it was appropriate to simplify the language while trying to remain faithful to the wording of

These verses are not listed in the *Bidāyat* but the essence of the *ikhtilāf* within this whole section is presented to us immediately after:

> In the case of other wines (*anbidha*),[11] they disagreed about the small quantity which does not intoxicate, and they agreed that the amount which intoxicates is prohibited (*ḥarām*).[12]

The *Bidāyat* then explains that the majority of the jurists of the Ḥijāz and the majority of the Traditionists say that any amount of an intoxicating substance, small or large, is prohibited, while the majority of the jurists of Kūfa and the majority of the scholars of Baṣra say that what is prohibited is the intoxication, not the drink itself (*sukr nafsihi la al-ʿain*). *Anbidha* does not include *khamr*, which is strictly wine made from pressed grapes. The *Bidāyat* explains the disagreement that is based on the 'conflict of traditions and analogies' on this subject. The jurists of the Ḥijāz have two approaches – to look at all the successive traditions on this subject or to designate all the *anbidha* – that is, intoxicating substances – as *khamr*. The *Bidāyat* does not give any reasons as to why intoxicating substances should be prohibited, nor does it seek to explore the variant terms and language in the Qur'ān that deal with wine, drink, and inebriety.[13] In the Qur'ān, there are words other than *khamr* used to imply an intoxicating drink. From the root *sakira*, we have the following:

> And from the fruit of the date palm and grapes, you obtain intoxicating drink (*sakar*) and also good nourishment. (Q 16:67)[14]
>
> They wander around in their state of intoxication (*sakrātihim*). (Q 15:72)
>
> O Believers, do not approach prayers while you are intoxicated (*sukarā*) until you know what you are saying. (Q 4:43)
>
> They would only say, Our vision has been intoxicated (*sukirat*) and we are a people bewitched. (Q 15:15)

Whereas *khamr* is used in both senses as wine to be shunned as well as wine that is a heavenly reward, it does not imply in itself a state of intoxication. *Sukr*,

the original Arabic. The verses cited are Q 2:219; Q 5:90–1; Q 12:36; Q 12:41; and Q 47:15 respectively.

11 *Anbidha* is the plural of *nabīdh*, a fermented drink made from dates, barley, or honey and a common beverage among the Arabs. Here, it would imply any intoxicating drink/wine that was not *khamr*, that is, not made from pressed grapes. However, *nabīdh* can also mean non-intoxicating fruit drinks.

12 Ibn Rushd, *Bidāyat*, vol. I, p. 578.

13 For an excellent study on wine in early Islam and the various sociological, theological, and legal approaches to prohibition see Kathryn Kueny, *The Rhetoric of Sobriety*, Albany: State University of New York Press, 2001.

14 Yūsuf Ali translates *sakr* here as 'wholesome drink', that is, non-alcoholic drink.

however, is used in the dominant sense of being in some state of inebriation, where the intellect has been distorted. Interestingly, in Q 4:43, being intoxicated (*sukarā*) is part of a longer list of natural bodily functions that defile. These are natural bodily functions, illness, travel, and sexual intercourse, all of which place the believer outside the realm of ritual purity. Only when the believer has either purified himself with water or earth can he be considered competent to perform sacred ritual like prayer. The intoxicated believer too needs to be purified from his state of 'defilement', that is, he needs to be sober again so that he can pray, fully aware of the words he is speaking. What we do not know is how the believer is 'defiled' as a result of being intoxicated and when the believer becomes sober enough to resume worship.

The Qur'ān, however, contains other names of drinks that are part of a sensual image referring to divine mercy or divine reward. The heavenly reward for the righteous makes mention of some form of wine on several occasions:

> They will be given to drink *raḥīq* sealed, whose seal is musk, and for this let those aspire, the ones with aspirations [for bliss] and whose mixture is of *tasnīm*, a spring from which drink the ones who are nearest to God. (Q 85:25)

Both *raḥīq* and *tasnīm* are interpreted as 'wines' that are not only pure – that is, devoid of any polluting effect – but reserved, especially in the case of *tasnīm*, for those who are nearest to God or the most beloved of God. The imagery here works on multiple levels to contrast heavenly wine with earthly wine and to portray a particular picture of heaven itself. First, in the case of *raḥīq*, this is drink sealed with musk. Musk is highly esteemed for its precious perfume and flavour, and a seal made with it contrasts with the seal of earthly wines, which are usually made of clay or molten wax. Second, *tasnīm* refers to springs of 'waters' or 'wine' that flow down from heaven, an image that parallels 'the rivers of wine (*anhār min khamr*), a joy to those who drink'.[15] In the Qur'ānic paradise, there will be various distinct flows of drinks and 'wines' in which *tasnīm* appears to enjoy the most elevated status. All these different drinks are beyond our earthly imagination but they are all united by being pure, which essentially means non-intoxicating, as is the effect with earthly wines. The Qur'ān presents no definitive understanding of the various drinks that are only partially encapsulated in the English translation 'wine'. Wine is associated with the possibility of intoxication whereas the heavenly 'wines' must be reminiscent of sweetness without the effects of clouded judgement. Despite the different names, one distinguishing factor is that all

[15] Qur'ān 47:15.

heavenly 'wines' are pure, that is, they will not lead to any kind of intoxication (*la yunzifūna*, Q 56:19 and Q 37:47), which is possible only with earthly wine.

The *Bidāyat*'s methodology is to quote two particular *ḥadīths* to support why the jurists of the Ḥijāz say that any amount of a drink that can potentially intoxicate is prohibited. It quotes two *ḥadīths* by Muslim and Bukhārī. The first is 'Any drink which intoxicates is prohibited (*ḥarām*),' and 'Each intoxicant is *khamr* and each *khamr* is prohibited (*ḥarām*)'.[16] The second argument is that all intoxicating beverages are called *khamr*. Their [the jurists'] reason is that *khamr* is called *khamr* because it veils the intellect (*khamīr al-'aql*) and that intoxicants are called *khamr* in the legal sense. Again he cites the Prophetic *ḥadīth* used by the jurists of the Ḥijāz who say that the Prophet had stated that *khamr* is from both the date palm and the grape vine, but also: '*Khamr* is from grapes. *Khamr* is from honey, *khamr* is from raisins and *khamr* is from wheat and I forbid you from every intoxicant.'[17]

The jurists of Kūfa, however, look at the Qur'ānic use of *sakar*, 'And from the fruits of the date palm, you obtain *sakar* and good nourishment,' (Q 16:67). They argue that *sakar* is an intoxicant and if God had prohibited it in its substance, he would not have designated it as 'good nourishment' (*rizq ḥasan*).[18] Again, a number of different *ḥadīths* are quoted for this stance:

> It is related from Abu Mas'ūd that he said, 'I witnessed the prohibition of *nabīdh* as you witnessed it, then I witnessed its permissibility; I remembered and you forgot.' They related from Abū Mūsā that he said, 'The messenger of God sent me and Mu'ādh to Yemen. We said, "O messenger of God, there are two drinks there they make from wheat and barley. One of them is called *mizr*, the other is called *bita*'; which one should we drink?" He replied, "Drink them both but do not get intoxicated."'[19]

The *Bidāyat* explains their reasoning that the *'illa* of prohibition of *khamr* is that it prevents the remembrance of God. This is substantiated by the Qur'ānic verse 'Satan seeks only to cast among you enmity and hatred through *khamr*, games of chance, and to turn you from the remembrance of Allah and prayer' (Q 5:90). As the *'illa* is found only in a particular quantity of the intoxicant, it is the quantity that should be prohibited except where consensus has been reached as in the case of *khamr*, where both small and large amounts are prohibited.

16 Ibn Rushd, *Bidāyat*, vol. I, p. 579.
17 Ibn Rushd, *Bidāyat*, vol. I, p. 580.
18 Ibn Rushd, *Bidāyat*, vol. I, p. 580.
19 Ibn Rushd, *Bidāyat*, vol. I, p. 580.

The *Bidāyat* then states that later scholars said that the argument of the jurists of the Ḥijāz is stronger with respect to transmission while the argument of the Iraqis is better by way of analogy. There is a detailed analysis about whether analogy should prevail over tradition or tradition over analogy and how one reconciles interpretation of a text with its apparent meaning. In the end it may be a matter of intellectual taste (*dhauq ʿaqli*) and extensive disagreement may need to prevail, so much so that some have said, 'each *mujtahid* is correct'.[20]

What follows is a detailed conclusion attributed to Ibn Rushd himself, who argues on the strength of two particular *ḥadīths*, 'Each intoxicant is prohibited (*ḥarām*)' and 'if something intoxicates in large quantity, its small quantity is also prohibited'. A persuasive argument is made for prohibition of any quantity of any intoxicant because the *ḥukm* of prohibition refers to the category rather than the quantity of the intoxicant. When one looks at Q 2:219, where in both *khamr* and games of chance there is 'great sin and some profit', God has not allowed small quantities and prohibited large quantities; rather, it is the harm that is prohibited and which must by analogy be prohibited in everything with this characteristic.[21]

Although the *Bidāyat* appears to be prohibiting any intoxicant in small or large quantities, it remains open to the variant legal distinctions. This is inevitable because of the ambivalence towards wine and other intoxicants in the Qur'ān itself. The selection of *ḥadīths* quoted in the *Bidāyat* also lends to various interpretations but the *ḥadīths* are generally more condemnatory of taking any intoxicants, and many define their intake as categorically *ḥ arām*, that is, absolutely forbidden. The Qur'ānic discourse on any drink that has the potential to intoxicate is poised between the appreciation of these very drinks, which were part of Arab cultural and social life, and a clear warning that intoxication leads to both forgetfulness of God and corruption of prayers. For the believing community, it was indeed the remembrance of God and obedience to his commands that defined them – wine as a substance was not sinful in itself, but intoxication would interfere with right conduct and proper ritual. As Katherine Kueny writes:

> The Qur'ān links together wine and gambling in Sūra 2:219, then adds idols and divination arrows to the list in Sura 5:90–1 to remind people to stay away from those things that interfere with God, prayer and the maintenance of a unified community of believers. The underlying purpose of stringing these items together in the Qur'ān is not to give a definitive statement on the legal

20 Ibn Rushd, *Bidāyat*, vol. I, p. 581.
21 Ibn Rushd, *Bidāyat*, vol. I, p. 582.

status of wine and other items in the natural realms, but rather to evoke the deeper, prophetic point that divisions within the community further separate the true believers from the one God.[22]

Again, in her analysis of Qur'ānic statements, Kueny concludes:

Generally speaking, the many references to wine and intoxication can be grouped together roughly according to topic: wine and its association with worldly order, and wine and its depiction of cosmic truth. In addition to being inclusive of all statements having to do with wine and intoxication, this taxonomical approach reveals how the Qur'an's rather brief and ambiguous references may not be understood simply as clipped legal statements stripped from their larger historical narrative, but rather as literary *topoi* used to underscore the limited repertoire of revelatory themes repeatedly restated with subtle variation throughout the text.[23]

When we look at the Qur'ānic statements about wine and intoxicants, there is indeed no definitive stance either about the substance or its consumption. The juristic tension reflects a questioning that is present also in the *tafsīr*:

Some note that in God's words 'They question thee concerning wine and games of chance,' exactly what the people have asked about is not made clear. It is possible that they have asked about the true character and nature of wine. Also they could have asked whether it is permissible to make use of wine. And they could have asked whether it is permissible or sinful to drink it. However, since God answers by indicating the sinfulness, the special emphasis of the answer provides proof that the questions concerned permission and sinfulness.[24]

Al-Rāzī (d. 1209) goes to great lengths to address all possible perspectives about permissibility and prohibition, quoting a wide range of *ḥadīth*s to support the different stances. In the following passage he deals with that most contentious issue – exactly what is meant by wine?

The second portion of evidence on which al-Shāfiʿī bases his opinion is this: Abū Dawūd relates that the Messenger of God said, 'Wine is made out of grapes, dates, honey, wheat and barley.' From this, one can draw two kinds of conclusions. The first is that this is an explicit explanation that these things fall under the designation of wine and thus are also included in the verse that establishes the prohibition against wine. The second is that it is not

22 Kueny, *Rhetoric*, p. 28.
23 Kueny, *Rhetoric*, p. 5.
24 Fakhr al-Dīn Muḥammad ibn 'Umar al-Rāzī, *al-Tafsīr al-Kabīr*, vol. 2. Beirut: Dār Iḥyā' al-Turāth al-'Arabī, 1999, pp. 395 and 396–7.

> the intention of the Lawgiver to give instruction concerning the various expressions [for wine and similar drinks]. Thus, in the present case, he cannot have wished other than to explain that the decision which applies to wine [made from grape juice] also applies to these [other kinds of wine]. If the known decision which is meant specifically for wine made from grape juice pertains to the wickedness of drinking, it must therefore be applied in like manner for these [other] types of drinks.
>
> Al-Khattābī said that that the reason the Messenger of God used the word 'wine' specifically for these five things was not because wine is produced only from these five. Rather, these are specially mentioned because they were well known at the time. Therefore, the decision concerning these five applies to all that are like them such as millet . . .
>
> [There are] two interpretations for the opinion from the Messenger of God that every intoxicating drink [*muskir*] is wine and that every type of intoxicating drink is forbidden. The first is that the word 'wine' designates all drinks that cause intoxication. The second is that every intoxicating drink is to be treated like wine regarding the sinfulness [of its use]. The Messenger of God is not referring to the literal meaning of this expression. The narrow interpretation of the word wine is not meant so one must take it as a figurative expression [*majāz*] for whatever is equivalent.[25]

In addition to anything that falls under the heading of an intoxicant, those substances that undergo some change, whether through mixing, storage, or ageing, are also dangerous. The majority of the jurists maintained the prohibition of mixing those things that were amenable to fermentation:

> A group of jurists said that such fermentation is disapproved (*makrūh*); another group said, it is permitted. Another group said . . . that a mixture of two things is prohibited even if they are not amenable to fermentation.
>
> The reason for their disagreement is that the Prophet prohibited the mixing of dried dates and raisins, of blossoms and ripe dates, and of unripe dates and raisins. In some versions, the Prophet said, 'Do not ferment blossoms and raisins together, or dates and raisins together, and ferment each separately.' On the basis of this there are three opinions: prohibition of mixing, permissibility along with the sin in fermenting and the opinion which sees this as an abomination.[26]

What emerges from this type of *ḥadīth* is the need to keep separate fruits that are good in themselves but through mixing may produce a kind of intoxicant. The question this raises is exactly what is being prohibited – the intoxicant or the mixing that leads to the intoxicant? Furthermore, there is

[25] This is a paraphrase in places of the text from Rāzī on Sūra 2:219/216 in *Tafsīr*, p. 397.
[26] Ibn Rushd, *Bidāyat*, vol. II, pp. 583–4.

no systematic view as to why certain fruits have been selected and not others. The varying opinions underlie a particular feature in the way *ḥadīths* are used for both permission and prohibition, that is, a general principle is assumed from lists that can never be exhaustive but are always illustrative, and that serve to underpin the fundamental message. In this case, the point being made is to ensure that intoxicants are not produced either deliberately or inadvertently.

Within the *tafsīr* and the later legal works, the opinions of the scholars were evidently inclining towards complete prohibition on all wine drinking and the use of analogy (*qiyās*) to thereby ban consumption of any intoxicant. It is worth mentioning by way of contrast to the legal works, where the subversive nature of wine is empahsised, that Ṣūfī literature used wine as a metaphor for establishing the mystic's desired relationship with the divine. As Enes Karic writes: 'While Muslim mystics sang songs glorifying the divine wine that does not intoxicate, Islamic theologians and jurists condemned, just as fervently the earthly wine that does.'[27] Of course, earthly intoxication was not the same as the true state of drunkenness, which led to loss of self and possible absorption into the divine. Ṣūfī piety and reverence for God did not advocate drinking any intoxicant, but they wanted to stress that a deeper knowledge of God lay well beyond legalism or literalism. As Kueny notes:

> The fact that a prohibited substance is used to express an awareness of God who vehemently opposes its consumption further strengthens the Ṣūfīs' authoritative voice, for they are suggesting that Divine Love transgresses all human boundaries, including those that theoretically establish his will. Using a condemned substance to make their point also allows the Ṣūfīs to use their experience of the two polar extremes as a means to penetrate divine truth not contemplated by ordinary believers who follow the literal meaning of the law.[28]

The *Bidāyat* mentions *khamr* on several occasions outside the discussion on foods and beverages. The following are examples of how *khamr* poses a problem.

THE DIVORCE OF THE INTOXICATED PERSON

Although the *fiqh* texts allude to intoxication in various places and present us with the theological debates around the concept, there is no definition of exactly what is meant by intoxication. This affects issues where legal

[27] Enes Karic, 'Intoxicants', in Jane Dammen McAuliffe, ed., *Encyclopaedia of the Qur'ān*, Leiden: Brill, 2002, vol. 2, pp. 555–7.

[28] Kueny, *Rhetoric*, pp. 114–15.

autonomy needs to be determined, as in the case of a man who pronounces a divorce. In the Book of Divorce (*Kitāb al-Ṭalāq*), the divorce pronounced by a man who is intoxicated comes into question:

> They agreed that the one who divorces must be the husband who is sane, of mature years, free and not under duress. They disagreed about the divorce of one who is coerced, intoxicated, ill and about the one about to reach maturity.
>
> About the divorce of the intoxicated person (*sukran*) the majority of the jurists say that it is effective. One group says it is not effective and among them is al-Muzānī and the followers of Abū Ḥanīfa. The reason for their disagreement is whether his order (*ḥukm*) is the *ḥukm* of the insane person or whether there is a difference between them. Those who said that the intoxicated person and the insane person are the same, for both have lost their senses and the condition of capability is sanity (*ʿaql*) said that it does not come into effect. Those who said that the difference between the two of them is that the intoxicated person has corrupted his senses of his own will and the insane person is different to that, said that the intoxicated person is liable for divorce.[29]

The distinction is one of legal capability and whether the intoxicated person still acts with legal capability or whether his loss of sense deprives him of the state of being *mukallaf*. The opinion 'each divorce is valid, except that of the idiot' equates the intoxicated person with the idiot, for he is an 'idiot of a sort'. Thus, his decisions are not legally binding for he is acting without the full faculty of his intellect. In forming such lists, the *fiqh* works are not concerned about why the composition of the list is as it is, but rather with the implications for anyone who falls within a category of such a list.

RITUAL ABLUTION

Within the legal works, *nabīdh* of dates presents a particular problem as it could be drunk as both an intoxicant and as an uninebriating drink. In the Book of Ritual Purification (*Kitāb al-Ṭahāra*), the *Bidāyat* mentions an opinion attributed to Abū Ḥanīfa which was opposed by all his disciples as well as the other jurists of the region.[30] The issue is the use of such *nabīdh* for the purpose of ritual ablution on a journey:

> On the tradition of Ibn ʿAbbās, which says, 'Ibn Masʿūd went out with the Messenger of Allāh on the night of the jinn and the Messenger of God asked him, "Do you have any water?" He said, "I have *nabīdh* in my container." The messenger of God said, "Pour out some," and he performed his ablutions with

[29] Ibn Rushd, *Bidāyat*, vol. I, pp. 101–2.
[30] Ibn Rushd, *Bidāyat*, vol. I, p. 51.

> it and said, "It is a drink and a purifying."' [In another tradition], the Messenger of God said, 'It is good fruit and purifying water.'[31]

Despite claiming that this opinion has been related to other Companions, the *Bidāyat* is of the opinion that this report was rejected by the Traditionists because of a weak *isnād*, that Ibn Masʿūd was not with the Prophet on the night of the jinn but also because of the Qur'ānic verse, 'And if you do not find water, then take for yourselves high clean sand or earth, and rub your hands and face with it' (Q 4:43). This verse means that God did not allow the use of anything other than clean sand/earth where water was not available. According to the *Bidāyat* those Ḥanafīs who allow the use of *nabīdh* may be using water in its absolute sense in this particular tradition. Here, the issue is one of essence – is the essence of an intoxicating *nabīdh* the intoxicant or the water from which the drink is made?

SALES THAT ARE PROHIBITED

In the list of things that have been prohibited for sale in the Book of Sale (*Kitab al-Buyu*ʿ), we are presented with *khamr*.

> God and His messenger have prohibited the sale of wine [*khamr*], carrion [*mayta*], swine [*khinzīr*] and idols [*aṣnām*] … The Prophet said about *khamr*, 'He who has prohibited its drinking, has also prohibited its sale.'[32]

This list is interesting for two reasons. First, it alludes to the Qur'ānic reference on the three things that are *ḥarām* – that is, blood, carrion, and swine – in this list blood is missing. Second, both idols and wine have been added as all these things are considered filth (*najasa*). The discussion is a complex argument about what can be legally owned, consumed, and sold. With respect to wine, it is considered filth, except for slight disagreement.[33] However, those who permit the sale of wine, carrion, and swine do so on the following principle:

> When a thing has more than one benefit, the prohibition of one of its benefits does not prohibit the rest of its benefits. Wine, carrion and swine … can lawfully be sold for those other benefits, that is, if they consist of benefits other than consumption. If they consist of benefits and are sold for such benefits, it is permitted.[34]

[31] Ibn Rushd, *Bidāyat*, vol. I, p. 51.
[32] Ibn Rushd, *Bidāyat*, vol. II, p. 158.
[33] Ibn Rushd, *Bidāyat*, vol. II, p. 158.
[34] Ibn Rushd, *Bidāyat*, vol. II, p. 160.

Interestingly, the *ḥadīth* from al-Tirmidhī, which seems far more definitive on the prohibition of all activities related to alcohol, has not been mentioned:

> God's messenger cursed ten people in connection with wine: the wine presser, the one who has it pressed, the one who drinks it, the one who conveys it, the one to whom it is conveyed, the one who serves it, the one who sells it, the one who benefits from the price paid for it, the one who buys it and the one for whom it is bought.[35]

Khamr becomes part of a longer list of things that are defined as *ḥarām*. Though the word *ḥarām* has not been used in the Qur'ān with respect to *khamr*, this distinction is no longer relevant in later legal works because conceptually it has been locked into a particular taxonomy, while still remaining the subject of complex legal qualifications. Although *najasa*, meaning filth, is used to categorise those things that cannot be lawfully owned or consumed, the sale of parts of such things appears to be permitted, for example, swine bristle in the Mālikī school. Similarly, regarding what is suitable and unsuitable *mahr*, it also places *khamr* along with *khinzīr* as belonging to the category of that which 'it is not permitted to own'. However, in such a case, Abū Ḥanīfa considers such a contract valid, if it contains a provision for *mahr al-mithl*:

> The reason for their disagreement is whether the principle of *nikāḥ* is the same as the principle of sale? Those who said that its principle is the same said that *nikāḥ* becomes defective with a defect of dower (*mahr*) just as sale becomes defective with a defect of price. Those who maintained that validity of dower is not a condition for the validity of marriage on the evidence that mention of dower is not a condition of the validity of the contract, said that the *nikāḥ* is effective and becomes valid with the *mahr al-mithl*.[36]

Within most *fiqh* texts, wine is a problem not only in terms of definition and prohibition but also in the context of penal law. Although we have looked at a selection of areas where *khamr* and intoxicants feature as problematic, consumption of intoxicants was understood as a crime for which punishment in some form had already been established. In the *Bāb fī Sharb al-Khamr*:

> They agreed that the cause [of the punishment] is the drinking of *khamr* in small or large quantities without coercion. They disagreed about intoxicants other than *khamr*. The scholars of the Ḥijāz said that the *ḥukm* is the same as

[35] al-Tirmidhī and Ibn Māja in http://www.muttaqun.com/alcohol.html.

[36] Ibn Rushd, *Bidāyat*, vol. II, pp. 33–4. *Mahr al-mithl* is a dower implicit in every marriage in which a fixed dower has not been specified at the time of the marriage contract.

> the *ḥukm* of *khamr*, with respect to prohibition and the liability of *ḥadd*, upon those who consume them in large or small quantities and whether they are intoxicated or not. The jurists of Iraq said what is prohibited is only the intoxication and it invokes the *ḥadd*.[37]

What is interesting is that it is in the discussion on punishments where we see an accusation of *fisq*, that is, sinfulness and profligacy, levelled at a person who drinks, unless the drinking is followed by repentance (*tawba*). Again, however, the legal distinction between *khamr* and other intoxicants remains so that a person is *fāsiq* if he drinks *khamr*, even if he is not intoxicated, whereas with other intoxicants it is only when the person is intoxicated that *fisq* is applied to him.[38]

The *Bidāyat* discusses the issue of flogging for a person who is intoxicated. Though it mentions variations, based on Prophetic practice and the growing concern in the community about alcohol, it states that the *ḥadīth* in which the Prophet awarded forty stripes is more authentic.[39] The multiple *ḥadīths* that deal with earthly punishment are essentially an implication of divine disapproval. What is being reinforced here is the sinfulness of drinking, not just its legal prohibition. Earthly punishment then becomes a precursor to divine punishment and the deprivation of heavenly blessings:

> Whoever drinks wine in this world will not drink it in the next.[40]
>
> Whoever drinks wine (*khamr*) in this world, then dies while he is addicted to it and does not repent, will not drink it in the hereafter.[41]
>
> Abu Hurairah: The Prophet said, 'If he is intoxicated, flog him. Then if he becomes intoxicated, whip him. If he becomes intoxicated again, whip him. Then if he becomes intoxicated, strike him in the neck.'[42]

Such *ḥadīths* condemn drinking as a serious crime in this world but leave open the opportunity for repentance; repentance from drinking may lead to redemption in the Hereafter. Heavenly wine is thus portrayed as the symbol of the ultimate reward for the believer.

In order to enforce the *ḥadd* punishment for drinking, the jurists had to prove that a person was intoxicated. This could be done either through a

37 Ibn Rushd, *Bidāyat*, vol. II, p. 573.

38 Ibn Rushd, *Bidāyat*, vol. II, pp. 573–4.

39 Ibn Rushd, *Bidāyat*, vol. II, p. 574.

40 Ibn Māja and Muḥammad b. Yazid, 'Kitāb al-Ashriba', in Muḥammad Fu'ād 'Abd al-Bāqī, *Kitāb al-Sunan*, ed., Cairo, 1953.

41 Aḥmad ibn Muḥammad Ibn Ḥanbal, *al-Musnad*, ed., Aḥmad Muḥammad Shakir, Cairo: Dār al-Ma'ārif, 1946 no. 4,916.

42 Ibn Ḥanbal, *al-Musnad*, 10,740.

personal confession or the testimony of two just witnesses. The Ḥanafīs and the Mālikīs, however, differ as to whether its smell on a person is enough to make him liable to the punishment. Though the *Bidāyat* does not explore this issue, it would appear that in classical law the smell of alcohol on a person could be construed as circumstantial evidence if corroborated by two witnesses; for the Mālikīs this is sufficient for *ḥadd* to be applied. However, being in possession of an object with which the offence might have been committed is not enough for a conviction. As Colin Imber shows in his study of legal traditions, it is imperative to show that the defendant drank voluntarily:

> Question: [What happens] if a wine jar is found in Zeyd's possession?
>
> Answer: it is related that Abū Ḥanīfa went on a Pilgrimage and that he, upon entering Medina, saw the people gathered a round a man. They said, 'We found him with a wine-skin, and we wish to inflict the fixed punishment on him.' Abū Ḥanīfa replied: 'He's got the instrument of fornication with him, too. So stone him.' And they left the man and scattered.[43]

In the *Bidāyat*, Ibn Rushd has given a systematic account of the inherent problem of defining intoxicants and then drinking intoxicants. Despite a certain ambivalence in the Qur'ān towards the issue of *khamr* and intoxication, legal works such as the *Bidāyat* have nevertheless understood the relevant verses in association with *ḥadīth* reports. It is the *ḥadīth* reports and early commentaries that saw wine and then all intoxicants as having the capacity to both corrupt personal piety and go beyond the boundaries of proper social and religious behaviour. The 'benefits' that may lie in wine were gradually eclipsed by repeating the problems that lay with consumption of wine. Layer upon layer of interpretation combined to magnify both drinking and the status of intoxication as subversive, ritually impure, and, most importantly, a crime against God. Nevertheless, defining the nature of this 'crime' continued to pose a challenge for the jurists for whom the ambiguous nature of wine remained a conceptual and legal problem. Today, the sale or consumption of wine or any other intoxicating beverage remains a contested issue, especially for many Muslims in the West. Some regard at least the sale of alcohol as a business necessity in a largely secular context. Others seemingly concur with the classical opinion that regards alcohol consumption the ultimate reflection of wickedness (*fisq*).

[43] Colin Imber, *Ebu's-Su'ud: The Islamic Legal Tradition*, Stanford: Stanford University Press, 1997, p. 211.

5

Islamic and Other Perspectives on Evil

> Evil is the point where the perpetual contradictions of our existence intersect: our knowledge that we are free, our knowledge that we are not; our knowledge that we are masters and creators, and our knowledge that we are frail and transitory beings, feeble, multiply conditioned, and that our works along with ourselves are condemned to bear the stigma of futility.
>
> (Gustave E.von Grunebaum)[1]

In contemporary philosophical and theological discourse there is a tendency to look at categories of judgement by pairing moral abstracts such as good and evil, justice and suffering or sin and salvation. While it is impossible to define such concepts in absolute terms, they are central in providing value judgements on human behaviour and the human condition. The monotheistic traditions of Islam, Judaism, and Christianity have explored these concepts within the God–man relationship and also in considering man's earthly paradigm of loss and struggle. While these terms are often considered within the philosophies of the ancient world, they do assume a particular poignancy in theological deliberation. In an article written in 1938 John Bennett said:

> Evil is the source of the most acute theoretical problem which Christians must face. Also, it is for many sensitive souls the most formidable practical obstacle to the religious life. But it must also be recognised that evil is the stimulus without which among men as they are there would be little religious faith at all. If there were no evil in the world the intellectual life of the Christian would run smooth but he would be so self-sufficient and would fit so comfortably in his environment that there would be little room for faith in

[1] Gustave E. von Grunebaum, 'Observations on the Muslim Concept of Evil', *Studia Islamica*, 31, 1970, pp. 117–34.

> anything but himself. The perspective that this fact provides is important as we face the problem of evil. A theology which does not take this problem seriously and throw all the light possible upon it must in time become bankrupt; but this perspective may give us patience as we discover that there are here dark places which no theology which has yet entered the minds of Christians can illumine.[2]

Around ten years earlier, the Muslim philosopher and thinker Muḥammad Iqbāl said in one of his most celebrated lectures:

> The two facts of moral and physical evil stand out prominent in the life of Nature. Nor can the relativity of evil and the presence of forces that tend to transmute it be a source for consolation to us; for in spite of all relativity and transmutation there is something terribly positive about it. How is it then possible to reconcile the goodness and omnipotence of God with the immense volume of evil in his creation? The painful problem is really the crux of Theism.[3]

Both of these thinkers were grappling with arguably the biggest problem for theistic world-views – the existence of evil in this world. To elaborate, the problem for theologians primarily is why is there so much evil in the world when the world has been created by an all-knowing and perfectly good God. Included in this question is the question of suffering – people suffer both physically and emotionally – and why there is so much injustice in the world and why natural catastrophes can take away so many innocent lives. From arguments of God's limitations of power to the existence of evil as an independent being from God, to the logical impossibility of a theistic God permitting evil, theologians from various religious traditions have throughout the centuries wrestled with the existence, meaning, and nature of evil. Theological perspectives are essentially about an intellectual approach to thinking about God. This issue has also been seen as an embarrassment to theism by some philosophers, who argue that the problem of theodicy is not resolved but dissolved by religious thinkers.

Concepts such as waste, suffering, meaninglessness, death and oppression, the Fall and sin are all themes used to define the existence or the origin of evil; but it is often difficult to be precise about the nature of evil, whether it be natural evil or moral evil. Classic examples of natural evil are evils that result chiefly from the operation of the laws of nature such as earthquakes, cyclones, floods, human disabilities, and illnesses. From the twentieth century onwards,

[2] John C. Bennett, "The Problem of Evil", *The Journal of Religion*, 18:4, Oct. 1938, pp. 401–21.

[3] Muḥammad Iqbāl, *The Reconstruction of Religious Thought in Islam*, Lahore: Muḥammad Ashraf Press, Lahore, 1954, reprinted 1960, pp. 80–1.

we have seen it in the form of tsunamis, 9/11, AIDS, the genocides in Rwanda, the fighting in the Middle East, and perhaps the most defining images of unspeakable human atrocities – the Holocaust. Much of natural evil however is also linked to individual and collective suffering of pain, deterioration, and danger. Moral evil is the deliberate misuse of our human freedom to carry out an act of wrongdoing such as murder or theft, though moral evil is also present in the defects in human character such as greed and dishonesty.[4] Moral evil is relational in character, for it is a wrong we do to another. Paul Ricoeur distinguishes by stating that 'suffering sets lamentation against reprimand, for if misdeeds make people guilty, suffering makes them victims'.[5] But Jovan Babić comments rightly that while 'natural evil exists independently of moral evil, yet it serves to produce conditions conducive to much of the moral evil we experience'. While scholars on the subject have often tried to create a typology of evil, there remains one fundamental demarcation:

> The evil that is most intimate to our experience is the evil that we ourselves do, active evil, not the passive evil we suffer. Of passive evils we know many. We undergo them in sickness, suffering and death, in being the victim of the active evil of others, as when we are deceived, cheated, dealt with cruelty in body and spirit, or tyrannised over by the powerful.[6]

One of the major challenges for Christian theologians has been to understand evil not just in terms of the Augustinian notion of the Fall and redemptive salvation but in the earthly and metaphysical dilemma posed by the relationship between an all-knowing, benevolent God, with conditioned or unconditioned omnipotence, and human freedom to resist God's goodness. For Augustine (AD 354–430), the curses of sin and death were the consequences of sex and sexual desire. Adam and Eve's Fall resulted in a basic disorder between the flesh and spirit, but Augustine tried to exonerate God from any blame by attributing evil to the choices of human will. For Augustine the moral life finds its meaning in the interpretive representation of God as love.[7] In the Irenaean

4 See the article by Nick Trakakis, 'Is Theism Capable of Accounting for Any Natural Evil at All?' *International Journal for Philosophy of Religion*, 57:1, Feb. 2005, pp. 36–66. Trakakis also talks about the interface between natural evil that can often be caused by human negligence. One other category of moral evil, often overlooked, is social evil or practices ingrained in the structure of society.

5 Paul Ricoeur, *Evil: A Challenge to Philosophy and Theology*, trans. John Bowden, London: Continuum, 2007, p. 37.

6 Albert Hofstadter, 'Reflections on Evil', The Lindley Lecture, University of Kansas, 1973, p. 3. This is explored further in Jovan Babić, 'Toleration vs Doctrinal Evil in Our Times', *The Journal of Ethics*, 8:3, 2004, pp. 225–50.

7 For an interesting take on the legacy of Augustine's theology of original sin, see Charles T. Mathewes, 'Original Sin and the Hermeneutics of Charity: A Response to Gilbert

type of theodicy, humankind did not emerge as finitely perfect, but as an immature being who needed to develop and mature within the challenges of this world. In the two-stage process of human development, mankind is not born perfect but rather perfection lies in the future. To grow into that perfect being while exercising genuine freedom requires a certain 'distance' from God in a world where God is not overwhelmingly evident but where humankind has the freedom to grow to know and love God. The translation of Aristotle's works into Latin during the twelfth and thirteenth centuries reopened the whole discussion between faith and reason in the West and greatly influenced Christian theologians such as Thomas Aquinas. Thomas wrote of evil being rooted in good and that the cause of evil is good:

> The cause of evil is good (III:10). That is because evil is not a being of its own; hence it cannot be a cause. But good causes evil only by accident because good can only produce good, but its active power may be deficient, and so the effect is also deficient . . . a moral evil consists in a defective act of the will.
>
> However much it multiplies, evil cannot totally overcome good (III:12), because as a privation it must always have a subject which is good. Even though sight, for example can diminish until it is totally gone, blindness remains in a subject.[8]

According to the seventeenth century-Leibnizian philosophical theodicy, God cannot be blamed for the existence of evil, for this world is the 'best of all possible worlds', where evils are essential to the superior goodness of the whole. During the twentieth century the scale and scope of human willingness and capacity to inflict death and suffering on other human beings has also led to a resurgence of philosophical reflection on the nature of evil. Richard Swinburne writes that the kind of evils we find on earth serve greater goods:

> If a perfectly good being is to allow evil to occur, he must have the right to do so and there must be some good which is brought about by allowing the evil to occur and could not be brought about by him in any better way, and so great that it is worth allowing the evil to occur. I believe that God does have the right to make humans and animals suffer for the sake of a greater good.[9]

Meilaender', *The Journal of Religious Ethics*, 29:1, Spring 2001, pp. 35–42. Mathewes writes, 'We ought to bury Augustine, not praise him . . . burial would recognise Augustine's humanity. Like us he struggled with clarity, changed his mind and operated within a fairly limited set of intellectual options whose parameters he did not set. Like us, that is, he worked under conditions of original sin . . . Ironically enough, it may be the extremity of our respect for antique minds that traps us in the habit of scolding them for not being more like us.'

8 Thomas Aquinas, *Summa Contra Gentiles, Books 1–III*, in Joseph Kenny, ed., *Christian–Islamic Preambles of Faith*, Washington: The Council for Research in Values and Philosophy, 1999, p. 110.

9 Richard Swinburne, 'Some Major Strands of Theodicy', in William Rowe, ed., *God and the Problem of Evil*, Oxford: Blackwell, 2001, 64, pp. 240–1.

The American Christian philosopher Alvin Plantinga has argued against Leibniz's view of the 'best possible world' by claiming that that there cannot be any best possible world because to any world can be added more pleasure or goodness to make it even. Plantinga puts forward the free will defence through the concept of *transworld depravity*. For Plantinga, it is possible that even an omnipotent God could not create a world with free creatures who never choose evil. Thus, it does not matter what kind of world God created, if God allows human beings to be free, then it is true that human beings will take at least one wrong action. Humanity cannot be significantly free yet at the same time have predetermined actions:

> What is important about the idea of transworld depravity is that if a person suffers from it, then it was not within God's power to actualize any world in which that person is significantly free but does no wrong – that is, a world in which he produced moral good but no moral evil.[10]

Most discussions on human freedom are premised on viewing it as inherently a good thing; human freedom is worth the risk and the pain inflicted in the world. This perspective has dominated at the expense of concentrating on the burden of freedom, the crushing weight of human choice, the ability and desire to often choose that which is not good. Ernst Troeltsch argued that if the image of God essentially consists in freedom, then evil could only be understood in terms of a genuine opposition:

> The Christian concept of evil thoroughly corresponds to the personal idea of God and the soul. Hence it is a purely religious concept, conceiving antimorality not in exclusively ethical terms, but also from a religious viewpoint: antimorality is construed as rejection of, or antagonism toward, God. It is this *religious* character of antimorality that constitutes its real roots and true depths. Hence the concept of sin, just like the concept of the image of God, is characteristically Christian; and it stands in the same relationship to the truly universal sense of evil that the concept of the image of God stands to the universal but vague struggle for higher life. Full knowledge of sin comes only with faith.[11]

Discussions on evil and suffering have assumed a more complex nature also because of the different kinds of evil and suffering that many see as the product of the modern age. But Peter Dews rightly questions why in a post-theological,

[10] Alvin Plantinga, 'The Logical Problem of Evil', in William Rowe, ed., *God and the Problem of Evil*, Oxford: Blackwell, 2001, pp. 111–12.
[11] Ernst Troeltsch, *The Christian Faith*, Minneapolis: Fortress Press, 1991, p. 242.

intellectual universe there should be philosophical difficulty in coming to terms with the concept and phenomenon of evil:

> It would seem that the problem of theodicy, of justifying the ways of God to a suffering world, should have disappeared for us who live after Nietzsche's proclamation of the death of God. And yet as the recent burgeoning of philosophical literature on the topic of evil suggests, the problem of theodicy seems in some sense to have outlived the explicit belief in a divine creator that first gave rise to it.[12]

Whether or not the use of the concept of evil can be disconnected from theological language to a more, secular, moral discourse is debatable. Modern theories of the specific contextuality of knowledge can be considered against the metaphysical speculation about the essence of human beings and the world in which we live and create, but any account of moral evil in the modern age requires 'recognition of the connection between evil and individual moral identity as a whole'.[13]

In recent years, many philosophers have drawn upon the works of Hannah Arendt in trying to understanding the specific complexity of the extent of human responsibility and moral evil. Before speaking of Arendt, the following passage by Elie Wiesel depicts the true horrors of a very man-made evil. The Holocaust was not simply the work of individuals, but whole institutions which supported the killing process. It was this evil that gave rise to most of Arendt's own reflections:

> Not far from us, flames, huge flames, were rising from a ditch. Something was being burned there. A truck drew close and unloaded its hold: small children. Babies! Yes, I did see this with my own eyes. Children thrown into the flames (is it any wonder that ever since then, sleep tends to elude me) . . . Never shall I forget that night, the first night in camp that turned my life into one long night seven times sealed.
>
> Never shall I forget that smoke. Never shall I forget the small faces of the children whose bodies I saw transformed into smoke under a silent sky. Never shall I forget those flames that consumed my faith for ever.[14]

In 1951 Arendt had written the *Origins of Totalitarianism* where her assessment of the regimes of Hitler and Stalin had led her to conclude that the evil of these regimes was a particularly twentieth-century phenomenon, a 'radical'

12 Peter Dews, '"Radical Finitude" and the Problem of Evil', in María Pía Lara, ed., *Rethinking Evil*, London: University of California Press Ltd, 2001, pp. 46–7.

13 Maeve Cook, 'Moral Evil and Moral Identity', in Maria Pia Lara, ed., *Rethinking Evil*, London: University of California Press Ltd, 2001, p. 115.

14 Elie Wiesel, *Night*, London: Penguin, 2006, pp. 32 and 34.

evil that was 'beyond the pale of human sinfulness'.[15] In 1961, however, Arendt attended the trial of Adolf Eichmann, a Nazi war criminal, in Jerusalem. This was an encounter that brought a perplexingly different dimension to her concept of evil. Arendt saw that evil deeds even committed on a gigantic scale could not necessarily be traced to a demonic person or ideology, and that there was an ordinariness in people like Eichmann who had committed huge atrocities; this led her to conclude that there was indeed a 'banality of evil'.[16] Doing terrible, degrading, and unspeakable things become normalised and systemised into everyday life. In her discussion of this banality, Arendt did not impute evil to the actual character of individuals. In responding to criticisms of her views in *Eichmann in Jerusalem*, Arendt wrote:

> It is indeed my opinion now that evil is never 'radical,' that it is only extreme and that it possesses neither depth nor any demonic dimension. It can overgrow and lay waste the whole world precisely because it spreads like a fungus on the surface. It is 'thought-defying' as I said because thought tries to reach some depth, to go to the roots and the moment it concerns itself with evil it is frustrated because there is nothing. That is its 'banality.' Only the good has depth and can be radical.[17]

In the Judaeo-Christian narrative on the moral approach to evil, the story of Job's suffering has led philosophers to question why the good and just should suffer and, more broadly, to understand evil as undeserved suffering. Paul Ricoeur wrote:

> The book of Job occupies its place in world literature primarily because it takes responsibility for the lamentation which has become a complaint, and for the complaint elevated to the status of a challenge. Taking as the hypothesis of the fable the condition of a righteous sufferer, a just man without faults who is subjected to the worst possible trials, it elevates the internal debate within wisdom to the level of a powerfully argued dialogue between Job and his friends, spurred on by the discord between moral evil and evil as suffering. But the book of Job perhaps moves us even more by the enigmatic and possibly deliberately ambiguous character of its conclusion. The final theophany does not give any direct reply to Job's personal

[15] Hannah Arendt, *The Origins of Totalitarianism*, New York: Harcourt, Brace & Co., 1951, p. 459. It was Immanuel Kant who first used the expression 'radical evil' in his *Religion within the Limits of Reason Alone*, trans. Theodore M. Greene and Hoyt H. Hudson, New York: Harper Torchbooks, 1960. Kant wrote that evil lay in man's freedom and the wickedness of human nature.

[16] Hannah Arendt, *Eichmann in Jerusalem: A Report on the Banality of Evil*, New York: Penguin Books, 1994.

[17] For more on this quote, see Henry E. Allison, 'Reflections on the Banality of Radical Evil', in Maria Pia Lara, ed., *Rethinking Evil*, London: University of California Press Ltd, 2001 p. 86.

> suffering; the speculation remains open in several directions: the vision of a creator with unfathomable designs, of an architect whose measurements are incompatible with human fortunes, can suggest that the consolation is differentiated eschatologically, that the complaint is out of place and inopportune, in respect of a God who is master of good and evil.[18]

Staying with the criticism of the fundamental Christian story, the French social theorist Jean Baudrillard imputes blame to God for the entire history of human wrongdoing and humiliation where God himself is the manipulator, 'in league with the principle of evil'. He writes:

> He who created the world and, as a result, took upon himself an infinite debt, and who has been constantly passing that debt onto mankind, the entire history of which since then is one of wrongdoing. And worse: to that enforced guilt he added humiliation. For mankind is faced with the impossibility of asking restitution and wiping away the debt. Being unable to take up the challenge it has to humble itself and give thanks. It is at this point that God chose to cancel the debt himself by sending his beloved son to sacrifice himself on the cross. He pretends to humble himself, and in so doing, inflicts an even greater humiliation on humanity by making it conscious of its impotence.[19]

Baudrillard laments that instead of taking advantage of the death of God to be free of this debt, human beings have deepened this debt.[20] Slavoj Žižek contests the traditional account of good and evil, the relationship between mortality and immortality where immortality is linked to the good and mortality to evil. He wrote that what makes us good is awareness of our immortality, God, our soul, 'while the root of evil is the resignation to our mortality'.[21] He presents an alternative:

> What if one wages the hypothesis that the primordial immortality is that of evil: evil is something which threatens to return forever, a spectral dimension which magically survives its physical annihilation and continues to haunt us. This is why the victory of good over evil is the ability to die, to regain the innocence of nature, to find peace in getting rid of the obscene infinity of evil . . . This is why Christ had to die – pagan gods who cannot die are embodiments of obscene evil.[22]

18 Ricoeur, *Evil*, pp. 44–5.
19 Jean Baudrillard, *The Intelligence of Evil or the Lucidity Pact*, trans. Chris Turner, Oxford: Berg, 2005, pp. 156–7.
20 Baudrillard, *Intelligence*, p. 157.
21 Slavoj Žižek, *Violence*, London: Profile Books, 2009, p. 56.
22 Žižek, *Violence*, p. 56.

In short, Western and Christian approaches to evil have been varied in their arguments for the existence of a good God, a manipulative God, human agency to act freely and the dilemma of natural evil, even eternal evil. Much of the depth in the Christian understanding of moral evil emerges through its understanding of human action and existential reality. Complex arguments about the nature of God and the nature of man go together. In Christianity the freedom of the human will is metaphysically necessary for the possibility of choice so that the very existence of freedom includes the option that evil could be chosen.[23] Many of these concepts have been reflected in the free will defence.

Islamic theology, both classical and modern, has been less occupied with this subject than its Christian counterpart. It could be argued that for the most part Sunnī theologians generally denied that humans have the freedom to act. Furthermore, while free will was understood as a necessary corollary for the power to choose good, and for some, reflected ultimately on a God who is good, it is very difficult to be exact about any ontological definition of a word like evil in Islam. The variety of words in the Qur'ān and later Islamic traditions to encompass the sense of human wrongdoing and human erring do not in themselves contain anything similar to the depth of differing but related views of terrible human actions and terrible human suffering that have occupied the minds of Christian and Western theologians and philosophers. With the exception of a few medieval thinkers, the issue of evil was not approached directly but rather subsumed within the larger discussions around the unity of God and the goodness of God. A dominant theme in Ṣūfī literature was to argue that there is really nothing in existence except God. God was the only Absolute (*ḥaqq*), the only manifest truth, and evil was really a name for not-being:

> The Beloved takes on so many different forms
> His beauty expresses itself in varied artistry
> Multiplicity is there to heighten the charm of Unity
> The one delights to appear in a thousand garbs
> The same idea has been referred to in the verse.[24]

Schuon also speaks of God causing evil not *qua* evil but indirectly as a fragment of a 'greater good':

> Every evil is a 'part' and never a 'whole'; and these negations or fragmentary privations which are the various forms of evil are inevitable owing to the fact

[23] For more detailed arguments on the subject see M. McCord Adams and R. Merrihew Adams, eds., *The Problem of Evil*, Oxford: Oxford University Press, 1990.

[24] Mīr Valīuddīn, *The Qur'ānic Ṣūfism*, Delhi: Motilal Banarsidass, 1997, p. 138. The 'verse' at the end of the quote by Jāmi' is Q 29:44, 'God created the heavens and the earth from *ḥaqq* (from/ in truth).

> that the world, not being God and being unable to be God, is of necessity situated outside God. But from the point of view of their cosmic function of being necessary elements of a total good, the various evils are in a certain way integrated into this good, and it is this point of view that makes it possible to say that metaphysically there is no evil; the notion of evil presupposes in fact a fragmentary vision of things, characteristic of creatures, who are themselves fragments; man is a 'fragmentary totality'.[25]

In both Christianity and Islam the story of human wrongdoing has been the basis for the origin of moral ambiguity or sin in the world. The ideal world or paradise was lost through human desire and must be regained. But even if we use this story as a starting point, however limited, for monotheism's account of evil or sin, the biblical Genesis 3 and Qur'ānic accounts of Adam's creation and Iblīs's temptation differ quite significantly in their account of human wrongdoing and the origin of evil in the world. An example of this is the nature of the forbidden tree itself. In the Bible the tree is regarded as the 'tree of the knowledge of good and evil' or the 'tree of conscience'. whereas in the Qur'ān the tree is the 'tree of eternity and possession' (Q 20:120). Certain exegetical readings of Genesis 3 have argued that the command not to eat of the fruit of the 'tree of knowledge of good and evil' suggests God's desire to keep humanity both innocent and also ignorant of any kind of empowering knowledge. In the Islamic tradition, Adam already had God-given knowledge, and his succumbing to Satan's whisperings is for the specific promise of immortality; Adam finally relents when Satan swears the promise of immortality in God's name.[26] Satan's repeated temptation is to make both Adam and Eve disobey the divine command because his knowledge of what the tree promises is greater than their human knowledge:

> Your God has forbidden you this tree in case you two should become angels or immortals. And he swore to them both, 'I am indeed your sincere advisor.' (Q 7:21–2)

25 Frithjof Schuon, *Dimensions of Islam*, trans. P. Townsend, London: Allen & Unwin, 1970, p. 26.

26 Despite this allusion to immortality, Muslim exegetes were divided over the nature of this tree. Some claimed that it was the tree from which the angels ate so that they could live forever while others say that it is not known whether the tree was grape, barley, or fig. Adam's physical appearance and his feelings of shame at seeing his genitalia are discussed at some length in Muḥammad ibn Jarīr Ṭabarī, *Jāmiʿ al-Bayān ʿan Taʾwil āy al-Qurʾān*, Beirut: Dār al Kutub, 1995, pp. 184–6. Ibn Kathīr gives details of Adam's shame and his subsequent entanglement with a tree (owing to his long hair) as he tries to run and hide from God. God still asks him why he ate from the tree when he had been forbidden, to which Adam replies that Eve had instilled this desire in him. See Ismāʿīl ibn ʿUmar Ibn Kathīr, *Tafsīr Qurʾān al-ʿaẓīm*, Cairo: Dār al-Ḥadīth, 1994, vol. 2, pp. 196 –7.

A similar temptation:

> Then Satan whispered to them, 'O Adam, shall I lead you to the tree of eternity and a kingdom that does not waste away?' (Q 20:120)

Satan's own pledge:

> 'I will lead them astray and I will arouse in them desires and I will command them so that they slit the ears of cattle and I will command them so that they change God's creation.' So whoever takes Satan as a guide instead of God he has certainly incurred a clear loss. (Q 4:119)

Followed by a warning:

> Satan promises them and arouses desire in them. But Satan does not promise them anything except delusion. (Q 4:120)

Satan's temptation of Adam in paradise is one act of deception; but for wrongdoing to prevail on God's earth, it is that Satan has been given a reprieve by God to *continue* leading humankind astray. It is Satan's agreement with God that he be allowed to 'whisper' constantly, to have the freedom to tempt humankind as long as he is able, not as a challenge to God but as a challenge to human goodness and to the goodness of God's creation. The concept of 'whispering' evokes an image of Satan working through subtle deceit and not bold gesture, of playing on the vulnerability of human desires. It is precisely because humankind is free to heed Satan that Satan has the defiant goal of persisting until 'God's creation' is itself changed. Satan himself cannot change God's creation on his own; he needs the weakness and vulnerability of humankind for creation to change. Satan neither owns the world nor humankind, but he does know that we humans have choice and that we are not bound by God to do the good. The assumption here is that creation is essentially good but open to the corrupting passions of humankind. However, as the Qur'ānic account of Adam's transgression is not fundamentally about the 'fall of man', some Muslim thinkers saw a positive ray in the first human act of disobedience. One of the few Muslim theologians of the modern period who has tried to reconcile a good God with the existence of moral and natural evil was the Indian philosopher poet Muḥammad Iqbāl. Iqbāl saw the creation of man as the creation of a being who, driven by desire and passion, would tear away all veils:

> Desire, resting in the lap of life
> And forgetful of itself,
> Opened its eyes, and a new world was born.
> Life said, 'Through all my years

I lay in the dust and convulsed
Until at last a door appeared
In this ancient dome.'[27]

For Iqbāl, Adam's transgression was not a loss and 'not an act of moral depravity: it is man's transition from simple consciousness to the first flash of self-consciousness, a kind of waking from the dream of nature'.[28] In Iqbāl's view, it is not that God desires to keep humankind from becoming more aware but Adam's inherent human impulse is to reach out for autonomous experience and knowledge; his sin is that of being too inquisitive. For Iqbāl good and evil fall within the same whole of creation because both are predicated on God's risk taking, faith in humanity and human freedom to choose:

> But to permit the emergence of a finite ego who has the power to choose, after considering the relative values of several courses of action open to him is really to take a great risk; for the freedom to choose good involves also the freedom to choose what is the opposite of good. That God has taken this risk shows His immense faith in man; it is for man now to justify this faith.[29]

The philosopher rather than the Ṣufi in Iqbal had faith in man's *khudī* or ego so much so that for Iqbāl, man had an independent capacity for his ultimate salvation. The onus is on man, not God. But Iqbāl was also aware of the dilemma that Satan's existence creates for the believer, and this frustration is exemplified in the following quatrain:

Who created the world out of his own self?
Whose unveiled glory does its beauty represent?
You say to me, 'Beware of Satan!'
But tell me, 'Who nurtured him? (*Armaghan-i Hijaz*, 394)

In becoming Satan, Iblīs is an incarnation of error and arrogance, of darkness, but even in this incarnation Iblīs is essentially doing precisely what he was created for; he does not act in his own right but as a divine creation. William Chittick writes:

> Without the powers that Iblīs represents, there could be no moral universe. We could not choose the right, because there could be no wrong, whereby the right could be distinguished. We could not be saved, because there would be no error and loss to define the nature of damnation and salvation. We

27 Muḥammad Iqbāl, *Tulip in the Desert: A Selection of Poetry*, trans. Mustansir Mir, London: Hurst & Company, 2000, p. 26.

28 Iqbāl, *The Reconstruction*, p. 85.

29 Iqbāl, *Reconstruction*, p. 85.

> could not enter the light because there would be no darkness to leave. We could not even exist because our existence depends upon the ambiguity of our situation. Our human status is defined by the fact that we hang midway between light and darkness, heaven and earth, spirit and body.[30]

While Adam's eating from the tree is, in Islam, the first human act of disobedience, it has been understood in Augustinian Christian doctrine as the very essence of the Fall, the entry of evil and sin into the world, an evil, inherent and contracted in humanity. Human beings could choose evil which had its origin in satanic temptation. However, Augustine's thinking could not account for the original fall of a good angel in Iblīs. Karl Barth tried a 'radical rethinking' of evil by describing evil as *das Nichtige* – a mysterious power of 'nothingness' which has its grounds in what God did not will in the act of creation. 'Nothingness' is that which contradicts the will of God.[31] Augustine's distinctive approach has nevertheless had a major impact upon Western theological thinking. The point is well made by von Grunebaum that in Christianity evil is both a structural and an accidental element, whereas in Islam evil is an accidental element only.[32] The sense of a 'fall' is also present in Islam but if a comparison must be made, Iblīs's 'fall' through his refusal to prostrate becomes a turning point in his life as well as heralding in a turning point in the lives of all of Adam's progeny. In the Islamic tradition, Iblīs worshipped God faithfully for years before he declined to prostrate in front of Adam and was rejected by God, the very being he had worshipped. The consequences of disobedience for Adam and Iblīs are that whereas Adam is in the first instance ashamed and wishes to hide, he asks for forgiveness; Iblīs merely asks for a reprieve. In the *qiṣaṣ* narratives, there are numerous accounts of how this drama unfolds and Iblīs's complaint and request to God:

> O Lord, you made me covetous. You led me astray and you made me a devil. All that was in your knowledge beforehand. Lord, respite me therefore until the day of judgement.[33]

As Iblīs's new destiny is earth, his future is now intertwined with that of humankind as the 'accursed Satan' vows to whisper temptation to humankind with the sole purpose of leading people away from God. With the creation of

30 Sachiko Murata and Willliam Chittick, *The Vision of Islam*, London: I. B. Tauris, 1996, p. 141.
31 Alistair E. McGrath, *Christian Theology An Introduction*, Oxford: Blackwell, 1994, p. 231.
32 Von Grunebaum, 'Observations', p. 120.
33 Muḥammad ibn 'Abd Allāh al-Kisā'i, *Qiṣaṣ al-Anbiyā'*, trans. Wheeler Thackston, Great Books of the Islamic World, 1997, p. 50.

human beings, Iblīs's fate also changes.[34] The Qur'ān does not explain why Iblīs was given the reprieve he asked for, but Iblīs becomes the personification of the source of both potential and real wrongdoing. Rejected by God, his nature and purpose is based on the intent to destroy goodness, beginning with the sexual innocence in Adam and Eve's relationship. The awareness he arouses in Adam and Eve is not an increased awareness of the divine but that of the profane. Frithjof Schuon expresses this as the passing from sacred love into profane desire:

> Loving each other, Adam and Eve loved God; they could neither love God nor know God. After the fall, they loved each other outside God and for themselves, and they knew each other as separate phenomena and not as theophanies; this new kind of love was concupiscence and this new kind of knowing was profanity.[35]

However one understands this narrative, at one level the Qur'ānic story is essentially a story of struggle but not alienation from a transcendent God. Firstly, evil is not absolute; for only God is absolute and therefore evil, appearing in time, can only be transitory and temporary, limited to this world. Secondly, Adam outranks Iblīs in creation's hierarchy and therefore, despite the power of evil as personified through Satan and his passions, all humankind has the potential to be victorious over Satan, i.e. over their own passions that lead them astray. Al-Ghazālī also uses the personification of Satan to talk of the dual nature of human beings where human nature is aligned to both angels and the devil. In doing evil (*sharr*) human beings are connected to the devil, and in doing good human beings are connected to the angels.[36] Iblīs showed Adam and his descendants the consequences of disobeying God so that they now know their real struggle is a struggle against denial of the divine command. Iblīs himself, in the words of Neil Gaiman's Lucifer, 'can never again be an angel ... innocence once lost can never be regained'.[37] Adam indeed beseeches God to help him avoid Iblīs's snares, to which God's response is 'Stretch forth your hands and call upon me, for I am

34 While Judaism, Christianity, and Islam share some close similarities about Satan, Satan is first mentioned in the book of Job where he asks God whether he can test Job's loyalty to God. In Genesis 3:1 of the Hebrew Bible, Adam and Eve are tempted by a snake, and there is no explicit mention of Satan here.

35 Frithjof Schuon, *Islam and the Perennial Philosophy*, London: World of Islam Festival Publishing Company Ltd, 1976, p. 191.

36 Abū Ḥāmid Muḥammad b. Muḥammad al-Ghazālī, *Kitāb Adāb al-Nikāḥ*, in *Iḥyā' 'Ulūm al-din*, Damascus: Ālim al-Kutub, 1992, vol. 2, p. 2.

37 Lucifer in Neil Gaiman, *Sandman: Season of Mists*, 1992, online quote.

near and responsive.'[38] Evil becomes equivalent to the things we do to ourselves and to one another which go against the wishes of a good God. However, disobedience alone does not lead to perdition, but through disobedience and arrogance, humankind might forfeit eternal happiness for eternal damnation. Iblīs's whisperings are the origin of human wrongdoing, and only God has knowledge of what will happen to those who continue to do wrong, including Iblīs, in the afterlife.

Islamic philosophy has also been concerned with divine freedom in relation to the problem of evil but, despite Iblīs's brief but dramatic entry into the human story, the Qur'ānic narrative is not built around the tragic consequences of any fall but human faith in the face of constant trial and temptation which will be sent by God; Satan's whispers are only part of this dilemma. Thus the Islamic emphasis on evil is built around humanity and evil rather than divinity and evil; for Muslim theology, like most theologies, is anthropocentric. God has created finite beings who have freedom and the capacity to disobey. Through Iblīs, Adam becomes more than what he was, he has an extended vision of himself and is conscious of the inner struggle between desire and good.

In this linear understanding of evil, the mystery of why there is an event that changes human destiny, and whether this is what God had intended through the medium of Iblīs, is not explained; Iblīs just becomes the defying force in our mortal existence. The sense of Adam's 'slip' is further softened by the Qur'ānic claim of Adam's vicegerency on earth. The Qur'ānic verse 'I am placing on the earth a vicegerent' (Q 2:30) already alludes to Adam's destiny in that Adam was created for the earth and not for the heavens. Adam's transgression is not a repeated theme in the Qur'ān, nor is he set up as the origin of all subsequent human wrongdoing because Adam is already forgiven for his 'slip'. Adam must now experience distance from God to understand what nearness was. It is through this distance that the problem of predestined acts and free acts becomes magnified. A Prophetic *ḥadīth* encapsulates this dilemma faced by Adam and all those who followed him:

> Moses said, ' My Lord, show me Adam who brought us and himself out of the Garden.' So God showed him Adam. Moses said, 'Are you our father, Adam?' He said that he was. Moses said, 'Are you the one into whom God blew his own spirit, whom he taught all the names, and before whom he commanded the angels to prostrate themselves, and they did so?' Adam replied that he was. Then Moses said, 'What made you bring us and yourself out of the Garden?' Adam replied, 'Who are you?' Moses told him. Adam

[38] al-Kisā'i, *Qiṣaṣ*, p. 52.

> said, 'Are you the prophet of the Children of Israel to whom God spoke from behind the veil and whom he appointed to be a messenger from among his creatures?' Moses replied that he was. Adam said, 'Did you not find that my slip was written in the Book of God before I was created?' Moses replied that it was. Then Adam said, 'Then why do you reproach me for something that God had decreed for me before my existence?'[39]

The problem of whether God acted arbitrarily or whether this was extreme divine calculation remains unresolved, but lies at the heart of the human condition. In the Qur'ān Adam is forgiven by God, but in his one act of disobedience, humankind becomes destined to a life of moral choices. The existential paradigm in Islam is not that of primordial sin but human capacity to commit all manner of sins. Sin is an act not a state of being, and the Qur'ānic theme of human salvation focuses more on repentance and deliverance from eternal punishment rather than on deliverance from sin.

In this regard the Qur'ān, whilst conveying God's merciful attitude to creation, does not in itself convey the early Christian debate of apocatastasis, a belief which began with Clement of Alexandria (*c.* 150–*c.* 215) but is associated more strongly with Origen (*c.* 185–*c.* 254). This was the conviction in the ultimate reconciliation between good and evil developed from the Pauline statement that ultimately God will be 'all in all' and the Johannine affirmation that 'God is love'.[40] God's love being inclusive would restore all things to their primal state of innocence. In the Qur'ān, there is no ultimate harmony of evil or Satan in God even though Iblīs did not always exist as the 'accursed Satan'. But as Iblīs worshipped God fully before his fall, what is to become of Satan remains with God. At times, the Qur'ān refers to the explicit existence of Satan as a real force working in the lives of believers even if his guile is weak:

> Those who believe, fight in the cause of God and those who deny faith, fight in the cause of evil. So fight against the friends of Satan even though the cunning of Satan is weak. (Q 4:76)[41]

39 This *ḥadīth* has been taken from Murata and Chittick, *Vision*, p. 143.

40 1 Corinthians 15:28 and 1 John 4:8. For an interesting analysis of the history of this controversial belief, beginning with St Clement through to Origen and Gregory of Nyssa, to its echoes in the Eastern Orthodox Church, see Constantinos A. Patrides, 'The Salvation of Satan' *Journal of the History of Ideas*, 28:4, 1967, pp. 467–78. Patrides concludes that the followers of Origen argued that God's infinite love would end the torments of hell for everyone including the fallen angel but that Protestant theologians over the centuries denied the possibility of Satan's restitution. This idea has been revived by the Eastern Orthodox Church and he quotes the Russian theologian Nicolas Berdyaev: 'One day Lucifer will be the most glorious archangel standing next to God; not Michael, Gabriel or Raphael – but Lucifer, after he has finally transubstantiated his terrible darkness into light': p. 478.

41 'Friends of Satan' is referred to as *auliyā' al-shaytān*.

In the Qur'ānic world, the focus is on humankind's wrestling with evil in this world, not the anxiety over the origins or the end of evil. God's wrath warns of a hell and yet his mercy promises a paradise, and this is a paradise without evil. Ultimately, a Prophetic *ḥadīth* does reflect an apocastasis when reconciling those who are damned to hell while still carrying an element of belief in God:

> Those who have merited paradise will enter it; the damned will go to hell. God will then say, 'Let those leave hell whose hearts contain even the weight of a mustard seed of faith!' Then they will be released although they have already been burned to ashes, or plunged into the river of rainwater or into the river of life; and immediately they will be revived.[42]

Faith in God is not an antidote to evil but faith kept alive can counteract all the passion and tragedy of evil. Evil in Islam did not appear in some original drama with its own force and beginnings. It is not illusory but real acts. Evil is not some objective malign force or, as Baudrillard says, 'a deliberate perversion of the order of the world'.[43] The Qur'ān itself does not give any abstract analysis of tragic evil and human loss, but repeats the theme of human propensity to do wrong and the divine essence to forgive.

The Qur'ān uses several words for wrongdoing/evil and many of these words appear to be interchangeable, but perhaps the closest we get to the notion of evil being that which is the opposite of good is contained in the word *sū'*. The word *sū'* occurs forty-three times in the Qur'ān as a noun.[44] The word captures the sense of that which is opposed to good but can be affected by good:

> The good deed and the evil deed are not equal. Repel evil with that which is most good then the enmity between whom and you would be as it he were a dear friend. (Q 41:34)

Below are some examples of how *sū'* or its plural *sayyi'a* have been used:

> When they disregarded what they had been warned about, we saved those who forbade evil but those who were wrongdoers we sent them a grievous punishment on account of their transgressions. (Q 7:165)

> Whoever works evil will be requited accordingly and he will not find besides God and protector or helper. (Q 4:123)

42 Cyril Glassé, *The New Encyclopaedia of Islam*, Walnut Creek, CA: AltaMira Press, 2002, p. 191.

43 Baudrillard, *Intelligence*, p. 160.

44 Brannon Wheeler, "Good and Evil", in Jane McAuliffe, ed., *Encyclopaedia of the Qur'an*, vol. 2. Leiden: Brill, 2002, p. 335.

> Those who have earned evil will have a reward like evil. (Q 10:27)

> Those who are patient seeking the face of their Lord, establish prayers, spend from what we have bestowed for their sustenance, secretly and openly and ward off evil with good, for those people the end is the eternal home. (Q 13:22)

> Evil will be the end of those who do evil. (Q 30:10)

These verses do not in themselves tell us what constitutes evil, except that evil is that which takes you away from God. There is also the strong sense in these verses that evil here refers to moral evil, the wrongdoings which we bring about intentionally, which we do to ourselves or to others. Natural calamities, the enormous suffering of innocents such as children, and physical pain are part of the larger debates on theodicy but do not relate to wilful wrongdoing. Evil or wrongdoing is the opposite of *ḥusn* and *ḥasan*, *ḥasanāt*, *khayr*, and *ṣāliḥ*, all words essentially meaning good, both religious good and worldly good, which are often used in contrast to evil. The word *sū'* is also used in the phrase 'evil design' in describing Joseph's rejection of Azīz's (Potiphar) wife's sexual advances. Joseph himself being one of the chosen prophets is saved from sin/*sū.'* Azīz's wife confesses to her desire to seduce Joseph and admits that the human soul 'incites sin/*sū'*'. The word *sū'* also has the sense of doing wrong to oneself but where seeking repentance from God can wipe out the wrongdoing:

> If anyone does evil or wrongs his own soul but afterwards seeks God's forgiveness, he will find God most forgiving, most merciful (Q 4:110)

This verse is immediately followed by a verse containing a different word for wrongdoing – *ithm*:

> If anyone earns sin, he earns it only against his own soul for God is full of knowledge and wisdom. But if anyone earns a fault or a sin and then throws it onto someone innocent, he carries on himself a false accusation and a clear sin. (Q 4:111–12)

The Arabic word used for sin here is *ithm*. But *ithm* and the collective noun for great sins, *kabā'ir*, are often paired in the Qur'ān:

> Those who avoid the greater sins and indecencies and when they are angry, forgive, those who respond to their Lord and establish prayers. (Q 42:37–8)

> If you stay away from the biggest sins which we have forbidden you, we will forgive you your evil deeds and will let you into a gate of honour. (Q 4:31)

The word *ithm* can also relate to concrete examples of wrongful practice such as eating that which has been prohibited:

> He has only forbidden you dead meat, blood and flesh of swine and that which has been slaughtered to any other than God. But if one is driven by necessity, neither craving nor transgressing, there is no sin for God is most giving and most merciful. (Q 2:173)

The Arabic *dhanb/dhunūb* is also used for sin:

> Say, o my servants who have transgressed against their souls, do not despair of God's mercy for God forgives all sins for he is most forgiving and most merciful. (Q 39:53)
>
> Those who say 'Our Lord we have believed, forgive us our sins and save us from the torment of the fire.' (Q 3:16)
>
> Our Lord, we have heard the call of one calling to faith, 'Believe in your Lord,' and we have believed our Lord. Forgive us our sins and take away from us our evils. (Q 3:193)

Al-Ghazālī also uses this term to define repentance when he says that 'repentance is [repentance] from sins' (*dhunūb*).[45] The Arabic *sharr* or evil is also used often as an antithesis to *khayr*:

> We test you with evil and good as a trial then you shall be brought back to us. (Q 21:35–6)
>
> Upon that day men shall come forth in separate groups so as to witness their own deeds. Whoso has done the weight of an atom of good shall see it, and who so has done the weight of an atom of evil shall see it. (Q 99:6–8)

The Arabic *khatī'a* and terms derived from the root *kh-t-'*, meaning mistake/crime, can also be found paired with *sū'* or *ithm*:

> Those who look for gain in evil and are surrounded by their crimes, they are the companions of fire and will live there. (Q 2:81)
>
> They said 'O our father, ask forgiveness for our sins for we were at fault.' (Q 12:97)
>
> Do not kill your children for fear of want. We shall provide for them and for you; indeed the killing of them is a great crime. (Q 17:31)[46]

45 al-Ghazālī, *Iḥyā'*, vol. 4, p. 2.

46 For a full list of words used in the Qur'ān for some form of human sin/wrongdoing see Muhammad Zaman, 'Sin, Major and Minor', in Jane McAuliffe, ed., *Encyclopaedia of the Qur'ān*, vol.5, Leiden: Brill, 2006, pp. 19–27. See also Toshihiko Izutsu, *Ethico Religious Concepts in the Qur'an*, Montreal: McGill University Press, 2002. Izutsu devotes a whole chapter looking at the vocabulary conveying good and bad in the Qur'ān which he states are evaluative rather than descriptive: see p. 203.

The word *ẓulm* meaning injustice or darkness is also equated with wrongdoing:

> It is they who believe and who do not mix their faith with wrong[doing]. For them there is safety and they are the rightly guided. (Q 6:82)

> When Luqmān said to his son, admonishing him, 'O my son do not take others in worship with Allah. Joining others in worship with Allah is indeed a great wrong[doing].

While the Qur'ān uses several words for different nuances for wrongdoing, it does not provide any clear ranking of what constitutes the worst sins or evils. In Q 17:23–38, a number of acts and commandments are mentioned, some to be observed, such as kindness to parents, humility, justice towards orphans, and some to be avoided as they are sins, for example, adultery, arrogance, and squandering of wealth, where spendthrifts are likened to the 'brothers of *shaytān*'. Evil is also that which leads to futility (*bāṭil*), something that does not benefit anyone. Very often the notion of seeking repentance and asking forgiveness from God follow verses of human wrongdoing. This did lead to a particular theological discrepancy, for there is one sin mentioned in the Qur'ān which God does not forgive:

> God does not forgive that any partner be associated with him. But he forgives anything else to whom he pleases. Whoever associates partners with God has devised a great sin. (Q 4:48)

This command is repeated again in Q 17:39 where the consequences for the sin of associating with God are rejection and hellfire. Yet Q 39:53 (above) tells us that God forgives all sins. The pairing of human transgression and divine forgiveness became a strong theme in Muslim literature alongside the idea of a God who can punish as well as forgive. One particular *ḥadīth* reflects this tension though its overriding image is that of a God whose very essence one might say is forgiveness:

> God Almighty has said: 'O son of Adam, so long as you call upon me and ask of me, I shall forgive you for what you have done and I shall not mind. O son of Adam, were your sins to reach the skies and were you to ask me forgiveness of me, I would forgive you. O son of Adam, were you to come to me with sins nearly as great as the earth and were you then to face me associating no partners with me, I would bring you forgiveness nearly as great as the earth.'[47]

[47] *Ḥadīth* number 37 related by al-Bukhārī and Muslim, cited in Ezzeddin Ibrahim and Denys Johnson Davies, *Forty Hadith Qudsi*, Cambridge: Islamic Texts Society, 1999, p. 116. I have slightly amended this translation. Both *dhunūb* and *khatāyā* are used in the Arabic.

The issue of major sins and human evils was the basis for many of the theological rivalries and tensions between the formative schools of Islamic philosophy such as those pertaining to the Khawārij, the Murji'a, and the Mu'tazila who all held onto their various positions about what constituted a grave sin and whether or not certain transgressions could lead to a believer being expelled from the community of Muslims even if the person continued to have faith. While faith (*imān*) is necessary, it is not the same as good deeds (*ṣāliḥāt*), and the question remains as to how the two are part of a conceptual whole.

These few examples of how evil is approached in the Qur'ān show that evil is simply one of the many translations for a human transgression, a human fault which goes against God's commands. While *ḥadīth* collections do list major sins, it remains uncertain which ones fall into this category and why. The eighth-century Shāfi'ī scholar al-Dhahābī contrasts major sins (*al-kabā'ir*) with minor sins (*al-ṣaghā'ir*), pointing out the difference between *ḥadīth* collections by al-Bukhārī and Muslim that list seven major sins and the tradition from Ibn 'Abbās that says that the major sins are closer to seventy in number.[48] For al-Dhahābī, the major sins are those that have been prohibited by God in the Qur'ān, by the Prophetic *sunna*, and by the traditions of the first righteous generation of the Prophet's Companions. Al-Dhahābī himself does not give any explanation as to why the seventy sins have been graded in this way, but the first sin is *shirk* and the seventieth sin is cursing/insulting (*sabb*) the Companions of the Prophet. Sin number sixty-nine is deception and treachery (*kadī'a* and *makr*). Amongst the examples used to denote deception, al-Dhahābī includes the verse from Q 4:142 alluding to the false prayers of the hypocrites: 'The hypocrites try to deceive God but it is he who deceives them.' Al-Dhahābī cites 'unlawful killing' as the second major sin, quoting Q4:93, but the emphasis of this verse is the unjust killing of a believer only (*mu'min*). Al-Dhahābī then quotes certain *ḥadīths* in which the killing of those who have made a covenant with the Muslim state, namely Jews and Christians, is also forbidden. Interestingly, the third major sin in al-Dhahābī's list is sorcery (*siḥr*). Al-Dhahābī is keen to point out that *siḥr* can lead people to the sin of *shirk* and that although some think it is only forbidden, it actually constitutes unbelief (*kufr*).[49] While most of the legal and moral vices listed in this text are those that one would expect from Muslim tradition, it is very difficult to see what system if any al-Dhahābī has applied to this list of gradation – exactly why are some sins/evils greater than others?

[48] Muḥammad b. Aḥmad al-Dhahābī, *Kitāb al-Kabā'ir (The major sins)*, trans. M. al-Selek, Beirut: Dār al-Fikr, 2007, p. 12.

[49] al-Dhahābī, *al-Kabā'ir*, pp. 23–9.

In al-Ghazālī's *Iḥyā'*, the section on *al amr bi'l-ma'rūf wa'l-nahy 'an al-munkar*, 'commanding right and forbidding wrong', provides a systematic doctrine of duties based on the Qur'ānic verses:

> Let there be one community of you calling to good and commanding right and forbidding wrong; those are the ones who prosper. (Q 3:104)
>
> And the believers, the men and the women, are friends one of the other; they command right and forbid wrong. (Q 9:71)

As Michael Cook says, there is no certainty that the Qur'ānic verses meant what later scholars took them to mean, i.e. the duty of one Muslim to intervene when another is acting wrongly.[50] However, Muslim scholars have for the most part understood wrong and sin as wrongdoing reflected in real acts. For our purposes here, it is interesting to note that after an introduction to the concept of wrongdoing, throughout most of his analysis al-Ghazālī retains the use of the word *munkar* for wrongdoing, rather than explore some abstract notion of evil or sin. He does however use the word *ithm* at the beginning of this whole treatise:

> God says, help each other in righteousness (*birr*) and piety (*taqwa*) and do not help in sin (*ithm*) and enmity (*'udwan*).[51]

Wrongdoing is specific things such as the following:

> If someone sees a young man or a mad man drinking wine, he must pour his wine out and forbid him just as if he sees a mad man commit adultery with a mad woman or with someone infatuated, he must forbid him from it.[52]

For al-Ghazālī, most wrongdoing is about wrongful acts that must be advised against or stopped. There is little understanding of forbidding wrong as meaning anything outside forbidding wrongful or unlawful acts. Evil therefore is not an existential state, it is the things we do, even when we have faith. We can always repent of wrongful acts because we as individuals are responsible for our acts. Perhaps one *ḥadīth qudsī* more than any other reflects this:

> God has written down the good deeds and the evil deeds. Then he explained it thus, 'He who has intended a good deed and has not done it, God writes it down with himself as a full good deed, but if he has intended it and done it,

[50] Michael Cook, *Forbidding Wrong in Islam*, Cambridge: Cambridge University Press, 2003, p. 3. This book is a condensed reflection of Cook's massive work, *Commanding Right and Forbidding Wrong in Islamic Thought*, Cambridge: Cambridge University Press, 2001.

[51] al-Ghazālī, *Iḥyā'*, vol. 2, p. 270.

[52] al-Ghazālī, *Iḥyā'*, p. 285.

> God writes it down with himself as from ten good deeds to seven hundred times or many times. But if he has intended an evil deed and has not done it, God writes it down with himself as a good deed, but if he has intended it and done it, God writes it down as one evil deed.'[53]

This *ḥadīth* illustrates that while good intention can count as a good deed, evil must be acted upon to count as evil, not merely intended or thought. The Islamic approach to evil and sin is based largely on a fundamental premise – that humankind has been made aware of evil and sinful acts through successive divine revelations and prophecies. God is a just God who has always sent prophets and revelation to humanity to give humanity the ability to discern between good acts and bad acts. Evil as an abstract entity has no place in the Qur'ānic vision of human destiny. The purpose of creation is to worship God by making the right choices in faith, morality, and human relationships; those who are righteous will enter the gates of paradise, and those who have denied God by making the wrong choices could be destined for the torments of hell. Observing the good and abstaining from the bad is essential for the attainment of ultimate salvation, though human repentance and God's mercy are constant reminders of our innate propensity to do bad things and God's power to forgive. Trust (*tawakkul*) and patience (*ṣabr*) must form part of righteous devotion. Humankind should remain optimistic because God is with us and we can all be guided by God if we 'turn to God in penitence' (Q 13:27). Good deeds create a benign earthly order, but are also tied to the salvation of the soul. Iblīs is a symbolic but necessary player in the human quest for salvation since without him there is nothing for intelligence to master. Unlike Adam, ordinary mortals have not experienced creation without evil, creation without suffering, but nor have humans experienced creation without love and joy and beauty.

From this perspective, the Muslim concept of evil or any kind of wrongdoing in Sunnī Islam is opposed to the kind of resignation found in secular existentialism; our actions are determined by individual choice, and they determine our own fate as well as the fate of others. Evil or sin always has a victim. The world is not absurd and a commitment to the good life in this world is our duty to God and to each other. The righteous Muslim cannot recognise himself in the evasion of responsibility that accompanies existential angst and to which as von Grunebaum says, there seems to be no real answer:

> Man is lost in a universe which he has not made and for which he is not made. Whatever direction he takes lacks ultimate justification, good and evil

[53] *Ḥadīth* number 37, cited in Ezzeddin Ibrahim and Denys Johnson Davies, *Forty Ḥadīth Qudsi*, Cambridge: Islamic Texts Society, 1999, p. 116.

are swept together in the grimace of the absurd. By branding it as absurd, the existentialist withdraws his responsibility from his society; the absurdities of its contradictions will be pointed to; but why replace one set of absurdities with another?[54]

However, conscious human effort to make the right moral choices will inevitably collide with the complex issue of God as the omnipotent ruler who determines the fate of all beings (*al qadar wa-l-qadā'*). The question of human free will and divine predestination arose in the second/eighth century by the proponents of free will called the Qadarites largely because of certain Qur'ānic passages that argued both in support of and against human freedom to determine action:

> If God had willed he could have made you all one people. God leads astray whom he wills and guides whom he wills. You shall be called to account for all that you have done. (Q 16:93)
>
> Those whom God wishes to guide, he opens their breast to surrender (*islam*) and those he wants to lead astray, he tightens their breast. (Q 6:125)
>
> It is not for any soul to believe except by the permission of God. (Q 10:100)

The various manifestations of the supreme command of God is crystallised in the earliest Ḥanafī creed that 'what reaches you could not possibly have missed you and what misses you could not possibly have reached you'.[55] Despite the complexities posed by certain Qur'ānic passages and creeds, wrongdoing is conceptualised largely in the Qur'ān as human wilful wrong-doing. But Muslim theologians were not averse to asking a variety of questions about why God allows evil and suffering and, if God alone is omnipotent, whether he alone is responsible for injustice. A history of *kalām* shows that fairly early on, the debate between the Mu'tazila and the predestinarians concentrated on the question of who creates man's acts – God or man.[56] As is well known in the history of Islamic thought, the Mu'tazila, who were proponents of human free will, wished to defend God's justice. They could not accept that God would create man to worship him and then punish man by making him an unbeliever; this would amount to defective justice. The Ash'arites got round the problem of preserving complete justice and complete omnipotence by developing the theory of *kasb* (acquisition) where God creates

54 Von Grunebaum, 'Observations', p. 132.

55 A. J. Wensinck, *The Muslim Creed*, Cambridge: Cambridge University Press, 1932, pp. 103 and 107–9.

56 For a good overview see Harry A. Wolfson, *The Philosophy of the Kalām*, Cambridge: Cambridge University Press, 1976.

man's actions and humankind appropriates them, thereby becoming responsible for individual actions.[57] For al-Ash'ari, God is the sole creator of man's actions. God creates in man his actions, his movements; but that does not mean that God himself is performing the action. God creates appropriation (*kasb*) in man and is its real agent but the act is performed in man, not in God. While it is not within the scope of this chapter to analyse in detail the philosophical and theological nature of the concept of *kasb*, in one of his most famous works, the *Kitāb al-Luma'*,[58] al-Ash'ari is asked specifically about the question of evil and who creates evil. The word used here for evil is *sharr*:

> Which is better, the good or he from whom good comes forth?
>
> He from whom the good comes forth and to whom is better than the good.
>
> Which is worse, evil or he from whom evil comes forth?
>
> He from whom evil comes forth making him unjust thereby and that is worse than the evil.
>
> Do you say that evil (*sharr*) is from God?
>
> Some of our companions say that all things are from God as a whole without saying of evil specifically that it is from God. I say that evil is from God in the sense that he creates it for another, not for himself.[59]

Later on in this polemic al-Ash'arī uses the word *qabīḥ* to convey the sense of that evil or that which is morally bad.

> Is God free to inflict pain on infants in the next life?
>
> God [is free] can do that and if he does that he is just. In the same way whenever he inflicts a never ending punishment for a finite wrong and some living things to others and blesses and not others and creates some with the knowledge that they will not believe, that is all just on his part. It would not be morally bad (*aqbaḥ*)[60] on God's part to create them in perpetual, painful punishment. It would not be shameful on God's part to inflict pain on the

[57] For an examination of al-Ash'arī's theory of *kasb* see Binyamin Abrahamov, 'A Re-examination of al-Ash'ari's Theory of "Kasb" According to "Kitāb al-Luma"', *Journal of the Royal Asiatic Society of Great Britian and Ireland*, 2, 1989, pp. 210–21. In his analysis, Abrahamov also draws on Frank's much earlier article on created causality in al-Ash'ari: see Richard M. Frank, 'The Structure of Created Causality According to al-Ash'arī An Analysis of the *Kitāb al-Luma'*, pars 82–164', *Studia Islamica*, 25, 1966, pp. 13–75.

[58] 'Alī ibn Ismā'īl Abū al-Ḥasan al-Ash'arī, *Kitāb al-Luma' fī al-Radd 'ala Ahl al-Zaygh wa'l-Bida': The Theology of Al-Ash'ari*, ed. and trans. Richard Joseph McCarthy, Beirut: Imprimerie Catholique, 1953.

[59] al-Ash'arī, *al-Luma'*, p. 47 of the Arabic. I have amended the translations where appropriate. Al-Ash'arī says that good and evil are by God's decision also in his treatise the *Ibana*, p. 241 in *Kitāb al-Luma'*.

[60] *Qabīh* can mean disgraceful, shameful, vile, or bad.

> believers and to allow the unbelievers to enter the gardens. We only say that he will not do this because he has told us that he will punish the unbelievers and lying in his knowledge [information] is not permitted.
>
> The proof that whatever he does it is for him to do is that he is the king, not subject to anyone. There is no one above him who can permit, or command or be an obstacle or prohibit or decree for him or fix boundaries for him. If this is so nothing can ever be morally bad from him. If a thing is so, it is only morally bad from our part because we transgress the limits and decrees set and bring about what we have no right to bring about. Since the Creator (*al-bāri'*) is subject to no-one and not under the command of anyone, nothing can be morally bad on his part.
>
> And if it is asked that lying is morally bad only because God has made it morally bad, then the answer is yes indeed and if he had made it good it would be good and if he commanded it, no one can oppose it.
>
> Then allow that God can lie just as you allow that God can command lying.
>
> Not everything which God can command can describe him. Do you not see that he has commanded us to pray, to submit and to move but he cannot pray, or submit or move for that is impossible for him. Thus he cannot lie not because it is shameful but because it is impossible for him to lie. So he cannot be described by the power to lie just as he cannot be described by the power to move or be ignorant.[61]

Al-Ash'arī's God is the creator of everything including evil but cannot be defined by that which is bad or unjust in the world. The focus of his theology was not so concerned with the consequences of human moral choices associated with any kind of freedom to act as with attributing complete omnipotence to God. From the arguments in the *Luma'*, the presence of evil and suffering in the world does not reflect negatively on a good God. Lying is bad only because God has declared it so, and for al-Ash'arī God can create lying for others but not lie himself, as this is an imperfection. The question still remains, 'why is it bad?' It would seems that in declaring that lying is bad only because God has declared it to be, God does not owe us any explanations. In his assessment of al-Ash'arī's theology, Frithjof Schuon attributes a 'mental weakness' to the intellectual argument of al-Ash'arī in that he tries to humanise the Absolute. Schuon states that 'What, in God is an overflowing of infinity, becomes for the Ash'arites and their like an unfathomable tyranny, at least in certain sectors of their thought.'[62]

[61] al-Ash'arī, *al-Luma'*, p. 73.
[62] Schuon, *Islam*, p. 129.

Albert Hourani gives an overview of the dominant discourse of 'theistic subjectivism' in the Muslim world in which he states that the theory of good and evil, justice and injustice are "defined entirely by reference to the commands of God as revealed to man in the *sharīʿa*".[63] Hourani writes that it was largely Ashʿarite thinking that prevailed and in which

> human acts are right only when God commands man or recommends to him to do them, without having any intrinsic character which would make them good in themselves.[64]

He argues that the main argument was 'simply the authority of scripture . . . and though this may not seem to us very convincing philosophically, it was hard to stand up in medieval Islam and argue that "good" had a meaning independent of scripture'.[65] Ibn Rushd was one of the many Muslim scholars who tried to use both reason and scripture to reconcile evil with an omnipotent and good God; he rejected this opinion in his work *Manāḥij*:

> This is extremely disgraceful because in that case there would be nothing which is good (*khayr*) in itself and nothing which is evil (*sharr*) in itself; but it is self-evident that justice is good and that injustice is evil. And associating [other gods] with God would not be unjust or wrong (*ẓulm*) in itself but only from the standpoint of the Law, and if the law had prescribed an obligation to believe in an associate of God, then that would have been just.[66]

However, George Hourani elaborates the notion of good as something that could be independent of divine command:

> Patience, gratitude, sincerity etc have their own moral content which can be understood by intelligence and cultivated by the good person . . . One reason why no certain conclusion can be attained is that the Qur'ān couples so closely two qualities of the good person; belief in God and doing right. The phrase 'those who believe and do right acts' is constant. Is it only those who believe that do right acts? If so, do they always do them? And when they do them, does it always follow from their belief and more particularly, from guidance derived from revelation? Or, on the contrary, does man start with right action and proceed from there inevitably to belief? We do not know the Qur'ān's answers to these questions, because it never faces them.[67]

[63] Albert Hourani, 'Averroes on Good and Evil', *Studia Islamica*, 16, 1962, pp. 13–40.
[64] Hourani, 'Averroes', p. 16.
[65] Hourani, 'Averroes', p. 16.
[66] Hourani, 'Averroes', p. 18.
[67] George F. Hourani, 'Ethical Presuppositions of the Qur'an', *The Muslim World*, 70, January 1980, pp. 1–28.

One of the most systematic attempts to defend God's omnipotence and attribute moral responsibility to humankind is contained in the famous letter of Ḥasan al-Baṣrī (AD 642–728) to the caliph 'Abd al-Mālik. In his recent work on early Islam, Suleiman Mourad refutes the view that the letters attributed to Ḥasan are actually his.[68] However, for the purpose of our discussion here, it is the content rather than the authorship of the letter that is of interest. The caliph had challenged Ḥasan al-Baṣrī to defend his particular theory on predestination (*qadar*) and Ḥasan's letter is a response to the caliph explaining the different meanings of *qadar*. The letter is premised on the basic idea of *qadar* in that it is essentially about the role and responsibility of God in human destiny.[69] Throughout the letter Ḥasan's aim is to reconcile God's *qadar* or determinism with the moral and religious freedom of human beings. God does not wrong man and since God had created man to worship him, he would not therefore predetermine disobedience and then punish man. The evidence for this defence is taken from revelation itself, and Ḥasan argues two fundamental principles, namely that God has created humanity to worship him and that evil does not come from God. In one passage from the letter, Ḥasan writes about the prophets themselves who never attributed their errors to God but took responsibility for their own wrongdoings:

> Consider our father Adam who was the most truthful of those who set an example, who said, when defying his Lord "We have wronged ourselves and if you do not forgive us and have mercy upon us, we shall be amongst those lost" (Q7:23). He did not say, "Your determination and your power." Likewise Moses said when he killed someone, "This is of Satan's work; he is a misleading, manifest enemy." He said, "My Lord I have wronged myself. Forgive me!" So God forgave him (Q28: 15–16). Moses said, "This is the responsibility of Satan and the ignorant while this is from the actions of the Merciful."[70]

In 1935, Julian Oberman's article analysing this letter criticises the letter for being 'void of the rationalism and schematism of the Mu'tazilites' for whom it was reason (*'aql*) that bound God to allow humankind freedom of action

68 See Suleiman A. Mourad, *Early Islam between Myth and History*, Leiden: Brill, 2006. After a lengthy analysis, Suleiman concludes, 'The corpus of anecdotes and letters attributed to al-Ḥasan is often contradictory and irreconcilable. His significance therefore is not to be measured by his historical role in the formation of particular trends, but rather by the ongoing expansion of his posthumous legacy as one of the founding fathers of Islam and the role that that legacy played in the legitimization of views and practices of competing religious movements': p. 240.

69 See Michael Schwarz, 'The Letter of Ḥasan al -Baṣrī', *Oriens*, 20, 1967, pp. 15–30.

70 This extract is a translation taken from Andrew Rippin and Jan Knappert, *Textual Sources for the Study of Islam*, Chicago: Chicago University Press, 1990, pp. 115–21.

and reason that required that human beings discriminate between good and evil regardless of revelation.[71] Obermann states that this particular treatment of '*qadar* is theocentric rather than homocentric', in that revelation alone is used to argue for the freewill defence.[72]

It would be right to conclude that the themes and discussions around the existence of evil in Islam are largely familiar problems for those who hold onto a conception of a good and omnipotent God. However, those Muslim thinkers who did consider human wrongdoing did not look at evil as the ultimate tragedy of creation, and human suffering as an abstract entity in the world; they did not speak of evil in some pure state because it seems, if not impossible, extremely difficult to define pure evil. Rather, they tried to reconcile the inevitability of human wrongdoing and the necessity of divine forgiveness in the face of a merciful and benign creator. Evil is problematic but wrongdoing definitely exists and wrongdoing is relational as it harms others and ourselves. Yet wrongdoing is closely associated with a God who forgives, and wants to forgive, for an unforgiving God is not God. The rationale for their thinking was that human society would suffer if it was not based on the rationale and goodness of divine laws and ethical directives. It was the function of Islamic law to eventually elaborate and work out the nuances of this obedience. But the nature of evil is fundamentally the wrong that we do to ourselves as well as to others. It can be manifest in a single act or a chain of acts. Either way, we act knowingly and freely. Evil is seen largely through the prism of human choice rather than divine damnation. Minus the tragic element of sin as evident in much of Christian theological reflection, evil loses its transcendental dimension and can appear to be reduced to the more prosaic, even the banality of human wrongdoing. But in Islamic thought, wrongdoing is corrosive, futile for the individual and society, and leads ultimately to an evasion of moral responsibility. It is through the possibility of wrongdoing, repentance, and subsequent discernment that humankind hopes to attain moral growth. Once committed, wrongdoing, wilful or inflicted, has the capacity to transform us into something better.

Bennett argued that many human qualities that we value most could hardly be possible without evil or the strong possibility of evil.[73] While he does not advocate that evil must be alive for us to develop the deeper levels of all virtues, he argues in relation to suffering:

[71] Julian Obermann, 'Political Theology in Early Islam: Ḥaṣan al-Basri's Treatise on Qadar', *Journal of the American Oriental Society*, 55:2, June 1935, pp. 138–62.

[72] Obermann, 'Political Theology', p. 156.

[73] Bennett, 'The Problem of Evil', p. 416.

> The greatest mystery of all is why some souls are able to transmute evil into good in their own lives and others are shattered by it. But when we have said all this, it still remains true that without suffering life is lived on a superficial level; we become self-sufficient, complacent and proud. Suffering deepens and strengthens every quality we have. It can purify us from preoccupation with trivial things. It raises love and friendship to the highest level. It forces us out of ruts and often gives life a new beginning.[74]

Why evil exists alongside an infinitely good God, and whether some evil is necessary, were not questions that occupied the world-view of the majority of Muslim thinkers. Why humans have to suffer natural disasters or be subject to unbearable pain are issues neither dissolved nor resolved within the arguments for an omnipotent and just God. While much of Islamic thought tried to absolve God of actively creating evil deeds and leading people astray, it recognised that human wrongdoing is part of the divine plan and that God has a stake in both the good that we do and the wrong that we do. There is no romanticising of evil in Islam. Human beings are part of the natural order and live with the struggle of choosing right over wrong for most of their lives. In this pursuit of the good life God's revelation guides but human conscience has always been vulnerable from the time of Adam. Adam's story is also the story of Iblīs who becomes Satan through disobedience. Yet does Satan exist or is it us human beings who keep the concept of Satan alive through our own wrongdoing? Doing wrong is an activity not a passive state of being. The sense of Satan standing back as we human beings reflect power, greed, and beauty in his name is encapsulated in a short tale, *These Are My Friends* by Paul Coelho:

> 'The reason the king is so powerful is because he's made a pact with the devil,' a very devout woman told the boy in the street and he was intrigued. Some time later, when he was travelling to another town, the boy heard a man beside him remark, 'All this land belongs to the same man. I'd say the devil had a hand in that.' Late one summer afternoon, a beautiful woman walked past the boy. 'That woman is in the service of Satan', cried a preacher angrily. From then on the boy decided to seek the Devil out and when he found him, he said, 'They say you can make people powerful, rich and beautiful.' 'Not really,' replied the devil. You've just been listening to the views of those who are trying to promote me.'[75]

There may not be a devil but there is a God. He may be utterly transcendent, but in order for humankind to make some sense of our relationship with him we

[74] Bennett, 'The Problem of Evil', p. 417.
[75] Paul Coelho, *Like the Flowing River*, London: HarperCollins, 2007, p. 75.

have to be able to make some judgement on his being. The believer acts knowing that God does not completely transcend human standards of good and evil, for what is wrong on earth is also wrong in the heavens; but neither can God be confined only to the human moral perspective. Human beings may try to understand God's ways but it is God alone who judges human beings. The story of Adam's 'slip' is not a story of alienation, a story of a remote past which has no relevance in our life; it is the story of the mixed blessings of human freedom and the capacity in every human being to do wrong but also to do right. God's forgiveness of Adam should not create a theology of false optimism in Islam but emphasise that the believer is morally bound by the resonance of the Qur'ānic verse 'To God do we belong and to him do we return.'

6

The Language of Love in the Qur'ān

> He who would know the Secret of both Worlds will find that the Secret of them both is love – Attar.
>
> Before all things, before the creation, before his knowledge of the creation, God in his unity was holding an ineffable discourse with himself and contemplating the splendour of His essence in itself. That pure simplicity of his self admiration is Love, which in his essence is the essence of the essence, beyond all limitations of attributes. In his perfect isolation God loves Himself, praises Himself, and manifests Himself by Love. And it was this first manifestation of Love in the Divine Absolute that determined the multiplicity of His attributes, and His names. Then God by His essence in His essence desired to project out of Himself His supreme joy, that Love in aloneness, that he might behold it and speak to it. He looked in eternity and brought forth from non-existence an image, an image of Himself, endowed with all the attributes and all His names: Adam. He created Adam in His own image, thus the human became the place of His manifestation.[1]

A question I have often asked myself is how did Islam come to be seen as a religion of law and Christianity a religion of love? When I read Christian theology, the word love is manifest in diverse ways and seems pivotal to any understanding of the divine being; God as love and God's unconditional love lie at the heart of Christian thought. In Islamic thought, other than in Ṣūfī literature, the love rhetoric has been virtually eclipsed by the rhetoric of obedience as the discussions around law gradually took pre-eminence in Islam's intellectual heritage as well as in popular piety. Even amongst the

[1] Louis Massignon, *The Passion of Hallaj*, trans. Herbert Mason, Princeton, NJ: Princeton University Press, 1982, vol. 1, pp. 103–4.

Ṣūfīs, systematic theories of divine love did not develop in early Islamic mysticism. There are few works that provide a complete theory of divine love.[2]

In his majestic trilogy on love, Irvine Singer wrote, 'In the philosophy of love, however, I am convinced that every discussion must start with Plato. Courtly love, romantic love, and major emphases in religious love, all take root in him.'[3] Throughout history philosophers and theologians have attempted to define the significance and essence of human love for God and God's love for humankind. The purpose of this chapter is to make some preliminary remarks on the language of love in the Qur'ān with a view to exploring how God's love for humankind is presented in the Qur'ān. Most theistic religions speak of God as loving in some way and, while it is acknowledged that scripture also contains a God who is also wrathful and punishing, it is most often his love and mercy that are recognised as the basis of his ultimate relationship with his creation, in particular with humankind. For most Muslims, the Qur'ān is where one comes to know something of God, for in the written word is contained the divine word. But in Islamic thought, the theme of God's cosmic love has been most poignantly felt through the rich and wide prism of Ṣūfī literature rather than being recognised as an overtly dominant discourse of the Qur'ān itself. Even for the Ṣūfīs, there remained a distinction between how God loves man and how man loves or should love God. Love in its various manifestations is part of the world order, the cosmic order, but there is no particular word that defines the relationship of love between God and man, so the concept of love carries within it the sense of both the divine and the profane. It was left to the exegetes and the Ṣūfīs to debate not only how God loves but also whether love, which implies a need amongst human beings, can be attributed to a perfect God who has no need. Furthermore, not all Ṣūfīs agreed with the conventional dichotomies posed by the distinction between *'ishq-i haqīqī* (love directed to God) and *'ishq-i majāzī* (love directed to human beings). It could be argued that the love verses in the Qur'ān have been interpreted in various ways, that there is no direct teleology between the Qur'ānic verses on love and Ṣūfī love interpretations. A mutual understanding of love between God and man can be inferred from the Qur'ān in a verse such as 'O You who believe, whoever from you turns back from your faith God will soon bring a people whom he loves [them]and they love

[2] For a useful introduction to the love motif in different religious and philosophical traditions see Binyamin Abrahamov, *Divine Love in Islamic Mysticism*, London: Routledge, 2003.

[3] Irvine Singer, *The Nature of Love, Plato to Luther*, 2nd edition, Chicago: University of Chicago Press, 2009, p. 47.

him' (Q 5:54). The emphasis on 'he loves them and they love him' is regarded by many as the focus for the whole of love mysticism in Islamic thought.[4]

Suleyman Derin writes that studying the nature of love is an intricate and complicated endeavour. Love is a phenomenon that falls into the ambit of many divergent disciplines such as psychology, literature, medicine, theology, biology, and so on. He states:

> All these disciplines attempt to define this concept from their own perspectives. To give a few examples, literature considers love as the driving force behind the finest poetry; medieval medical sciences perceives it as a kind of disease; theology sees it as a way of approaching and nearness to God; and in philosophy it is the desire of the imperfect to attain perfection.[5]

When one glances at the Qur'ānic verses that explicitly mention God's love, the expression of this love is varied, situational, often logical to the human mind, but it is one Qur'ānic motif, among many others. The language of love, affection, or desire appears in various contexts but despite the plurality of words that command an affinity between God and his creation, there is no defining moment when God seals his love for human beings. Furthermore, from the human perspective, there is no commandment to *love* God. Unlike the biblical commandment 'You shall love the Lord your God with all your heart, and with all your soul, and with all your mind, and with all your strength' (Mark 12–30), there is no one command directed to human beings to love God in the Qur'ān. When one looks at the verses describing how God loves humanity and his creation, they can appear quite different, even timid, in comparison with their biblical counterpart. And yet, it is these same Qur'ānic verses that inspired the exuberance of Ṣūfī love poetry celebrating human and divine love reflecting all the time the universal longing and the living reality of the love for God and God's love for humankind. My purpose here however is not to draw any systematic comparisons between biblical and Qur'ānic manifestations of divine love or, more crudely put, 'which religion has the more loving God or the more loving relationship between man and God?' I aim to show rather how the vocabulary of love in both scriptures points to two different divine discourses about God and the story of his relations with humankind. The concept of love is far ranging and covers different aspects of human relations, but in this chapter

4 See the writings of William Chittick including *Ṣūfism: A Short Introduction*, Oxford: Oneworld Publications, 2000.

5 Suleyman Derin, *Love in Ṣūfism*, Istanbul: Insan Publications, p. 13.

I have not dwelt on the charitable expressions of love such as social justice, caring for the poor, the widow, and the orphan or extending hospitality to the stranger in both religious traditions. There is however no doubt that these are ethical expressions of the bonds tie humankind to one another and are divine requisites for a just and flourishing society; however, these expressions remain outside the scope of this particular study.

During my many years of teaching Islamic Studies to undergraduates, I have often used comparisons between Christian theology and Islamic theology as a way of inviting students to think of words and their meanings in different theological and scriptural contexts. Using the word theology here is itself problematic, for the word has for most of its life been regarded as a largely Christian discipline in the academy. This traditional understanding of theology does not translate neatly into a scholarly activity for all world religions, including those commonly defined as the monotheistic/ Abrahamic traditions. In 1976 Frithjof Schuon drew attention to this issue in his assessment of the discipline of theology within the Christian and Islamic scholarly traditions:

> Theology does not have and cannot have the same function or the same dignity in Islam as in Christianity. In Christianity it has majestic prototypes in the Gospel of St John and in the Epistles, followed by venerable models in the writings of the Fathers of the Church, including Denys the Areopagite, and on this foundation it gave rise to the great scholastics and, in the East, to the Palamitic doctrine; but theology in Islam has no sacred prototype. Neither the Qur'ān nor the *sunna* contain any such thing, and the first theological attempts met with a categorical rejection on the part of the traditionalists, so that in fact the legitimacy of *kalām* remains open or at least not entirely settled; it would consequently be unjust to wish to compare the two theologies – the Christian and the Muslim – given that their respective roles are by no means equivalent except in a completely extrinsic respect.[6]

Schuon is right to an extent, particularly if one searches for an Islamic theological equivalent to the richly complex Christian doctrines of God. But I understand theology at its simplest level to mean human attempts to talk about God. In doing theology we are attempting to define and respond to God

[6] Frithjof Schuon, *Islam and the Perennial Philosophy*, London: World of Islam Festival Publishing Company Ltd, 1976, p. 144. St Gregory Palamas (1296–1359) was a monk of Mount Athos in Greece and later the archbishop of Thessaloniki. His theology distinguished between God 'as He is in Himself '*(kath' 'eautón*) or the 'divine essence' (*hyparxis*) and 'God as Being' (*ousía*) or the 'Divine Energies' (*dynameis*), the latter being the uncreated powers or acts through which being acts. See William Stoddart, 'Lossky's Palamitism in the Light of Schuon', at www.sacredweb.com/online_articles/sw6_stoddart.pdf.

in some way. God has spoken and we must respond. Scripture is always the beginning without an end. Scripture demands reading and re-reading, it demands interpreting through a variety of voices that continue to give meaning to our relationship and understanding of God. In this way, *kalām*, *falsafa*, *fiqh*, and *taṣawwuf* are therefore all examples of theology. They are all ways of reflecting upon God, his will, and his nature. The intellectual response to God is no less than worship itself:

> For scholars in religious studies, revelation can never be perceived directly as an act of God, or a fact of history. God's self-revelation to a community can only be accessible to scholarship as a historical process, effectively a literary one, and one in which the community partakes creatively. Irrespective of the degree of metaphor discovered in the notion that God writes himself, it is the writings of God's mediators that are available for analysis. Not even of the Qur'ān is it claimed that God dictated, and merely dictated it. God's revelation is not different from the effort of the community to express its understanding of God, and since that (in all its highest forms) is necessarily a literary achievement, it will be subject to the usual conventions of literary type and genre. To know God, it is reading skills that are required. But the act of reading is a creative one: the message depends on the readers' interaction with the text. God is what the reader makes of his (God's) texts.[7]

Even if this passage overstates the 'reading' of God to know God, belief in God demands an obligation to talk of God; silence, even contemplative silence, may not be enough. In this attempt to talk of God we respond to a God who chooses to 'reveal' something of his infinite self in finite time. However we understand revelation and whether God 'reveals' directly or indirectly, he intercedes in human history at some level to communicate with humanity about humanity and about himself. Nowhere is this more explicit than in the famous *ḥadīth qudsī* 'I was a hidden treasure then I desired to be known, so I created a creation to which I made myself known; then they knew me.'[8] The very purpose of creation is for God to reveal himself. For Ṣūfīs such as Ibn 'Arabī and Hallāj this is not because God needs creation in any way to realise his fullness but because God's creative love is so strong that it triggers off the whole process of creation. God's self-identity is timeless, he does not become less God or more God in the act of creation, but something within God inspires a movement of creative freedom. The Qur'ān however, focuses largely on human worship of God as the reason for creation:

[7] Norman Calder, 'Method and Theory in the Study of Religion', *Journal of the North American Association for the Study of Religion*, 1997, pp. 47–73.

[8] Badi'al-Zamān Foruzanfar, *Āḥadīth-Masnavi*, reprint, Tehran: Amir Kabir, 1987, p. 29.

> I created jinn and mankind only to worship me. I want no sustenance from them nor do I want them to feed me. (Q 51:56–7)

In different ways in the Qur'ān, the emphasis on human worship of God remains the principal if not only explanation as to why human beings were created. Ibn 'Arabī however drew a connection between love and worship so that worship of God was not about knowing God or obedience to him, but essentially about loving him. For Ibn 'Arabī, love becomes a universal principle encompassing the actions of all creation, the basis by which all phenomena are explicable. Human beings may not be able to attribute a beginning or purpose to God's love but, he writes,'We came from love, we are created in love.'[9]

Traditional theistic interpretations of God's omnipotence do not place any obligations on either God's essence or his attributes but God chooses to 'reveal'. The most dominant Qur'ānic discourse of a direct engagement with humanity is through God's signs (*ayāt*) in the natural world and God's messengers. God wants to be known, to remind, and to be remembered. Revelation is to be understood as a process of God communicating in the concreteness of events, reigniting in humankind a new awareness of themselves and their relation to the world. In Islam God has done this throughout history by sending messengers from Adam to Muḥammad who all bring the same primordial truth anchored in the heart of humanity. Revelation in Islam sends us back to the unconditional proclamation of the oneness of God. The Qur'ān proclaims God's sovereignty and the truths of the afterlife and the angels; it stresses the world that remains an invisible reality. All the prophets and messengers are chosen above others in their communities with messages and books but they remain human. Their mission is to transform the society around them, but in the process they themselves are never divinised. Revelation belongs to the history of the manifestation of God and is present in the history of those sent by God. Revelation not only communicates the truth of God in himself but the truth of man and of history by telling humankind something different from what it knows. In this way, the Qur'ān sees itself as both the *furqān*, the criterion of right and wrong, and as a historical oral process recalling past history. One particular way of showing this is that the Qur'ān presumes that its audience is familiar with the stories and beliefs in the scriptures of Jewish and Christian communities, and it is within this context that one of the major Qur'ānic themes becomes the continuity of message and messenger in human history:

[9] Muḥammad ibn 'Alī Muḥyī al-Dīn Ibn 'Arabī, *Tarjumān al-'Ashwāq: A Collection of Mystical Odes by Muḥyiuddīn ibn al-'Arabī*, ed. and trans. Reynold A. Nicholson, London: Oriental Translation Fund, 1911, vol. 2, p. 318. Ibn 'Arabī defines God's love for man as *al-ḥubb al-Ilāhī*.

> To every people was sent a messenger. (Q 10:47)
>
> We have sent you inspiration as we sent it to Noah and the messengers after him. We sent inspiration to Abraham, Ismāʿīl, Isaac, Jacob and the tribes, to Jesus, Job, Jonah, Aaron, and Solomon and to David we gave the Psalms. (Q 4:163)
>
> Remember your Lord much and glorify him in the evening and in the morning. (Q 7:41)

The Christian term 'revelation' is complex in terms of a 'manifestation' of God by God. In the Christian theological context, in the person of Jesus Christ the word became flesh and the incarnation became a more technical term, prompted by the prologue to the Fourth Gospel, 'And the Logos was made flesh' (John 1:14). But however one understands incarnation, either literally or as a metaphor, revelation refers to God's presence in the message and life of Jesus. Carmelo Dotoli explains this at the beginning of his book as following:

> To understand revelation as the word of God, means to affirm that listening is a decisive experience, without which existence is incapable of opening itself to the encounter with God and with other human beings: a difficult encounter, certainly, that requires readiness to move and to search but also a seductive one and rich with promise because it is capable of transforming the way of seeing life in its reality if God would not settle in history as Lord of history, he could not be seen as the God free and provident, tender and love of life, close to man and yet totally other from him.[10]

Dotoli ends his book with the following view of revelation:

> The Christian novelty is in the fact that revelation has reached its highest point in the self-communication and historical self-giving of God in the person of his Son, Jesus Christ. It is here that the pretension of revelation is placed: to be the revealer of the promise of God already realized in the Easter mystery but still in the making 'until God has put all enemies under his feet' (1 Cor 15:25). This not-yet belongs without doubt to the project of God, but also to the free decision of man to make his own truth, that is Jesus Christ, whose ultimate and definitive role meets with a reality of recognition that lives in the rhythms of history and its unveiling.[11]

In Islam the Prophetic role of Muḥammad is essential to the transmission of the Qur'ān, and his words and actions, encompassing the *sunna*, are

[10] Carmelo Dotoli, *The Christian Revelation: Word, Event and Mystery*, trans. Cavallo Domenica, Aurora, CO: Davies Group Publishers, 2006, pp. i–ii.

[11] Dotoli, *Christian Revelation*, p. 137.

understood as part of the revelatory process. Although the word became book, the book is not God; the book only provides a glimpse of the various possible natures of God. Yet even to talk of God's nature and thereby God's essence and his attributes posed a problem for speculative theologians in the Muslim world. Were his attributes the same as his essence, and could divine attribute or essence be known to human beings?[12]

In Islam, the process by which God and his will are known is commonly acknowledged in the notion of *waḥy*. While the noun *waḥy* conveys the sense of God communicating with humankind through a process of inspiration, 'Remember your Lord inspired the angels [with the message]' (Q 8:12), it does not capture the full sense of the descent of divine communication. Here, the word *nuzūl*, while not Qur'ānic, captures the sense of coming down or sending down, vital for a correct understanding of the Qur'ānic hermeneutics of God speaking to man.[13] In the Qur'ān only Moses has been singled out as one who spoke directly with God. In all other cases, contact with God has been mediated, and in the case of Islam Gabriel is God's mediator:

> Say, whoever is an enemy to Gabriel, for he brings down [revelation] to your heart by God's will, a confirmation of what went before and guidance and good news for those who believe. (Q 2:97)

But for Muslims there is a prehistory of the Qur'ānic text, between the word which was with God in the *lawḥ al-maḥfūẓ* and the word sent down by God, a 'text to be recited in Arabic and to be read as an Arabic book'.[14] The Qur'ān makes reference to the word that is with God:

> This is a glorious Qur'ān, in a guarded tablet. (Q 85:21–2)

It is the process by which the word that is with God and that is conveyed in earthly form to human beings through the angel Gabriel that Schuon describes as the three hypostatic degrees of revelation:

> In Revelation one must distinguish three aspects, which are first the Eternal Word in God; secondly its specification – on the archangelic level – for a

[12] For a detailed discussion of these themes see Binyamin Abrahamov, 'Fakhr al-Dīn al-Rāzī on the Knowability of God's Essence and Attributes', *Arabica*, T.49, Fasc. 2, April 2002, pp. 204–30.

[13] Stefan Wild, 'We Have Sent Down to thee the Book with the Truth', in Stefan Wild, ed., *The Qur'ān as Text*, Leiden: Brill, 1996, p. 137.

[14] For more on the relationship between the recited Qur'ān and the written text see William A. Graham, *Beyond the Written Word: Oral Aspects of Scripture in the History of Religion*, Cambridge: Cambridge University Press, 1987.

> particular human receptacle; thirdly its manifestation on earth and in time to meet circumstances which while being no doubt providential, are nevertheless human and terrestrial. The second or intermediate degree presents two aspects, one essential and the other specific; thus the Qur'ān having descended to the seventh heaven, remains on the one hand the absolute and the undifferentiated Divine Word while on the other it becomes the specific Divine Order or particular Message. It is in the third degree that the Qur'ān flows into human language and manifests its intentions of perspective, equilibrium, and salvation by means of human contingencies which determine a particular expression.[15]

Revelation is thus manifest in speech. Human beings need speech to communicate with one another and they need speech to talk of God. Yet while religious texts provide a glimpse of the possibility of God and language provides the metaphors of our relationship to him, our language and the limits of our understanding will always remain deficient. The Qur'ān talks of God in a specific language and to a specific time, but God cannot be monopolised by any faith nor imprisoned through any form of language. Human beings respond to God through words and worship but reflection on God can never be exhausted. The Qur'ān itself claims that for all our efforts to talk of God, we will never be able to do true justice to God:

> And if all the trees on the earth were pens and the seas were its ink, with seven more seas to back it up, the words of God will not be exhausted for God is the most mighty, the most wise. (Q 31:27)

Revelation has been mediated through different books and prophets throughout history, including those prophets with whom God has shared exceptional intimacy such as Abraham, Moses, Jesus, and Muḥammad, but revelation is construed fundamentally as messages from God to humankind about the truthfulness of God. History has been a process of disclosures, however veiled, between God and humankind For this reason, revelation must be understood in the wider context of transcendence and immanence.

While a major philosophical theme came to be the absolute transcendence and oneness of God as the fundamental core of Islamic monotheism, Muslim theology from the second/eighth century onwards wrestled with how transcendence could be reconciled with immanence and how God, who does not reveal himself in his interaction with humankind, could be known. How could human beings understand a transcendent God who exists in pre-eternity as well as

[15] Schuon, *Islam*, pp. 62–3.

post-eternity whereas human life, intellect, and perception are all finite? Islam and Christianity have their own historical contexts in which their scriptural texts and their successive theologies emerged. Contexts give some insight into why certain doctrines become more dominant within a community and across religious communities. Much of the interreligious polemics of the eighth to ninth centuries between Muslims and Christians focused on the complexities of the divinity of Christ and the Christian Trinity. Islamic theology has for the most part argued against these doctrines as a corruption of the true meaning of *tawḥīd* – 'he does not beget nor is he begotten' (Q 112:3). The Muslim concept of unity is more concerned with the unicity of God, i.e. God is unique and transcendent in his oneness. The creation of humanity is simultaneous with a given status for humanity, for this is part of the gradual unfolding of the divine plan. But in the act of creation, God himself remains transcendent and untouched. In the Qur'ān at least, human beings carry an inherent dignity and honour conveyed in the very manner of their creation but God's love (*ḥubb*) is not expressed as a reason for human creation. Furthermore, while the divine breath is an essential element in the completion of humankind, it does not explain how and if this makes humanity godlike in any way. This is not because there is no reference to images of God in the Qur'ān but because the dominant message of the Qur'ān is that 'nothing is like him [God]' (Q 42:11). There can be no confusion between the Creator and the Created.

It is worth noting here that while such views about God's transcendence remain dominant, this was not always the case. Theologians and philosophers struggled with God's transcendence, immanence, and anthropomorphist ideas which could be attributed to God. God does not reveal himself to humanity nor does he resemble humanity. In his treatise on God, Baydāwī wrote:

> The first topic is that the reality of God most high does not resemble any other being; that is to say his reality in its total quiddity has no commonality with any other being. This is because if his reality should resemble that of any other being, then the factor by which each of the two natures would be distinguished from the other would be both external to their realities.[16]

Yet, in his conclusion to these ninth–tenth-century debates on the visual conceptualisation of God, Adams writes:

[16] 'Abd Allāh ibn 'Umar Baydāwī, *Tawāli'al-Anwār min Matāli'al-Anzār*, ed. and trans. E. Calverley and James Pollock, Leiden: Brill, 2002, p. 751. The Arabic *māḥīya* has been translated as quiddity.

> The God of 9th–10th-century Sunnism was theophanous and corporeal. It was widely believed that an encounter with the divine inaugurated Muḥammad's prophetic career. Such a God would eventually be replaced by an invisible, non-theophanous deity, as it was in Judaism, but not before making a significant contribution to the development of Islamic orthodoxy, which has shown itself to be remarkably fluid over the years.

In both our beleaguered and our strident attempts to attribute meaning to God and his revelatory process, the theistic religions have developed a common vocabulary of terms where words such as prophecy, salvation, revelation, and the hereafter carry mutual significance and some overlap. In Islam and Christianity, even though these words can mean different things in their respective traditions, many of the dialogical discussions are premised on the assumption that we are talking about the same God, the one God of Christians and Muslims who chose to reveal something of himself through the oral medium of the Qur'ān, and in human form through Jesus Christ. This God is omnipotent, transcendent, and good. He exists and acts as the Infinite in the finite and the Absolute in the relative. It can of course be argued that even within one faith, believers have different understandings of God, his laws, and his will; but there is nevertheless an essential core of creeds and doctrines which point to some agreed idea of God in both religions, an idea in which the majority of believers have an emotional and intellectual stake.

The Qur'ānic God is intimately but not openly tied to the lives of his creation. God retains the element of secrecy of self by speaking only through inspiration or from behind a veil, never revealing himself directly to humankind. The secrecy motif is presented throughout the Qur'ān in various ways; God hides and reveals; God knows the secrets of our hearts but human beings do not know the secrets of God:

> To God belongs all that is in the heavens and on earth, whether you know what is in yourselves or conceal it, God calls you to account for it. (Q 2:284)
>
> And he is God in the heavens and the earth. He knows your secret and your disclosure and he know what you earn [by your deeds]. (Q 6:3)
>
> Indeed he knows what is open, uttered in speech and he knows what you conceal. (Q 21:110)
>
> Whether you keep secret your saying or say it openly and aloud, he knows full that which is hidden in the breasts. (Q 67:13)

The multiple verses that refer to chest (*sadr*) or heart (*qalb*) as the places where secrets lie have as an underlying theme God's knowledge of all things human and human inability to keep any secret in the reality of divine omniscience.

God sees, watches, and hears in the Qur'ān and the sense of his panoptic gaze is encapsulated most eloquently in the *ḥadīth* that '*iḥsan* is to worship God as if you see him for if not, to know that he sees you'.[17]

When God does choose to reveal to his prophets and messengers his secrets or that which is hidden (*al-ghayb*), they speak clearly about this to their communities even though they announce that they are only the bearers of the message; they have no knowledge of the unseen:

> Say, 'I do not say to you, I possess the treasures of God, nor do I know that which is hidden/unseen (*al-ghayb*) nor do I say to you I am an angel. I follow only that which has been revealed to me'. (Q 6:50)
>
> 'If I had knowledge of the unseen, I would have multiplied all good and no evil would touch me. I am only a warner, and a bringer of good tidings to a people who have faith'. (Q 7:188)[18]

This concept of the unseen or the realm of the unseen (*al-ghayb*) is reiterated in the Qur'ān, for God has the keys to the unseen (*mafātīḥ al-ghayb*). But even though God is the unseen who sees all, his love for creation cannot be revealed in its fullness on this earth; it remains veiled.

Yet the question of how Muslims and Christians conceive God's love for human beings remains a fertile ground for theological and ethical exploration. For many Christians, a Trinitarian understanding of God emphasises the manifestation of divine love over the polemics of divine unity. In the Trinity we encounter the essence of divine love in Christianity, for it is here that we see relational love, the loving relationship between the Father, Son, and the Holy Spirit. In this relational love lies the expression of God's love when no creation yet existed. But God's love is also eternal: he is love before the existence of creation; his love is not contingent on creation even if it is given to creation:

> And in this love he has done all his works, and in this love he has made all things profitable to us, and in this love our life is everlasting. In our creation we had beginning, but the love in which he created us was in him from without beginning. In this love we have our beginning, and all this shall we see in God without end.[19]

[17] For more on this concept of secrecy and revelation see an interesting study by Ruqayya Yasmine Khan, *Self and Secrecy in Early Islam*, Columbia: University of South Carolina Press, 2008, chs. 1–2.

[18] The concept of God knowing all things but remaining unseen and invisible himself is maintained consistently throughout the Qur'ān.

[19] Julian of Norwich, *Showings*, trans. Edmund Colledge and James Walsh, New York: Paulist Press, 1978, pp. 342–3.

God's love resides in the fellowship of the Trinity. Christians emphasise triunity to emphasise that God is love and acts freely out of love in this relationship. The focus is on the language of divine love whereby the Gospels reflect on the particular issue of love as the defining element of the Christian faith. In Christianity, God is a God of love; indeed, God is love (1 John 4:8) and God's unconditional love (1 John 4:19) for humanity is what defines him. But as David Burrell writes:

> The precise sense in which God's creating can be an aid to be free will escapes us. Once that life is revealed, then it will be necessary that such a One act freely, out of love, yet the manner whereby that loving free consent to the divine goodness allows it to overflow into creation will utterly escape us. God is free in creating is not for us to know. So the Christian revelation may offer a glimpse, but never a demonstration, of that initiating and sustaining love of God, in whose very current we are invited to participate.[20]

Even though theologians have wrestled with what is meant by 'God is love', there remains in Christianity a fundamental conviction that God cannot be understood outside the pluriform expressions of love. Here God's love is his being and this love, manifested through Jesus Christ, is an active, not static, love, directed towards humanity. It is a love that invites human beings to live in love with one another. God's love is such that God gives of God's own self so that each hypostasis of the triune God gives and opens itself to the others. The eternal love of God and the eternal word of God are linked as reflected in the Johannine Prologue:

> In the beginning was the Word, and the Word was with God and the Word was God. He was with God in the beginning. Through him all things were made and without him nothing was made that was made. In him was life and that life was the light of men. The light shines in the darkness and the darkness did not comprehend it. There came a man sent from God whose name was John. He came as a witness to testify about the Light so that all might believe through him. And the word became flesh and dwelt among us, and we saw his glory, glory as of the only begotten from the Father, full of grace and truth.

This eternal love is ultimately manifest on the cross in the redemptive death of Christ:

20 David Burrell, 'Transforming Love', in Miroslav Volf, Ghazi bin Muhammad, and Melissa Yarrington, eds., *A Common Word*, Grand Rapids, MI: Eerdmans Publishing Co., 2010, pp. 153–6, p. 155.

> This is how we know what love is: Jesus Christ laid down his life for us. And so we ought to lay down our lives for one another. How does God's love abide in anyone who has he world's goods and sees a brother in need and yet refuses help. (1 John 3:16)

Paul also speaks of the radical presence of love in two different ways:

> Love is patient; love is kind; love is not envious or boastful or arrogant or rude. It does not insist on its own way; it is not irritable or resentful; it does not rejoice in wrongdoing, but rejoices in the truth. It bears all things, believes all things. Hopes all things, endures all things. Love never ends. (1 Cor. 3:4–8)

He also admits to being possessed by love and its transformative power, as in Galatians:

> I have been crucified with Christ and I no longer live, but Christ lives in me. The life I live, in the body, I live by the faith in the Son of God, who loved me and gave himself for me. (Gal. 2:20)

While it is not within the scope of this chapter to explore all the biblical reflections on love and sacrifice that have inspired Christian theology, it is worth noting that New Testament writers, while bearing witness to the divine origin of love, drew various conclusions. Furthermore, there was also a concern similar to that shared by their Muslim counterparts to stress the distinct nature of God's love from human love, as God does not need love. In his classic work, *Agape and Eros*, Anders Nygren wrote:

> We cannot speak of loving God in precisely the same sense as we speak of loving one another. Human love includes the motive of enriching and developing other's lives. This meaning is absent from the thought of love for God.[21]

God's love for humankind and human love for God became a central feature of Christian theological speculation. Nygren argued that God's love for humankind is unmotivated, a spontaneous gift, prompted by the very nature of God to love:

> We have therefore every right to say that agape is the centre of Christianity. Agape comes to us as a quite new creation of Christianity. Its sets its mark on everything in Christianity. Without it, nothing that is Christian would be Christian. Agape is Christianity's own original basic conception.[22]

21 Anders Nygren, *Agape and Eros*, trans. Philip S. Watson, New York: Harper & Row, 1969, pp. 94–5.

22 Nygren, *Agape*, p. 85.

For Nygren, God's spontaneous love is for all, not a love merited only by the righteous or those who pertain to godliness; God loves generously and unconditionally. Our value and worth come from God loving us. If God loves us unconditionally, then our love for our neighbour is also unconditional and impartial. Here, Nygren has problems with the Johannine concept of love where one detects a tension between universalist aspirations and community limitations. While a fellowship and intimacy of love can be found in the Christian community's faith in God, Nygren saw in John's neighbourly love a particularistic love, a love for those who share the Christian faith. Nygren writes that love in John 'loses something of its original, all-embracing scope; it becomes love for those who bear the Christian name'.[23] *Agape* cannot become a preferential love, it must retain its universal expression. Paul also felt that his conversion was caused by God's love and identified the theology of the Cross with *agape*. But it could also be argued that Paul placed the love of neighbour higher than the love of God, summed up in the commandment, 'You shall love your neighbour as yourself' (Rom 13:9). In his recent work on love, Werner Jeanrond writes about the ambiguity and at times sectarian tendencies that are also part of the Christian story of love:

> The Johannine discourse on love centres on a particular Christian community's own inner life – including the call to pay attention to those 'brothers' who require help and assistance. The equality of the (male?) members of the Christian community may thus be stressed. However the shift from a love that is actively concerned about all the others now to a love that is primarily directed towards the inner circle of a particular Christian church cannot be over looked. In this community love functions first of all in terms of internal loyalty over against a societal context experienced as threatening. The fact that the Johannine community celebrates God's overall love for the world in the sending of the Son should not mask this narrowing of the community's overall horizon of love.[24]

Whatever the tension between the abstractions of spiritual love and the actual praxis of love, biblical accounts of divine love are linguistically extraordinarily powerful. Such dramatic expressions of love are not explicitly present in the Qur'ān. In addition, the Christian God is not a solitary God. The filial love as expressed in the fatherhood of God is not just a metaphor of an earthly relationship – it points to an eternal relationship that together with the spirit constitutes a threefoldness in God and where salvation has a triune structure. This metaphor has no place in the Qur'ān or in Islamic theology.

[23] Nygren, *Agape*, p. 154.
[24] Werner Jeanrond, *A Theology of Love*, London: T&T Clark International, 2010, p. 37.

The Muslim invocation of God is always accompanied by reference to God's majesty or mercy, but the Qur'ān contains no reference to an intimate relationship as reflected in the concept of 'father'. When Islamic thought refers to any intimacy in the relationship between God and man, it is linked with the maternal, for example, 'God's kindness towards his creatures is more than a mother's towards her baby.' God is loving in being *al-wudūd*, but God's goodness and expression of his relations with humankind do not lie in redemptive love. In Islam, prophets, by virtue of being human, have their limits; it is ultimately God's grace that reconciles humankind to God.

When one examines Qur'ānic verses where love is expressed in the negative such as 'God does not love those who do wrong' (Q 3:57 and Q 3:140), 'God does not love transgressors' (Q 2:190), and 'He will cause people to come whom he will love and who will love him, (Q 5:54), one can be left with the image of a God who draws near to man only when man draws near to him. This reading would imply a contingent and bilateral element in God's love, a love that is seemingly earned through right conduct, piety, or obedience to divine laws and commands. There is also an element of fear implied in obedience, a fear that does not wipe out love but enforces obedience. This is often contrasted with the concepts of Christian grace through Christ, which shows that God's love is spontaneous and has no expectations of us and that faith in Christ replaces or fulfils the law:

> The Law was our guardian until the Messiah came so we might be justified by faith. (Gal. 3:24)
>
> For sin shall not be your master for you are not under law but under grace. (Rom. 6:14)

While Paul's views on the place of law in the ritual and moral life of the new Christian community are complex, a Christ-centred soteriology emphasises God's grace and his unconditional love for all of humanity. God does not just love, he loves unconditionally, for he is love. God's love for humanity results in God becoming man so that man might become God. God sends Christ 'to seek and save that which was lost' (Luke 19:10). God in Christ and the self-sacrificing love of God for humanity expounded in *agape* is a central dimension of Christian faith; Christians who search for this ultimate sacrifice do not find this in Islam. In the Bible, God loves because it is in his nature to love and he must be true to his nature. Love not only refers to the nature of God but as a consequence must therefore be the basis for all human relationships. The double love commandment proclaimed by Jesus in the Gospels of Matthew, Mark, and Luke are central to the Christian belief:

> You shall love the Lord your God with all your heart, and with all our soul, and with all your mind. This is the greatest and first commandment. And a second is like it: You shall love your neighbour as yourself. (Matt. 22.37–9; cf. Mark 12.29–31; Luke 10.27–8)

Despite the absence of similar verses in the Qur'ān, the Qur'ān contains its own images of God's love and mercy and the ethical obligations of human justice. But the fundamental difference is that in Islam neither God's relationship with humanity nor his love for humanity is dependent on self-revelation or self-sacrifice; God remains veiled or hidden. The Qur'ānic discourse on God demands that we turn to God and is replete with a soteriology fixed on divine forgiveness. Human freedom inevitably means human sin but remembrance of God entails forgiveness however many sins are committed. The Qur'ānic verses on love are not concerned with redemptive love expressed through Christ's crucifixion and resurrection; the Qur'ānic story is different. Here, God is near to man but does not become man to show divine forgiveness. Conversely, Pannenberg writes that, for the Christian,

> Faith in Jesus depends on a conviction of the presence of God in him. Only that presence lends the figure of Jesus universal significance.[25]
>
> For the love of God was for Jesus visible in his own mission to proclaim the nearness of the kingdom of God, both because this proclamation is God's offer of participation in the salvation of his rule and above all because it made Jesus' unconditional promise of forgiveness possible.[26]

In both Islam and Christianity, God gives of himself in his power and potential to transform our lives. Thus, love becomes a central feature of the discussions between Islam and Christianity, and the topic of God's love presumes some commonalities in the understanding of God and love as well as acknowledging fundamental doctrinal differences.

In the Qur'ān there are various words used for love which define all aspects of human love and divine love. The most common word for love is *ḥubb*, from the verb *ḥabba*, which encapsulates the different dimensions of human desire and divine love. Here, there is no effort to keep the boundaries between *eros* and *agape* as distinct kinds of love. A persistent theme in the Qur'ān is the reflection on human desire for this world rather than the next world. This is reflected both in human desire to prefer the earthly life and in the desire for the wealth of earthly life:

[25] Wolfhart Pannenberg, *The Apostles' Creed*, London: SCM Press Ltd, 1972, p. 16.
[26] Pannenberg, *Apostles' Creed*, p. 52.

> Those who love (*yastaḥibbūna*) the life of this world more than the Hereafter, who hinder [men] from the path of God and seek therein something crooked. They are astray by a long distance. (Q 14:3)
>
> You love (*tuḥibbūna*) the temporal life and leave alone the Hereafter. (Q 75:20–1)
>
> And you love (*tuḥibbūna*) wealth with a great love. (Q 89:20)

The word is also used for specific things in our earthly life, which we should love and that which we should not love:

> Those who love (*yuḥibbūna*) to see scandal spread among the believers, will have a grievous penalty in this life and in the Hereafter: God knows, and you know not. (Q 24:19)
>
> Fighting is prescribed for you, and you dislike it. But it is possible that you dislike a thing which is good for you, and that you love (*tuḥibbu*) a thing which is bad for you. But God knows and you know not. (Q 2:216)
>
> Yet there are men who take [for worship] others besides God as equal to God. They love them (*yuḥibbūnahum*) as they should love (*ḥubb*) God but those of faith are overflowing in their love (*ḥubban*) for God. (Q 2:165)
>
> Do not think that those who exult in what they have brought about, and love (*yuḥibbūna*) to be praised for what they have not done. Do not think that they can escape the penalty; for them is a grievous penalty indeed. (Q 3:188)
>
> So Ṣāliḥ left them, saying: 'O my people! I did indeed convey to you the message of my Lord. I gave you good counsel, but you do not love (*la tuḥ ibbūna*) good counselors'. (Q 7:79)
>
> O you who believe! Do not take for protectors your fathers and your brothers if they love (*istaḥabbu*) unbelief over faith. If any of you do so, they do wrong. (Q 9:23)

The love for earthly life is reflected in our love for material goods, and also for each other, including those with whom we have close intimate relationships:

> Fair in the eyes of men is the love (*ḥubb*) of things they covet: Women and sons; heaped-up hoards of gold and silver; horses branded [for blood and excellence]; and [wealth of] cattle and well-tilled land. Such are the possessions of this world's life; but in nearness to God is the best of the goals [to return to]. (Q 3:14)

The notion of *ḥubb* is also used to depict different forms of love between people; it can be used to convey false affection:

> Ah! you are those who love (*tuḥibbūnahum*) them, but they do not love you (*yuḥibbūnakum*), though you believe in the whole of the Book. When they meet you they say, 'We believe,' but when they are alone, they bite off the

> very tips of their fingers at you in their rage. Say: 'Die in your rage, God knows well all the secrets of the heart'. (Q 3:119)

Ḥubb also conveys a violent and erotic human passion, as conveyed in the narrative of Potiphar's wife's desire for Joseph:

> The ladies in the city said, 'The wife of Aziz is seeking to seduce her slave from his [true] self. He has indeed inspired her with a passionate love (*ḥubb*). Indeed we see her clearly going astray'. (Q 12:30)

But the word is also used consistently to refer to God's love for believers and for certain qualities among the believers. In this way, *ḥubb* is used frequently to describe God's love and those who receive God's love:

> God loves (*yuḥibb*) those who keep themselves pure. (Q 2:222)
>
> Do good for God loves (*yuḥibb*) those who do good. (Q 2:195)
>
> Say, 'If you love (*tuḥibbūna*) God, follow me for God will love you (*yuḥibbukum*) and forgive you your sins. God is most forgiving and most merciful. (Q 3:31)
>
> God loves (*yuḥibb*) those who are patient. (Q 3:146)
>
> And God gave them a reward in this world and the excellent reward of the hereafter; for God loves (*yuḥibb*) those who do good. (Q 3:148)
>
> God loves (*yuḥibb*) those who trust in him. (Q 3:159)
>
> If you judge, judge with justice between them for God loves (*yuḥibb*) those who act justly. (Q 5:42)
>
> O you who believe! If any from among you turn back from his faith, God will produce a people whom he will love (*yuḥibbuhum*) as they will love him (*yuḥibbūnahu*). (Q 5:54)
>
> On those who believe and do deeds of righteousness there is no blame for what they ate [in the past], when they are God fearing and believe, and do deeds of righteousness, or are God fearing and believe, and are God fearing and believe for God loves (*yuḥibb*) those who do good. (Q 5:96)
>
> The treaties are not dissolved with those pagans with whom you have entered into alliance and who have not failed you in anything, nor aided any one against you. So fulfil your engagements with them to the end of their term, for God loves (*yuḥibb*) the righteous. (Q 9:4)
>
> If two parties among the believers fall into a quarrel, make peace between them. But if one of them transgresses beyond bounds against the other, then fight against the one that transgresses until it complies with the command of Allāh. But if it complies, then make peace between them with justice, and be fair, for God loves (*yuḥibb*) those who are fair. (Q 49:9)

The word *ḥubb* and its derivates are also used for the love that God will not show to humanity. There are a variety of human ills that are not loved by

God. These ills can range from denying God and the rejection of faith to those who waste and squander:

> God will deprive usury of all blessing, but blesses charitable acts with multiple increase. He does not love (*lā yuḥibbu*) the wicked sinner. (Q 2:276)
>
> Fight in the cause of Allāh those who fight you, but do not transgress limits for God does not love (*lā yuḥibbu*) the transgressors. (Q 2:190)
>
> When he turns his back, his aim everywhere is to spread mischief through the earth and destroy crops and cattle. But God does not love (*lā yuḥibbu*) mischief. (Q 2:205)
>
> Say, 'Obey God and his messenger.' But if they turn back, God does not (*lā yuḥibbu*) love those who reject faith. (Q 3:32)
>
> As to those who believe and work righteousness, God will pay them their reward but God does not love (*lā yuḥibbu*) those who do wrong. (Q 3:57)
>
> Serve God and do not join any partners with him. Do good to parents, kinsfolk, orphans, those in need, neighbors who are near, neighbors who are strangers, the companion by your side, the wayfarer, and what your right hands possess. For God does not love (*lā yuḥibbu*) the pompous and the arrogant. (Q 4:36)
>
> God does not love (*lā yuḥibbu*) that evil should be made public in speech except where injustice has been done for God is he who hears and knows all things. (Q 4:148)
>
> O you who believe! Do not make unlawful the good things which God has made lawful for you, but commit no excess. For God does not love (*lā yuḥibbu*) those who commit excess. (Q 5:87)
>
> It is He who produces gardens, with trellises and without, and dates, and tilth with produce of all kinds, and olives and pomegranates, similar and different. Eat of their fruit in their season, but render the dues that are proper on the day that the harvest is gathered. But waste not by excess, for God does not love (*lā yuḥibbu*) the wasters. (Q 6:141)
>
> O Children of Adam! Wear your beautiful apparel at every time and place of prayer. Eat and drink, but do not waste for God does not love (*lā yuḥibbu*) the wasters. (Q 7:31)
>
> If you fear treachery from any group, throw back [their covenant] to them, on equal terms. God does not love (*lā yuḥibbu*) the treacherous. (Q 8:58)
>
> Qarūn was of the people of Moses but he acted insolently towards them. Such were the treasures we had bestowed on him that their very keys would have been a burden to a body of strong men. 'Behold,' his people said to him, 'Do not exult for God does not love (*lā yuḥibbu*) those who exult in riches.' (Q 28:76)
>
> The recompense for an injury is an equal injury. But if a person forgives and makes reconciliation, his reward is due from God for God does not love (*lā yuḥibbu*) those who do wrong. (Q 42:40)

Another word for love in the Qur'ān is *mawadda*, often used to denote affection and friendship between people which God himself has placed:

> You will find the Jews and Pagans strongest among men in enmity to the believers; and nearest among them in love (*mawadda*) to the believers you will find those who say, 'We are Christians,' because amongst these are men devoted to learning and those who have renounced the world, and they are not arrogant. (Q 5:85)
>
> And he said, 'For you, you have taken [for worship] idols besides God, out of mutual love (*mawadda*) and regard between yourselves in this life'. (Q 29:25)
>
> And among his Signs is this, that he created for you mates from among yourselves, that you may dwell in tranquillity with them, and he has put love (*mawadda*) and mercy between you. (Q 30:21)
>
> O you who believe! Take not my enemies and yours as friends, offering them love (*mawadda*) even though they have denied the truth that has come to you, and have driven out you and the Messenger because you believe in God your Lord – not if you have come out to strive in my way and to seek my good will. You secretly show them love (*mawadda*). I know full well all that you conceal and all that you reveal. And any of you who does this has strayed from the straight path. (Q 60:1)
>
> It may be that God will grant love (*mawadda*) between you and those whom you [now] hold as enemies. (Q 60:7)

The word *mawadda* is not confined to any specific kind of love, or love that is specific to any group of people. It is a sentiment that can be granted by God to human beings or which human beings may feel for each other. The noun *wadd* is also used, as in 'On those who believe and do righteous work, God will bestow love (*wadd*)' (Q 19:96) and 'He is the Forgiving, the Loving (*ghafūr al-wudūd*)' (Q 85:14).

> Yet there are men who take [for worship] others besides God, as equal with God. They love them as they should love God (*yuḥibbūnahum ka ḥubb bi-lāhī*). But those who have faith are overflowing in their love for God. If only the unrighteous could see, they would see the punishment. To God belongs all power and God will strongly enforce the punishment. (Q 2:165)
>
> It is not righteousness that you turn your faces towards the East or West. But it is righteousness to believe in God and the Last Day, and the angels, and the Book, and the messengers and to spend of your wealth out of love for him [*'ala ḥubbihī*] for your kin, for orphans, for the needy, for the wayfarer, for those who ask, and for the ransom of slaves; to give prayers and to give to charity; to fulfil the contracts which you have made; and to be firm and patient, in pain and adversity, and throughout all periods of panic. Such are the people of truth, those who fear God. (Q 2:177)

> We listened to him and we granted him Yaḥyā. We cured his wife for him. They were ever quick in doing good works and they called on us with desire (*raghban*) and reverence and humbled themselves before us. (Q 21:90)

The concept of *ḥubb* also occurs in the *ḥadīth* canons and the *ḥadīth qudsī*.[27] The following are taken from Bukhārī's *Ṣaḥīḥ* to convey a range of contexts in which the word love is used:

> Narrated Abū Hurairah, 'God's Messenger said, "By him in whose hands my life is, none of you will have faith till he loves me (*akūna aḥabba 'alaihī*) more than his father and children."'[28]
>
> Narrated Abū Hurairah, 'The Prophet said, "If God loves (*aḥabba*) a person he calls Jibrīl, 'God loves (*yuḥibbu*) so and so Jibril, love him (*fa-aḥbibhū*)' and Jibrīl would love him (*yuḥibbuhū*) and call amongst the inhabitants of heaven, 'God loves (*yuḥibbu*) so and so, so you love him (*fa-aḥibbuhū*) also.' So the inhabitants of heaven would love him (*fa-yuḥibbuhū*)and then the pleasures of the people on earth are made clear to him."'[29]
>
> Narrated 'Abdullāh bin Mas'ūd, "A man came to God's Messenger and said, "O God's Messenger, what do you say about a man who loves (*aḥabba*) some people but cannot catch up with their good deeds?" God's Messenger said, "Every person will be with those whom he loves (*aḥabba*)."'[30]
>
> Narrated Anas b. Mālik, 'A man asked the Prophet, "O God's Messenger, when will the hour be established?" The Prophet said, "What have you prepared for it?" The man said, "I haven't prepared much for it by way of prayers, fasting or charity, but I love God and his Messenger." The Prophet said, "You will be with those whom you love."'[31]
>
> A man came to the Prophet (may the blessings and peace of God be upon him) and said, 'O Messenger of God, direct me to an act which if I do it [will cause] God to love me (*aḥabbanī*) and people to love me.' He said, 'Renounce the world and God will love you (*yuḥibbaka*) and renounce what people possess and people will love you (*yuḥibbaka*).'[32]
>
> God the Almighty has said, 'Whoever shows enmity to a friend of mine, I shall be at war with him. My servant does not draw near to me with anything more loved by me (*aḥabba ilaiyyī*) than what I have made

27 A *ḥadīth qudsī* is generally understood to be a *ḥadīth* in which the words uttered are by the Prophet although they are inspired by God.

28 Muḥammad ibn Ismā'īl Bukhārī, *Ṣaḥīḥ al-Bukhārī: The Translation of the Meanings of Ṣaḥīḥ al-Bukhārī, Kitāb al-Nikāḥ*, Saudi Arabia: Maktaba Darrussalām, 1997, *ḥadīth* 14, p. 61.

29 *Bukhārī, Ṣaḥīḥ*, vol. 4, *ḥadīth* 3209, p. 276.

30 *Bukhārī, Ṣaḥīḥ*, vol. 4, *ḥadīth* 6169, p. 110.

31 *Bukhārī, Ṣaḥīḥ*, vol. 4, *ḥadīth* 6171, p. 111.

32 Ezzedin Ibrahim and Denys Johnson Davies, trans., *an-Nawawi's Forty Ḥadīth*, Damascus: Holy Koran Publ. House, 1976, *ḥadīth* 31, p. 104. Where I have considered appropriate to do so, the translations have been modified slightly.

obligatory upon him and my servant continues to draw near to me with supererogatory works so that I shall love him (*uḥibbahū*). When I love him (*aḥabtuhū*) I am his hearing with which he hears, his seeing with which he sees, his hand with which he strikes and his foot with which he walks. Were he to ask [something] of me, I would surely give it to him; and were he to ask me for refuge, I would surely grant him it.'[33]

The concept of trying to draw near to God evokes God as a God in waiting, a God almost desperate to respond to human longing. He does not just listen to us, he becomes the ears with which we listen, the sight with which we see, the hand with which we strike, and the foot with which we walk.

While the varying notions of love contained in the Qur'ān through the vocabulary of *ḥubb* or *wadd* allude to God's love, these concepts on their own are only a partial reflection of God's relationship with his creation. The love vocabulary compliments that which lies at the core of divine engagement with creation. The fundamental term that allows us a glimpse of God's nature is in the principle of mercy or loving compassion (*raḥma*). The Qur'ān is replete with the vocabulary of compassion as the defining essence of God:

> God the Most Compassionate (*al-raḥmān*)! It is He who taught the Qur'ān; He who created man and taught him speech. (Q 55:1–4)
>
> Say, 'O my servants who have transgressed against themselves, despair not of the mercy of God (*raḥma Allāh*), for God forgives all sins: for he is oft-forgiving, most merciful (*ghafūr al-raḥīm*). (Q 39:53)
>
> My mercy (*raḥmati*) extends to everything. (Q 7:156)
>
> God is truly compassionate and merciful to mankind (*ra'ūf al-raḥīm*). (Q 22:65)
>
> He has at heart that which you suffer, he has care for you, for the believers, compassionate and merciful (*ra'uf al-raḥīm*). (Q 9:128)

Abū Ḥāmid al-Ghazālī (d. 1111), the foremost scholar and theologian of the medieval Islamic world, analyses love in many of his works but presents a systematic appraisal in the *Iḥyā'* in the *Kitāb al-Maḥabba wa'l-Shauq wa'l-Uns wa'l-Riḍā'* (The book of love, yearning, intimacy and satisfaction). Al-Ghazālī focuses on man's love for God. It is an intellectual rather than emotional exploration of love. Al-Ghazālī does not offer any heavy exploration of the Qur'ānic language and concepts on love, though he mainly uses the word *ḥubb*, but begins by describing the mystical states and stations towards God by concluding that the love of God is the highest in rank and the last stage in drawing towards God before repentance and patience. For al-Ghazālī,

33 Ibrahim and Johnson Davies, *an-Nawawi's Forty Ḥadīth*, *ḥadīth* 38, p. 119.

the theory of love is religious and mystical, for it is always directed to God. Love is not a means to God, love is the end station for the acquisition of the love of God is the end. He emphasises that loving God and loving the Prophet are compulsory and that the meaning of faith is the love for God and his Prophet more than anything else. Al-Ghazālī like Augustine stresses that real love is love of God, not love of self. But al-Ghazālī defines a powerful connection between knowledge and love where precedence is given to knowledge– i.e. spiritual knowledge. Without spiritual knowledge there can be no love; the stronger the knowledge the stronger the love because love is not merely an emotion but the highest form of cognition.

But what are the servant's signs of his love for God when obedience to God conflicts with our own desires? Al-Ghazālī admits that we all say we love God but actually love is a very difficult thing. The book is full of traditions that stress this devotion: a desert Arab tells the Prophet that he had not prepared for the Day of Judgement by way of fasting or prayers but that he did love God and his Prophet. The Prophet replies, 'He who loves one will be with him.'[34]

Al-Ghazālī also devotes a whole book to the concept of hope in God's mercy, exploring the therapeutic influences of hope on humankind. Human beings are all too aware of their propensity to sin but hope in God's mercy is dominated by love for God and the awareness that God loves us human beings.

> According to the tradition, when the servant commits a sin and asks God for pardon, God Almighty says to his angels, 'Look at my servant, he has committed a sin and he knows that he has a Lord who will pardon and take away the sin. I testify to you that I have pardoned him.' And according to the tradition, 'If my servant were to sin so that his sins were to reach the clouds of the skies, I would pardon him them in so far as he asked pardon of me and hoped in me.' And according to the tradition, 'If my servant were to meet me with sins the equal of the earth, I would meet him with pardon the equal of the earth.' And according to the tradition, 'Surely the Angel holds up the pen against the servant when he sins for six hours and if he repents and asks for pardon, he will not record it against him and if he does not repent he will record it as an evil deed.' And according to another tradition, 'If he performs a good deed after he has recorded it against him, the Angel of the right hand says to the Angel of the left, "Throw away the evil deed [so that one multiple of

[34] Abū Ḥāmid Muḥammad b. Muḥammad al-Ghazālī, *Kitāb al-Maḥabba*, in *Iḥyā' 'Ulūm al-Dīn*, Damascus: Ālim al-Kutub, 1992, pp. 252–4. There are two other philosophical works which Abrahamov refers to in the above mentioned work, p. 17. The first is the thirty-seventh epistle of *Rasā'il Ikhwān al-Ṣafā'* called *Fī Māhiyyat al-'Ishq* (On the essence of love) by the 'Bretheren of Purity'; the second is Ibn Sīnā's *Risāla fi'l-'Ishq* (An epistle on love).

ten is cast away from his good deed] and give him nine good deeds, so the evil deed is thrown away from him."'[35]

> Anas reported in a tradition that the Prophet said, 'When the servant commits a sin it is recorded against him.' So a nomad said, 'And if he repents of it?' He said,' It is erased from him.' He said, 'If he returns to it?' The Prophet said, 'It is recorded against him.' The nomad said 'If he repents?' He said, 'It is erased form his page.' He said, 'Until when?' He [the Prophet] said, 'As long as he asks for forgiveness and repents towards God. God does not become weary of forgiving until the servant becomes weary of asking for forgiveness. When the servant intends a good deed, the master of the right hand writes it down as a good deed before he performs it. If he performs it it is written down as ten good deeds. Then God Almighty adds to it seven hundred times. When he intends a sin, it is not written down against him and when he performs the sin, it is written down as one sin only and beyond it is the goodness of God's pardon.'[36]

This overwhelming mercy is a mystery, for it is essentially a plea from God to humankind not to despair of God's mercy. Mercy, unlike love, is not bilateral – human beings cannot have mercy on God, but God chooses, indeed desires, to be merciful to human beings. Indeed, al-Ghazālī also quotes a tradition where a believer implores God to keep him away from sin. God's response is 'All my believing servants ask this from me. But if I should keep them away from sin, upon whom will I bestow my blessings and to whom will I grant forgiveness?'[37] God expects, indeed wants, human beings to commit sin so that he can forgive; herein lies a mutual dependency between the divine and the human, a dependency that does not limit God but allows him constant opportunities to show the full magnitude of his love. God demands unswerving loyalty to his unique being, but in return his mercy knows no bounds. In those Qur'ānic verses and *ḥadīth*s that speak so profusely about God's mercy, we find an Islamic doctrine of eternal hope; there is no room for nihilism in Islam.[38] In humankind's eternal need for God lies the recognition that hope is alive in this world and that religious faith in a good God is not an illusion or a projection of one's own dreams. God is real, our sins are real, and divine forgiveness is real. The following *ḥadīth* is poetic in its imagery of the spaciousness of God's mercy:

[35] Ghazālī, *Kitāb al-Khauf wa'l Rajā'*, in *Iḥyā'*, vol. 4, p. 129. Elsewhere al-Ghazālī has explored the issue of loving God and the challenges faced by the believer.

[36] Ghazālī, *Kitāb al-Khauf*, in *Iḥyā'*, pp. 129–30.

[37] Ghazālī, *Kitāb al-Khauf*, in *Iḥyā'*, p. 132.

[38] See Mona Siddiqui, 'Between God's Mercy and God's Law: Human Dignity in Islam', in Paul Middleton, ed., *The God of Love and Human Dignity: Essays in Honour of George Newlands*, London: T&T Clark, 2007, pp. 51–64. Persistent references to the images of divine mercy reveal a God desperate to forgive.

> And according to a tradition, truly God possesses a hundred mercies. From these, he has put away ninety-nine beside himself and revealed only one mercy in this world. By virtue of it people show compassion to each other and the mother is compassionate to her child, and the beast is humane with its offspring. On the day of resurrection God will join this mercy to the ninety nine and will spread them out over the whole of his creation and every single mercy will be in conformity with the heavens and the earth.[39]

By implication God's blessings too are an extension of his love even though the word *ḥubb* is not specifically mentioned:

> He gives you from all which you ask him for and if you were to count the blessings of God you would not be able to number them. (Q 14:34)
>
> Do you not see how God has made serviceable to you all that is in the heavens and on earth and made his blessings flow to you in abundance both outwardly and inwardly? (Q 31:20)

Here again there is the strong sense that humankind with its limited appreciation of the divine does not always see these blessings, and they can remain closed to our sensory world.

It is often argued that it is in Ṣūfī literature where the most dynamic and beautiful expressions of love and mercy come together. While some would regard the Qur'ānic material as relatively scant on the vocabulary of love, the poetry of the Ṣūfīs is inspired by the Qur'ān. Ibn 'Arabī cites the saying of Abū Madyan, the twelfth-century Maghribī spiritual authority:

> The spiritual aspirant (*al-murīd*) is not a true aspirant until he finds in the Qur'ān everything to which he aspires.[40]

Inspired by the Qur'ānic vocabulary of *ḥubb* and *raḥma*, as well as the divine names such as *al-laṭīf* (the kind), *al-walī* (the friend), *al-ḥalīm* (the gentle), *al-ra'ūf* (the merciful), and *al-ghafūr* (the forgiver), many Ṣūfīs see the whole of the cosmos as pulsating with the love that flows from God and the ecstasy of desiring God:

> You have infused my being
> Through and through,
> As an intimate friend must
> Always do.
> So when I speak I speak of only You

[39] Ghazālī, *Kitāb al-Khauf*, in *Iḥyā'*, p. 132.

[40] Muḥammad ibn 'Alī Muḥyī al-Dīn Ibn al-'Arabī, *al-Futuhat al-Makkīyya*, Cairo: 1972–89, vol. 3. I am grateful to Reza Shah Kazemi for this quote from 'God, "The Loving"', in Miroslav Volf, Ghazi bin Muhammad, and Melissa Yarrington, eds., *A Common Word*, Grand Rapids, MI: Eerdemans Publishing Co., 2010, p. 100.

And when silent, I yearn for You.[41]
I swim in the sea of Love,
Tossed up and down by waves
They lift me up at times,
At others in them I drown.
Till this Love brought me to
Where there was no shore in sight.[42]

The voice of love
Each moment comes
From everywhere
We were in heaven once
We were friends to angels once,
To that place let us return,
That is our country, our home.
Higher than heavens, we are.
Greater than angels, we are.
Why not leave them both behind?
Our goal is Majesty, divine.[43]

The sickness of love is from other illnesses apart;
Love is the barometer of God's mystery in our hearts.
Love whether it be of this world or the others
Leads us to the Lord who is the Lord of all!
However must I describe Love's qualities?
When I am in it my words aren't adequate
The tongue can throw some light on it
But Love is most illumined by silence
When the pen was busy writing, it was fluent
When it reached the word of Love, it broke down.[44]

One plunges the depth of love in Ṣūfī poetry and yet, as Rūmī says, the pen broke when it reached the word of love. Love remains indefinable, ineffable even though it is a universal experience, for in the end love is a reality that transcends whatever one writes or says about it. If this is so, it may be even more difficult to define the extent of God's love based on the usage of 'loving' terms in the Qur'ān when the Qur'ān tells us that it contains that which is hidden and which remains with God.

[41] Rābi'a Baṣrī in Mahmood Jamal, ed. and trans. *Islamic Mystical Poetry: Ṣūfī Verses from the Early Mystics to Rūmī*, London: Penguin Books, 2009, p. 7.

[42] Mansūr Hallāj, in Jamal, *Islamic Mystical poetry*, p. 33.

[43] Jalaluddīn Rūmī, in Jamal, *Islamic Mystical poetry*, p. 133.

[44] Rūmī, in Jamal, *Islamic Mystical poetry*, p. 145.

However, this did not preclude Muslims from understanding the Qur'ān as saying something about God and viewing the Qur'ān as a glimpse into God's being and mercy revealed in human language. The words, while open to multivalent meanings, remain accessible to some order of human interpretation; but human interpretation tends to reduce rather than enlarge God's love. In the Qur'ān, the vocabulary of divine and human love is found largely in words such as *wadd* or *ḥubb* which conceptualise love as an emotion or act between human beings or between God and human beings. It can be given by God to whomsoever he wishes, love can be contingent upon right action and it can be bestowed upon the righteous or the penitent by God. Love can be withheld from those who are wicked and showered on those who are just. Love here is about knowing those whom God likes, for example, the righteous and the patient and those whom God does not like, such as the wasters, the unrighteous, the arrogant. Love here is concerned with the ethical behaviour of humankind to each other to which God responds. In acting upon those virtues that God encourages we are honouring God's preferences for human behaviour. God's dislike for certain human characteristics are the traits that human beings should not like in themselves as they take us away from God, for example, arrogance, waste etc. Yet while the Qur'ān says unambiguously that God does not love the arrogant or the wasters, we do not know how this absence of love is manifest on earth. How does God's grace and forgiveness work in the lives of the good and the bad?

In the Gospels the dramatic power of love has to some extent already taken place with Christ's crucifixion and resurrection. In the Qur'ān the drama is yet to unfold, for the promise of forgiveness has been made. The Qur'ān does not speak of one act by God or one defining expression of God's love. Perhaps this is Islam's biggest parting with Christian doctrine: that it does not have those defining moments of both alienation from God as in the Fall nor subsequent reconciliation with God, redemption through the death and resurrection of Christ.

The Qur'ān does not convey explicitly the primacy of God's love, i.e. God loves us first, as is found in the passage from John's Gospel on love.

> Beloved, let us love one another, because love is from God; everyone who loves is born of God and knows God. Whoever does not love does not know God, for God is love. God's love was revealed among us in this way; God sent his only Son into the World so that we might live through him. In this is love, not that we loved God but that he loved us and sent his Son to be the atoning sacrifice for our sins. Beloved, since God loved us so much we also ought to love one another. No one has ever seen God; if we love one another God lives in us and his love is perfected in us. We know that we live in him and he in us, because he has given us of his Spirit. And we have seen and testify that the

> Father has sent his Son to be the Savior of the world. If anyone acknowledges that Jesus is the Son of God, God lives in him and he in God. And so we know and rely on the love God has for us. God is love. Whoever lives in love lives in God, and God in him. In this way, love is made complete among us so that we will have confidence on the Day of Judgment, because in this world we are like him. There is no fear in love. But perfect love drives out fear, because fear has to do with punishment. The one who fears is not made perfect in love. We love because he first loved us. If anyone says, 'I love God,' yet hates his brother, he is a liar. For anyone who does not love his brother, whom he has seen, cannot love God, whom he has not seen. And he has given us this command: Whoever loves God must also love his brother. (1 John 7:21)

God's love in this Gospel is reflected ultimately in a story of divine presence and divine atonement intimately linked with God's sending of his Son to the world. For their part human beings must acknowledge that God lives in Jesus Christ. Jesus' salvific role is based on a love that graced the world because God loved his creation first. Loving one another is an expression and extension of this divine love. In loving one another, one abides in God and preserves the unity of the community. While in Islam God does not reveal himself through any visible or human form, Islam accepts in its own way a sense of the divine in Jesus, for he is the spirit (*rūḥ*) of God. The Immaculate Conception of Mary and the virgin birth of Jesus are also testament to the spiritual mystery associated with both Mary and Jesus but the Christic element of Jesus is seen as one more example of God's omnipotence only. The primacy of God's love is repeated in the Gospels as our earthly paradigm whereby God has now brought us into a new relationship with the cosmos. God loves us radically not because of our worth but because we are. In the Qur'ān, however, God's love is about desire: desire for the believer to return to him from any place or any distance. God urges constant movement and devotion towards him. At some level the attempt to draw any comparison between the redemptive, kenotic love exemplified in Christ's crucifixion and resurrection and the various dimensions of divine love as reflected in the Qur'ān is flawed. For divine love took on human form and became the essential structure at the very basis of a Christian understanding of God. To be close to Jesus Christ is to be close to the embodied love of God. While both Islam and Christianity talk of a loving God, Islam relying on the concept of mercy for a more comprehensive and expansive definition of love, there is, in my view, a profound structural difference in the way love is conceptualised in Christianity and Islam. In Christianity one dwells on the nature of the divine being by focusing primarily on its human manifestation in Christ. God has interceded in the mystery of Christ's suffering, crucifixion, and resurrection, allowing for love to walk this earth and transform human existence. In Islam, God's love is both hidden and visible in this world, it flows from his transcendent being and his constant mercy inviting us to transform ourselves and our lives. In Islam, the merciful God inspired the *eros* and the *agape* of Ṣūfī poetry where the Ṣūfī is the lover desperately desiring some kind of relationship– even identification– with the beloved, God. Perhaps no Ṣūfī has made this more manifest than al-Hallāj, who cried out: 'I am the Truth.' In his work on Ṣūfī piety Franz Rosenthal explains how Jalāl al-Dīn Rūmī understood this cry from al-Hallāj:

> Take the famous utterance that 'I am God.' Some men reckon it as a great pretension, but 'I am God' is in fact a great humility. The man who says' I am the servant of God' asserts that two exist, one himself and the other God. But he who says, 'I am God': that is, 'I am not, He is all, nothing has existence but God, I am pure nonentity, I am nothing.' In this the humility is greater.[45]

But the merciful God also inspired the discipline of jurisprudence, a rigorous intellectual feast engaging generations of scholars whose primary concern was the possibility of reflecting ad nauseam so as to know God's will. The Qur'ānic discourse on love is not about redemption but the transformation of man in his worship of God. Prophets reflect certain truths, but their purpose is to point to the ultimate truth. Truth and meaning remain hidden in God but we must act knowing that God is present and that he desires to show mercy, to give hope from both near and far. As human beings we cannot conceive of a distant God, only a transcendent God who remains near to human thoughts and prayers, whose love is a passion, a promise, and a force for hope, even though, like the most intense love, it may remain veiled and, to our human senses, forever a secret.

[45] Franz Rosenthal, '"I am You" – Individual Piety and Society in Islam', in Amin Banani and Speros Vryonis, Jr., eds., *Individualism and Conformity in Classical Islam: Fifth Georgio Levi Della Vida Biennial Conference*, Wiesbaden: Otto Harrassowitz, 1975, pp. 33–60, pp. 50–1.

7

Virtue and Limits in the Ethics of Friendship

> On that day friends will become enemies of each other, except for those who are righteous.
>
> (Q43:67)

> Each friend represents a world in us, a world possibly not born until they arrive, and it is only by this meeting that a new world is born.
>
> (Anaïs Nin)

Growing up as Muslim in the United Kingdom, I have lived most of my life not thinking in any systematic way about the friendships or relationships I have formed outside those of my immediate family. Friendships just happened; sometimes they were good and sometimes they were short-lived. I grew up in a nuclear family with no near or distant relatives and less than a handful of trips to Pakistan where I was born. My social milieu was made up of British people largely of non-Muslim origin. My parents, who would be categorised as first-generation immigrants to the United Kingdom, were from educated backgrounds and in the main became friends with other middle-class Muslims. We socialised with them and their children were our peers. Yet, looking back on these years, I confess I never really forged what I would call true friendships with the children. My friends were people with whom I went to school, college, and then university. And today in my professional context my friends are still largely from non-Muslim backgrounds. They are nominal and practising Christians and Jews as well as agnostics and humanists. This has not happened through any deliberate intent but as a result of the nature of my employment, the environment where I work, and, consequently, the kind of people I meet. Many of these people have become friends in whom I choose to confide and put my trust.

Indeed, in my personal and professional life, I realise that intellectual intimacy, which is built partly on the gradual disclosure of one's own thinking and views on a range of subjects, lies at the basis of the most profound friendships; here differences of race, gender, or religion could not become obstructions to forming meaningful friendships. As Waddell states, 'so much of our life is a history of our friendships'.[1] But friendships are not perfect, nor should they be idealised. They rely on the constancy of spending time together, of sharing one's thoughts and daily life, and at times they demand working through the consequences of uncomfortable closeness and declarations. Yet, I have never really thought that my deeper friendships could be based on anything other than the mutual emotional and intellectual enjoyment of another's company. I have felt compelled to examine this issue through my personal experience of forming relationships and friendships with a whole variety of people to whom I feel emotionally connected largely because I have grown up in the liberal, social milieu of a Western society. Here, I have resisted the rigorist conceptions in Muslim piety that Muslims should not be friends with non-Muslims, that religion alone should be the defining premise of any friendship. In this way I have never regarded my own friendships as posing a moral dilemma. Today, my children's friendships with boys and girls of varying backgrounds has prompted me to think on the very nature of friendship and how it shapes who we are as children and our identity as adults. This is significant for me because friendships can become defining points in our lives. They involve risk, they can take us away from the comfort of religious and psychological convictions, for they involve making choices about relationships and often staring at life's uncertainties and ambiguities. Friendships demand that we evaluate who we are as people and how and in whom we seek happiness and wisdom.

One other event that caused me to deliberate on the varying concepts of friendship was the death of a friend, a friend who remained outside my faith, culture, and family but whose absence from my life has not diminished memories of how transformative a real friendship can be. Sometimes a friendship creeps up on a person and presents itself as a wonderful and life-changing event; such a friendship is rare, and may even be difficult, but it is proof that we may not be able to rationalise or understand the deepest kind of friendship; it just is. Furthermore, I agree with the view that one of the proofs of a true friendship is that it can survive the absence created by death, even if it is in memory only. In his work on lawyers, law, and friendship, Peter

[1] Paul Wadell, *Friendship and the Moral Life*, Notre Dame, IN: University of Notre Dame Press, 1989, p. 7.

Goodrich writes that in death 'the departed friends – *mortui vivunt* – become images, living spirits, the continuation of the surviving friend in the soul of the departed':

> Indeed all the great meditations on friendship were occasioned by the death of a friend and this commonality of death to the declaration or avowal of friendship, to explicit reflection upon friendship, needs to be noted and at some later point contested.[2]

Friendship is both a gift and a task, often an intense relationship based on love and companionship. In this chapter, I would like to reflect on the richness of different perspectives on friendship, a topic that Ralph Emerson described as 'like the immortality of the soul … too good to be believed'.[3] Friendship is an irreducible and varied relationship, but it is often declared as the defining relationship of the modern age. Friendship is difficult and ambiguous, crossing boundaries of love, affection, and virtue. It can be fragile and solid with its own demands of loyalty and magnanimity, trust and sincerity. Human beings need friends in their search for emotional and intellectual well-being, and friendship like love can be transformative in its effects. The terms 'friend' and 'friendship' can be used in a number of ways, described or cased in the language of altruism or egoism; but when classical philosophy gave it consideration, it regarded friendship as the most important constituent of a worthwhile and happy life. Friendship in the ancient world enjoyed a social standing and philosophical deliberations considered the value of friendship in creating the moral framework of a good society. The significance of friendship has reappeared in contemporary times as a political and sociological question. Today, however, friendships are considered mainly private relationships which matter to us as individuals in our private space and time.

Despite the relevance of friendship to the quality and meaning in our lives, only a small number of philosophers and theologians have written on the subject of friendship at any length. In contrasting the prominence of friendship in Greek philosophy and moral thought to its relative neglect in modern philosophy, Hans Gadamer claimed that because friendship is not a value or belief, it does not fit easily within modern thought, largely premised on a self-conscious modern subject.[4] For Gadamer, friendship is a good rather than

2 Peter Goodrich, 'Laws of Friendship', *Law and Literature*, 15:1, 2003, pp. 23–52.

3 Ralph Waldo Emerson, 'Friendship', in *Essays: First Series*, Boston: J. Munroe & Co., 1841 (http://www. emersoncentral.com/friendship.htm).

4 Hans-Georg Gadamer, 'The Ethics of Value and Practical Philosophy (1982)', in *Hermeneutics, Religion and Ethics*, trans. Joel Weinsheimer, New Haven: Yale University Press, 1999, p. 117. Gadamer explains that he noticed this difference when he *first*

a value. It is a good that comes into being when shared, not demanded nor willed, between two people, 'No more than love can friendship be summoned on demand.'[5] However, Gadamer distinguishes having good will towards someone or a feeling of sympathy towards another, from friendship. Having a good disposition towards is not the same as friendship:

> Even if this sympathy or good will were actually to occur on both sides and to that extent constitute reciprocity, it would be mere friendliness so long as the two people were not really openly bound to each other. The common condition of all 'friendship' is more than that: the true bond that – in various degrees – signifies a 'life together'.[6]

Friendships are an important aspect of the texture of communal human life. Concepts – indeed, typologies – of friendship are implicit in many of the central sociological and ethical questions of today and have a stake in defining who we are as individuals and also who we are as communities in a multi-racial, multi-faith, and multi-cultural environment.

From a religious perspective there seems to be no dominant narrative on friendship nor is scripture itself overtly concerned with the way friendship is essential to our humanity. There are some references to friendship; for example, Jesus says to his disciples, 'I call you servants no longer but friends' (John 15:15). But if anything friendship is about preferential and selective love whereas most scriptural traditions extol the universality of love and the relationship of love between human beings and God. *Agape*, the distinctive Christian love, demands that we love our enemy even though we know there is no reciprocity to this love. Paul Waddell compares the relationship of friendship with Christian love:

> Friendship is a necessary good in any life but it is not a specific good. It is a powerful love, but it is not the love by which we imitate Christ. Given the relationship between *agape* and *philia*, to begin to be friends is not to begin to be Christian. Friendship is one life, *agape* another. Friendship is good love but it is not redemptive love, and that explains why the relationship between *philia* and *agape*, even if not inalterably conflictual, is inalterably strained.[7]

Wadell himself critiques the arguments of those who say that friendship and Christian love are opposed by examining the writings of Søren

lectured on the role of Greek ethics and saw 'two extensive books of the *Nichomachaen Ethics* deal with the subject – whereas Kant's moral philosophy merits only a single page!'

[5] Gadamer, 'Ethics', p. 117.

[6] Hans-Georg Gadamer, 'Friendship and Self-Knowledge: Reflections on the Role of Friendship in Greek Ethics (1985)', in *Hermeneutics, Religion and Ethics*, trans. Joel Weinsheimer, New Haven: Yale University Press, 1999, p. 128.

[7] Wadell, *Friendship*, p. 71.

Kierkegaard and Anders Nygren. While Kierkegaard displayed more nuance in his later writings, both writers saw *agape* as the distinctive Christian love that taught love for all, in which there were no outsiders. This was in contrast to friendship, which was viewed as preferential and exclusionary love, and could even be selfish love. Waddell recognises the compelling nature of their arguments but concludes:

> When friends are bought together by a mutual love for God and a desire to follow Christ, their friendship is a relationship in which they learn the ways of God, imitate Christ and thus learn to embrace those they hitherto ignored. In this context, *agape* is not something other than friendship, but describes a friendship like God's, a love of such generous vision that it looks upon all men and women not as strangers but as friends.[8]

While Christian perspectives on biblical love allow for different narratives on love and friendship, the Qur'ān does not consider friendship as an emotional need or desire and commitment between people. It seeks to address friendship primarily in the political context of forging alliances. In the Qur'ān the virtue of friendship is seen largely as a commitment to solidarity with people who have submitted to the new faith. Thus, the Qur'ān appears to prohibit any alliance with those who reject the new revelation:

> O you who believe, do not take my enemies and yours as your allies, showing them friendship when they have rejected the truth you have received and have driven you and the Messenger out simply because you believe in God. (Q 60:1)

In the Qur'ān friendship is not an abstraction but assessed largely through the narrative of the new faith in its political environment. The Qur'ān encourages friendship between those whose alliances are for God and for the Prophetic message.

Nevertheless, where philosophical inquiry has explored friendship, there is in general approval of friendship as being a good thing for individuals and for wider society. This discussion on friendship is based on the select writings of certain classical and Renaissance scholars as well as Qur'ānic and Islamic reflections on friendship. I have concentrated in the main on Western philosophical and belletristic literature sprinkled with some more modern insights. It is not because the Islamic belletristic literature does not contain accounts of friendship, but rather that in the Islamic context I wanted to explore a more systematic approach. This chapter does not attempt to explore all facets of

[8] Wadell, *Friendship*, p. 96.

friendship, nor does it discuss in any detail the blurring of different love boundaries. The analysis of classical and medieval works serves to shed light concerning the various interests in friendship as a philosophical question but also a deeply personal encounter which shapes our histories and our futures.

I should add that I am not concerned so much with the ambiguities of friendship created by feelings of sexual attraction, love, or erotic and homosexual love, which may all be consequences of a strong friendship but are not friendship in themselves. Both the relationships of deep friendship and romantic love are ones that we enter voluntarily and, in some sense, both are relationships that 'happen to us'. However, even if the demarcation lines may fade, there remain distinctions:

> It might be said that friendship is calm, reasonable, calm and sober, whereas erotic love is spontaneous, irrational, wild and orgiastic. Or that friendship tends towards the mind, conversation and the spiritual, whereas erotic love is nothing without the body, touch and lust. Alternatively, friendship seems to develop over time: it loves to dwell on what has passed and to ponder what is to come. But erotic love delights in immediacy; it exclaims, 'Now!'[9]

It is probably true to say that friendship remains unspoken when it is working but nevertheless, reflection on friendship shows how important friendship is to the individual's quality of life as well as to the well-being of society. It has both a political and emotional dimension, for though love and affection are ethical and theological virtues, they form the basis of the human bond and are the fundamental ingredients of communal cohesion and solidarity. There are many friends with whom I have lost contact over the years, some through distance and some through negligence. For friendship is a commitment that needs patient nourishing to grow.

Friends as opposed to family are people with whom we choose to share our lives, either partially or wholly. They are people whose particular company we seek as opposed to seeking company in general. However, on this issue of choice, Laurence Thomas is right:

> As a rule we do not self-consciously choose our friends in the way that we, say, choose the clothes that we wear. One does not shop for a friend in the way that one shops for an article of clothing. There is a very clear sense that we grow into friendships; indeed we can even be surprised that our interaction with someone has given rise to such companion friendship. We are

[9] Mark Vernon, *The Philosophy of Friendship*, New York: Palgrave Macmillan, 2005, p. 30.

surprised in that it would never have occurred to us that so deep a friendship would have developed. There is a sense in which friendships happen to us.[10]

However hard it may be to define friendship, friendships are something that most of us live and remember. In many ways our friends have the most significant impact and influence on our beings as they help us to be who we are and yet more than ourselves; close connections with others helps us to feel a whole variety of emotions:

> Friendship enlarges our knowledge . . . through out the whole gamut of human experience by enabling us in some measure to adopt the viewpoint of another person through our sympathetic identifications with him. Through friendship we can know what it is like to feel or think or do certain things which we do not feel, think or do ourselves. And our knowledge is not merely knowledge by description, but knowledge by acquaintance, derived from our sympathetic sharing of this experience.[11]

Friendship may be included as one of life's most simple pleasures, and yet it can be a complex matter in terms of defining who we are and our place in any society. There is individualism in friendship, not an anti-social or asocial individualism but an exclusivity in that we are not seeking through friendship any social cooperation, only selective cooperation with others. As C. S. Lewis points out:

> The outlook which values the collective above the individual necessarily disparages friendship; it is a relationship between men at their highest level of individuality. It draws men from 'collective' togetherness as surely as solitude itself could do; and more dangerously, for it withdraws them by two's and three's. Some forms of democratic sentiment are naturally hostile to it because it is selective and an affair of the few. To say, 'These are my friends' implies 'Those are not.'[12]

In the ancient world the special bond of friendship constituted an essential department of ethics. *Philia* entailed a fondness for another, and in the Greek world *philia* did not just mean a voluntary friendship but a basic sociability in human beings that was demonstrated in loyalty to one's family and to a wider community; *philia* enabled us to live together. The English concept of friendship is contained in Aristotle's notion of *philia*, regarded as the pinnacle of

10 Laurence Thomas, 'Friendship', *Synthese*, 72:2, Kurt Baier Festshcrift, Part two, August 1987, pp. 217–36, p. 218.

11 Elizabeth Telfer, "Friendship." *Proceedings of the Aristotelian Society*, New Series, vol. 71, 1970–1971, pp. 223–41, p. 240.

12 C. S. Lewis, *The Four Loves*, New York: Inspirational Press, 1991, p. 60.

social relations. Aristotle claimed that human beings were political animals who sought out the company of each other and that humanity could not realise itself as humanity without social cooperation. Friendship was what kept cities together and the reason lawmakers gave more attention to friendship than justice was because they wanted to eliminate faction which is enmity:

> There is no need for rules of justice between people who are friends, whereas if they are just they still need friendship – and of what is just the most just is thought to be what belongs to friendship.[13]

Thus friendship is the first law of community without which justice between communities would be difficult. Friendship is an ingredient to the moral life, the life of a civic community. There are few phrases more often repeated in literature on friendship than Aristotle's claim:

> Friendship is a kind of excellence, or goes along with excellence, and furthermore, is very necessary for living. For no-one would choose to live without friends, even if he had all the other good things; for even the wealthy or those who rule over or dominate others are sought to need friends more than anything.[14]

Like Socrates and Plato Aristotle took virtue to be central to the well-lived life. Aristotle writes that in all kinds of misfortune people think of their friends as their only refuge and that 'friendship is good will between reciprocating parties'.[15] Friendship motivates us to regard the interest of others. But for Aristotle, there were three kinds of friendships: friendships of pleasure, friendships of utility, and friendships of virtue. In a rather lengthy explanation Aristotle describes each of these:

> Those who love each other for the useful do not love them for themselves, but in so far as some good accrues to each of them from the other. Similarly too, with those who love each other because of pleasure: people do not feel affection for the witty for their being of a certain character, but for the pleasure they themselves get from them. And and those who love because of the useful feel fondness because of what is good for themselves, and those loving because of pleasure because of what is pleasant to themselves; they do not love by reference to the way the person loved is, but to his being useful or pleasant. And in fact these friendships are friendships incidentally . . . such

[13] Aristotle, *Nichomachean Ethics*, trans. Sarah Broadie and Christopher Rowe, Oxford: Oxford University Press, 2002, 115a25.
[14] Aristotle, *Nichomachean Ethics*, 1155a5.
[15] Aristotle, *Nichomachean Ethics*, 115b30.

> friendships are then easily dissolved if the parties become different; for if they are no longer pleasant or useful, they cease loving each other.[16]

For Aristotle reciprocity of wanting what is good for another and feelings of benevolence between men of virtue towards each other lie at the basis of a true friendship:

> It is the friendship between good people, those resembling each other in excellence, that is complete; for each alike of these wishes good things for the other insofar as he is good, and he is good in himself... For every kind of friendship is because of some good or because of pleasure, either without qualification or for the person loving, and in virtue of some sort of resemblance between the parties; and to this kind of friendship belong all the attributes mentioned, in virtue of what the friends are in themselves, since in this respect they are similar and in the others, and the good without qualification is also pleasant without qualification.[17]

His understanding of a genuine friend is someone who loves or likes another person for the sake of that other person. Wanting what is good for another is what he calls 'good will' (*eunoia*), which must be a reciprocal desire. Aristotle insists that friendship must be between good people who do good for each other for only good is lovable.[18] This is not because friends of virtue need each other so that each brings to the other something significant to the relationship that was not there initially. Friends who are virtuous and good already possess the best qualities and self-sufficiency of character. In Aristotle's view, those friends who need each other are relegated to the category of 'friendships of utility'.[19] This is not to say that bad people cannot be friends with one another, but that kind of friendship does not last because 'the bad get no gratification from each other, unless they might get some benefit'.[20] The true and best friendship is one where benefits are a consequence of rather than reason for the relationship.

However, if true friendship is reserved only for the virtuous, what of ordinary people who have virtues and vices and may have friendships of usefulness and pleasure? Do these friendships not count as friendships and be seen merely as exploitative relationships? If friendships of virtue are the 'perfect' friendships requiring 'perfect' people then *eudaimonia*, Aristotle's

16 Aristotle, *Nichomachean Ethics*, 1156a15.
17 Aristotle, *Nichomachean Ethics*, 1156b5, 1156b20.
18 Aristotle, *Nichomachean Ethics*, 1165b10.
19 Douglas J. Den Uyl, 'Friendship and Transcendence', *International Journal for Philosophy of Religion*, 41:2, 1997, pp. 105–22.
20 Aristotle, *Nichomachean Ethics*, 1157a20.

vision for the complete life is a possibility for only a few, if any, and his ethic is elitist.[21] But Aristotle's argument is that virtue is essential to a good life and we cannot be good by ourselves or in solitude. We need friends to know ourselves and to do good in life, for the moral life is what happens to us in relation to others. Friendships based on pleasure and advantage would only be exploitative if each person aimed solely at their own pleasure or advantage and not at that of the friend.

> The fact that Aristotle delineates three kinds of friendship suggests each human life needs to include all three... Each type of friendship is good because each contributes to our well being and is an element in a fulsome life, but friendships based on moral goodness are better, because of what they can do for the friends. These friendships make people good... friendships formed from virtue have greater moral possibilities than friendships formed from usefulness or pleasure.[22]

The goal of the moral life is not just the virtuous person but the virtuous community. In his analysis of Aristotle's plea for virtue, Waddell states that the connection between ethics and politics is that the moral life aims to achieve a certain kind of society, namely a society of virtue, but it also requires a certain kind of society, 'the society of men and women dedicated to the same *telos*, working for and with one another to make each person's achievement of the good possible. In this sense, the polis of the city-state is both the prerequisite of the moral life and its ultimate aim.'[23]

Friendship is structured to an attraction of the image of the same so that 'all the features of friendship start with one self and are extended to others'. For Aristotle, the self (*autos*) and self love (*philautia*) are not objective and impersonal notions but describe the human being's sense of themselves, their choices and actions. 'Self' is what one is when being a genuine friend to another so that a person can recognise themselves in their friends. Via another, a person becomes one with himself so that the other becomes like a mirror of self-knowledge.[24] In Aristotle's view, to be aware of one's friend is in effect to be that friend by means of one's own activity of knowing him; one must therefore know oneself.[25] Friends cannot conceal themselves from one

[21] For an inciteful discussion of this see John M. Cooper, 'Aristotle on Friendship', in Amelie Oksenberg Rorty, ed., *Essays on Aristotle's Ethics*, Berkeley: University of California Press, 1980, pp. 301–40.

[22] Wadell, *Friendship*, p. 57.

[23] Wadell, *Friendship*, pp. 46–7.

[24] See Gadamer's comments on Aristotle in 'Friendship'.

[25] For a detailed discussion of this see Anne Marie Dziob, 'Aristotelian Friendship: Self Love and Moral Rivalry', *The Review of Metaphysics*, 46, 1993, pp. 781–801.

another. Acting for the good of another does not in itself demand self-sacrifice for, in caring abut someone else, we do not have to lose care of ourselves. When we recognise others as friends, we can enjoy their existence in the same way that we can enjoy our own existence.[26] As he says, 'friendship in its superior form resembles one's love for oneself'.[27]

However, Aristotle is of the view that friendships can be dissolved when friends fail to stay the same. On this point Cicero also agrees that at times it was better to break off a friendship and, if discord had developed between friends, friendship should die out gradually so that 'friendship dies a natural rather than violent death'.[28] Cicero's *De Amicitia* was written by a lawyer and takes the form of a dialogue with Quintus Mucius Scaevola, Cicero's tutor in law and one of Rome's most famous lawyers. Cicero's view, expressed through Laelius, the main speaker of the treatise, regards friendship as the 'greatest thing given to man by the immortal gods' for friendship penetrates into all our lives, even the lives of those shun the company of mankind.[29] Cicero sees the person of wealth and prosperity but no friends as foolish. He saw a life where one was neither loved nor loving as the kind of life that tyrants endure.[30]

Cicero saw friendship as existing only between good men, men who cultivate virtue which is the greatest of all things.[31] For Cicero friendship was what made life worth living:

> To begin with, how can life be worth living, to use the words of Ennius which lacks that repose which is to be found in the mutual goodwill of a friend? What can be more delightful than to have someone to whom you can say everything with the same confidence as to yourself? Is prosperity not robbed of half its value if you have no one to share your joy?[32]

The need for companionship, for relationships that allow individual and open expression, are an essential component of human life. But Cicero stresses the importance – though difficulty – in being worthy of friendship, and that most people seek friends only to profit by them. He laments:

26 See Oliver Leaman, 'Secular Friendship and Religious Devotion', in Oliver Leaman, ed., *Friendship East and West: Philosophical Perspectives* Richmond: Curzon, 1996, pp. 251–62, p. 252.

27 Aristotle, *Nichomachean Ethics*, 1166b1.

28 Marcus Tullius Cicero, *De Amicitia*, 21, trans. E. S. Shuckburgh, web resource: http://ancienthistory.about.com/library/b/b1_text_ciceo_deamic.htm.

29 Cicero, *De Amicitia*, 23. Here Cicero mentions Timon of Athens, who still needed company to release his anger.

30 Cicero, *De Amicitia*, 15.

31 Cicero, *De Amicitia*, 5–6.

32 Cicero, *De Amicitia*, 6.

> Accordingly they never possess that most beautiful and spontaneous friendship which must be sought only for itself without any ulterior object.[33]

Character and goodness are fundamental pillars of a good friendship in that we should endeavour to be good ourselves and seek goodness when choosing our friends. Here respect for oneself and respect for the friend is essential and virtue is what creates, sustains, and gives meaning to a friendship:

> But most people unreasonably, not to speak of modesty, want such a friend as they are unable to be themselves, and expect from their friends what they do not themselves give. The fair course is first to be good yourself, and then to look out for another of like character. It is between such that the stability in friendship of which we have been talking can be secured; when, that is to say, men who are united by affection learn, first of all, to rule those passions which enslave others, and in the next place to take delight in fair and equitable conduct, to bear each other's burdens, never to ask each other for anything inconsistent with virtue and rectitude, and not only to serve and love but also to respect each other. I say 'respect'; for if respect is gone, friendship has lost its brightest jewel. And this shows the mistake of those who imagine that friendship gives a privilege to licentiousness and sin. Nature has given us friendship as the handmaid of virtue, not as a partner in guilt.

The word respect is complex, for how is respect determined amongst friends? Is it through an acceptance of each other's characters without criticism, or is it an appreciation of the value inherent in each person as an individual and as a friend? One could even argue that respect taken to a certain point instils an element of anxiety, so that we may not really be who we want to be even amongst our closest of friends. Perhaps every friendship contains a level of dissimulation, a level of feigning, if only to preserve the friendship. But for Cicero, a real friend is as it were 'a second self'.[34] Friends are alike and bound by resemblance and act in reciprocity. For Cicero, there was always the possibility that friendships could be sought for ulterior or material advantages but he writes that true friendship is 'an inclination of the heart' springing from a natural impulse:

> But friendship by its nature admits of no feigning and no pretence: as far as it goes it is both genuine and spontaneous.[35]

33 Cicero, *De Amicitia*, 21.
34 Cicero, *De Amicitia*, 21.
35 Cicero, *De Amicitia*, 8.

Indeed, for Cicero, 'genuine friendships are eternal'.[36]

While Aristotle was not a lawyer, he placed his treatise on friendship in the context of law and ethics. Cicero stressed the concept of self-recognition in the bond of friendship. However, the French Renaissance essayist Michel de Montaigne wanted his essays to act as a self-portrait of the writer and said in his preface to the first volume of essays that 'I am myself the matter of my book.' Montaigne dedicated his book 'to the private conscience of my relatives and friends, so that when they have lost me (as soon they must), they may recover here some features of my habits and temperament'.[37] In his biographical note on Montaigne, Frame writes that Montaigne wished to be recognised in his work as the man he was. However:

> Rousseau resented the fact that the *Essays* were not frank enough to suit him; but Montaigne was not writing confessions. When he started his book he had lost a dear friend, Etienne de la Boétie, to whom he had been able to express, as he never could to any one person again, his every thought, view and feeling. Self-sufficient though he was, he had an imperious need to communicate. The *Essays* are his means of communication; the reader takes the place of the dead friend.[38]

Montaigne's reference to La Boétie's work, *La Servitude volontaire*, which Montaigne had seen long before he knew La Boétie, is mentioned as the medium of their first acquaintance. He sets the scene for his discourse on friendship, which he wrote after La Boétie's death, by remembering passionately the strength of this friendship:

> [It] gave me my first knowledge of his name, thus starting on its way this friendship which together we fostered as long as God willed, so entire and so perfect that certainly you will hardly read of the like and among men of today you see no trace of it in practice. So many coincidences are needed to build up such a friendship that it is a lot if fortune can do it in three centuries.[39]

36 Cicero, *De Amicitia*,

37 *The Complete Essays of Montaigne*, Michel de Montaigne, trans. Donald Frame. Stanford: Stanford University Press, 1965.

38 Montaigne, *Essays*, p. v.

39 Montaigne, *Essays*, p. 136. Montaigne was a close associate of the Protestant king of Navarre. He had many enemies and had to exercise a level of prudence in his public life. La Boétie was the author of a treatise called 'On Willing Slavery', a controversial work that led him to be accused of republicanism and a work that Montaigne had read before he met La Boétie. In his short biographical note on Montaigne, Vernon says: 'When they did meet, it was therefore almost to be expected that they would fall into a friendship based upon the relief of being able to share their passionate nonconformity' (p. 151). Montaigne therefore put his

Montaigne's exaggerated note about the probability of such friendships is not to belittle friendships generally but to claim that when such a friendship as the one he shared with La Boétie does come about, it can neither be matched nor replicated. Montaigne cites Aristotle's view that nature inclines human beings to nothing more than it does to society but he disagrees that the four ancient types of friendship – natural, social, hospitable and erotic – translate into real friendship:

> From children towards fathers it is rather respect. Friendship feeds on communication, which cannot exist between them because of their too great inequality. For neither can all the secret thoughts of fathers be communicated to children, lest this beget an unbecoming intimacy, nor could the admonitions and corrections which are one of the chief duties of friendship be administered by children to fathers.[40]

While Montaigne extols the relationship between brothers, which is full of affection, he writes that 'since brothers have to glide their careers along the same path and at the same rate, it is inevitable that they often jostle and clash with one another'.[41] Thus the element of competition between brothers will not allow this relationship to be defined as a friendship.

Montaigne distinguishes love for a woman from friendship in that in love 'there is nothing but a frantic desire for what flees from us' whereas:

> Friendship on the contrary, is enjoyed according as it is desired; it is bred, nourished, and increased only in enjoyment, since it is spiritual, and the soul grows refined by practice.

Montaigne does not regard women as having the capacity to form the intense but platonic fellowship that men can share, for he writes that a woman's soul 'is not firm enough to endure the strain of so tight and durable a knot'.[42] Indeed, Montaigne bases his whole essay on friendship inspired and moved by the friendship he cherished with La Boétie. The friendship is a soul friendship, it is an exceptional friendship and, while most friendships may not reach such heights, there is, in Montaigne's reflections, a sense of mournful pride that he was fortunate enough to have experienced both the love and loss of such a relationship. He describes this in quasi-mystical language of love:

trust in someone whose betrayal would have cost him his life. It was a short friendship as La Boétie died four years after they met.

40 Montaigne, *Essays*, p. 136.

41 Montaigne, *Essays*, p. 136.

42 Montaigne, *Essays*, p. 138.

> In the friendship I speak of, our souls mingle and blend with each other so completely that they efface the seam that joined them, and cannot find it again. If you press me to tell you why I loved him, I feel that this cannot be expressed, except by answering: Because it was he, because it was I.[43]

Montaigne writes about his personal friendship with a passion but does not pretend that this model of friendship is based on any other model, nor can it serve as a model for anyone else. Montaigne is too aware that this friendship was so intense that 'neither of us reserved anything for himself nor was anything either his or mine'.[44] The perfect friendship of which Montaigne speaks of is indivisible. Unlike common friendships, which can be divided between different people, there is a strong impression of self-emptying rather than self-discovery in Montaigne's view of the perfect friendship:

> Each one gives so wholly to his friend that he has nothing left to distribute elsewhere; on the contrary, he is sorry that he is not double, triple or quadruple and that he has not several souls and several wills, to confer them all on this one object.[45]

When one has found the perfect friendship, the other becomes myself for 'a single dominant friendship dissolves all other obligations'.[46] Montaigne's views on friendship are influenced almost completely by his friendship with a Boétie. Like Aristotle and Cicero he too recognises that there are many superficial kinds of friendships, but in his own experience of friendship, where 'we act from the very bottom of our hearts', motivation and action must be true. Montaigne's very personal account of a very close friendship leaves no room to see the other as the other; there is no distance between him and La Boétie. And yet there is no idealising of friendship from a distance or romanticising its memory. He insists that it was formed and developed very quickly between them as they were grown men who realised that they may not have the luxury of time to linger on a gradual relationship. This confirms again the element of reciprocity vital to any flourishing, even intense, friendship. Friendship is not unilateral. It is not like erotic love, which can quicken regardless of whether the love is returned; indeed, unrequited love can produce "eross' most exquisite passion – infatuation". While the tone maybe seen as masculinist, there is no fear of intimacy here. Yet there is a paradox in Montaigne's reflection whereby he recognises not only the uniqueness of his

[43] Montaigne, *Essays*, p. 139.
[44] Montaigne, *Essays*, p. 140.
[45] Montaigne, *Essays*, p. 141.
[46] Montaigne, *Essays*, p. 142.

friendship but also what he considers its superiority. His friendship is perfect and yet there is no other friendship with which to compare it.

Another great essayist of the sixteenth century who was also a lawyer, scientist, and a statesman was Francis Bacon. In his introduction to Bacon's *Essays*, John Pitcher writes that though the essays look unbelievably easy to write:

> The fact is that the writing in the *Essays* took Bacon almost thirty years to perfect, and that by the time he had finished with it (in 1625) it was one of the major achievements in prose to have come out of the Elizabethan academies and courts of law.[47]

Bacon also wrote on friendship by beginning with Aristotle's quote from *Politics*, 'Whoever is delighted in solitude is either a wild beast or a god.'[48] Bacon sets the scene for his discourse at the very beginning by comparing what soothes the heart to that which soothes other bodily organs:

> A principal fruit of friendship is the ease and discharge of the fullness and swellings of the heart, which passions of all kinds do cause and induce. We know diseases of stoppings and suffocations are the most dangerous in the body, and it is not much otherwise in the mind: you may take sarza to open the liver, steel to open the spleen, flowers of sulphur for the lungs, castoreum for the brain; but no receipt openeth the heart but a true friend, to whom you may impart griefs, joys, fears, hopes, suspicions, counsels, and whatever lieth upon the heart to oppress it, in a kind of civil shrift or confession.[49]

Bacon goes through the three 'fruits of friendship'. He describes the first:

> The communicating of a man's self to his friend works two contrary effects, for it redoubleth joys, and cutteth griefs in half. For there is no man that imparteth his joys to his friend, but he joyeth the more, and no man that imparteth grief to his friend, but he grieveth the less.

Thus, for Bacon, sharing each other's joys and grief is an essential aspect of a good friendship. As human beings we need to be able to relate to others in order to be ourselves, and indeed to be able to communicate the extremes of emotions. For Bacon, the second fruit is an extension of this communication whereby in seeking counsel from a friend, a person's own thoughts are better distilled:

47 Francis Bacon, *The Essays*, ed. John Pitcher, Harmondsworth: Penguin, 1985, p. 14.
48 Bacon, *Essays*, p. 138.
49 Bacon, *Essays*, p. 139.

> Whosoever hath his mind fraught with many thoughts, his wits and understanding do clarify and breakup, in the communicating and discoursing with another; he tosseth his thoughts more easily; he marshalleth them more orderly; he seeth how they look when they are turned into words; finally he waxeth wiser than himself; and that more by an hour's discourse than by a day's meditation.[50]

Bacon stresses the importance of wise counsel from a friend, which can be counsel concerning manners or business. Friendship is indispensable for self-reflection, and direct counsel from a friend can help a person's life and work:

> The calling of man's self to a strict account is a medicine sometimes too piercing and corrosive. Reading good books of morality is a little flat and dead. Observing our faults in others is sometimes unproper for our case. But the best receipt is the admonition of a friend.[51]

Bacon describes the last 'fruit of friendship' as the 'pomegranate, full of many kernels'.[52] Bacon's key point here is that he thought the ancients were sparing in their speech to say that a 'friend is another himself', for in fact a 'friend is far more than himself'. Bacon argues this by explaining that the individual does not mange to complete all his work or fulfil all his desires in life. However, if a person has a true friend:

> He may rest almost secure that the care of those things will continue after him. So that a man hath as it were two lives in his desires. A man hath a body, and that body is confined to a place; but where friendship is, all offices of life are as it were granted to him and his deputy, for he may exercise them by his friend.[53]

Bacon saw in friendship a unique relationship that allowed friends to be truthful to each other, and even possibly continue the work of one another. His fundamental disagreement with the classical, especially Aristotelian, view of friendship lay in saying that friends are useful and that we need them for a whole variety of circumstances in life. The classical view recognised usefulness in friendships but the highest type of friendship was defined neither by benefit nor utility.[54]

Today conversations about friendships and the rights and wrongs of certain friendships have become a more contested social phenomenon.

50 Bacon, *Essays*, p. 142.
51 Bacon, *Essays*, p. 143.
52 Bacon, *Essays*, p. 144.
53 Bacon, Essays, p. 144.
54 Den Uyl, 'Friendship', p. 107.

Over the last few decades as societies in many Western European countries appear more fragmented, pluralist, and where loyalties to groups and communities have shifted somewhat, who we are friends with has become a much larger political affirmation of identity and rights. In this landscape we often assess ourselves and our political as well as spiritual affiliations through the ties we form with those around us. This can lead to a conscious exercise in forming friendships with those who amongst other characteristics share the same faith as us. From a Qur'ānic perspective, friendship is envisaged largely through the spectrum of right belief and therefore the right kind of alliances. The Qur'ān contains around forty verses referring to some form of friendship which may or may not correspond to the definition of a friend in Western philosophical writings. Yet there is little exploration of this theme outside *adab* literature. Scriptural texts do not offer any kind of treatise on friendship, as one often finds in philosophical and other writings, other than to warn against hypocrisy and deception through association with false or unbelieving friends.

Friendship is not discussed in any explicit way in the Qur'ān though the words *walī*, *khalīl*, and *sādiq* all correspond to the English word 'friend'. In the Qur'ān, friendship and social ties are envisaged largely within the theme of forging alliances. These alliances can be on the human plane between individuals, politically between communities, or between human beings and God. In the former context, the Qur'ān's reference to friends is those whom the fledgling Muslim community looks to as becoming allies of the new faith. The Qur'ān repeatedly advises against forming bonds of protection or alliance with those who are not from the new category of believers. This category of people can consist of Jews and Christians though even a cursory reading of the Qur'ān reflects its variant perspectives on this particular group:

> O you who believe, do not take the Jews and Christians as protectors; they are protectors only to each other. Anyone who takes them as an ally becomes one of them – God does not guide such wrongdoers. (Q 5:51)[55]

The Qur'ān also stresses the wrongs of making alliances with those who ridicule the Prophet's message:

> O you who believe, do not take as allies [friends] those who ridicule your religion and make fun of it, whether people who were given the scripture before you, or believers, and be mindful of God if you are true believers. (Q 5:57)

[55] The word *walī* or *walīy* (pl. *awliyā'*) can mean supporter, protector, friend, or a legal guardian.

In fact the Qur'ān uses the word *bitāna*, 'that which is inside'. In Ibn Kathīr's *tafsīr*, *bitāna* refers to a friend with whom one shares secrets, and such friendship can only be had with those who accepted Islam. The believer is commanded not to seek friendship or take as advisers those who are non-Muslims, as they will only have enmity towards Islam.[56]

> You who believe, do not take into your intimacy outsiders who spare no effort to ruin you and who want to see you suffer. Their hatred is evident from their mouths but what their hearts conceal is much worse. We have made our Revelations clear for you. Will you not then use reason? (Q 3:118).
>
> It is not for the Prophet and for the believers to ask forgiveness for the idolators even if they are related to them – after having been shown that they are the inhabitants of hell-fire. (Q 9:113).
>
> O you who believe! Take not my enemies and yours as friends, offering them love (*mawadda*) even though they have denied the truth that has come to you, and have driven out you and the Messenger because you believe in God your Lord – not if you have come out to strive in my way and to seek my good will. You secretly show them love (*mawadda*). I know full well all that you conceal and all that you reveal. And any of you who does this has strayed from the straight path. (Q 60:1)

In terms of friendship with God, several Qur'ānic verses stress the concept of God as helper (*naṣīr*) or friend (*walī*):

> Your friends are God and his Messenger and those who believe, who establish prayer, give *zakāt* and bow down in worship. (Q 5:55)
>
> Unto God belong the dominion of the heavens and the earth. He gives life and he takes life. Except for him we have no protector nor helper. (Q 9:116)
>
> Say, 'Who is it that can screen you from God if it be his wish to give you punishment or to give you mercy?' Nor will they find for themselves beside God, any protector or helper. (Q 33:17)
>
> There is no fear upon the friends of God nor shall they grieve. (Q 10:62)
>
> Who is better in his religion than one who submits his whole self to God, does good and follows the way of Abraham, the true in faith? For God took Abraham for a friend. (Q 4:125)

In the Qur'ān, God is a friend of the believer and the believers are friends amongst themselves. Believers can come closer to God by being closer to each other. Their friendship however should not be construed as a passive state of

56 Ismā'īl ibn 'Umar Ibn Kathīr, *Tafsir Qur'ān al-'Aẓim*, Cairo: Dār al-Hadīth, 1994 vol. 2, p. 372.

being; the alliance and friendship between believers is expressed through 'enjoining the right and forbidding the wrong' (Q 9:71). A consistent theme of the Qur'ān is that those who become friends and protectors of each other are active members of the community:

> Those who believe, emigrate and strive with their wealth and themselves in the way of God, and those who give shelter and help, they are friends of one another. (Q 8:72)

In his analysis of formal friendships in the medieval Near East, Shelomo Goitein writes that friendship had a negligible role in pre-Islamic Arabia owing to the pre-eminence of the bonds of blood and kinship, and that

> Formal friendship, *ṣubḥa*, came into the Arab world with religion, with the Islam of Muḥammad. Conversion was conceived as a personal bond between the new believer and the founder of the religion. It was symbolized by a handclasp, the joining of hands by which the ancient Arabs used to confirm a contract or a covenant.[57]

In the *ḥadīth* canons, we find notions of friendship heavily embedded in ideas of brotherhood and a common faith:

> Some people asked God's messenger, 'Whose Islam is the best?' He replied, 'One who avoids harming the Muslims with his tongue and hands.'
>
> None of you will have faith until he loves for his brother what he loves for himself.[58]

From the religious perspective, society becomes divided between those who believe and those who do not believe for all sorts of political, religious, and social reasons where friendship is encouraged with the former group and not the latter. Furthermore, in scripture, one senses that true friendship lies with God alone as only God himself is the true friend. Friendship must be sought for God and rooted in God and for the new community, which is commanded to submit to God. One might be tempted to argue that religious faith places a distinct value on particular friendships where God is not just present but the focus. An example of this tension from the Christian tradition relates to Book IV of Augustine's *Confessions*. Augustine is thinking sorrowfully about the death of a dear friend whom he describes as 'sweet to me above every sweetness of that life of mine'. As Augustine reflects on the cherished memories of

57 Shelomo Goitein, 'Formal Friendship in the Medieval Near East', *Proceedings of the American Philosophical Society*, 115: 6, 1971, pp. 484–89.

58 Muḥammad ibn Ismā'īl Bukhārī, *Ṣaḥīḥ al-Bukhārī: The Translation of the Meanings of Ṣaḥīḥ al-Bukhāri, Kitāb al-Nikāḥ*, vol. 7, Saudi Arabia: Maktaba Darrussalām, 1997, p. 60.

this friendship through childhood and youth, he states that theirs was not truly a friendship because Christ had not been its centre and God had not been its goal:

> But in childhood he was not such a friend as he became later on, and even later on ours was not a true friendship, for friendship cannot be true unless you solder it together amongst those who cleave to one another by the charity poured forth in our hearts by the Holy Spirit, who is given to us.[59]

Even when we explore the vast literature of Islamic law, we find that although Islamic law regulates many different kinds of relationships, it does not deal systematically with friendship or typologies of friendship. The relationship between husband and wife, parents and children, masters and slaves, believers and non-believers are just examples of human ties and bonds that are assessed in legal language. Much of the legal language of classical texts deals with social, political, moral, and financial obligations between the individuals or two parties. The law books touch on aspects of affection and loyalty in different human relationships, but friendship does not come under scrutiny in the examination of private or civic life.

One could argue that friendship is one area of human relationships that has been given little systematic discussion in the pre-modern Islamic legal and theological texts. This not to say that it has not been analysed, especially in *adab*.[60] The ninth-century teacher and philologist Ibn Qutayba devoted a whole book to friendship in his encyclopaedia, *Kitāb ʿUyūn al- Akhbār* (The book of choice narratives). In a similar type of work, the tenth-century Andalusian scholar Ibn ʿAbd Rabbih of Cordoba wrote the sophisticated treatise *al-ʿIqd al-Farīd* (The unique necklace)[61] but it contains only one specific reference to friendship:

> Abu ʿAbd Allāh, al-Mahdī's secretary, said, "How needy the powerful ruler is of a friend who would restrain him, of modesty that would curb him, of intelligence that would control him, and of long experience, perspicacious mind, noble descent, and personal ethics that would facilitate matters to

59 Augustine, *The Confessions*, IV:4, trans. John K. Ryan, New York: Image Books, 1960, p. 97.

60 *Adab* is often used to refer to the elegant prose and poetry of belles-lettres in modern times. In earlier times, its meaning included all that a person needed to know to pass as a cultured and refined individual in society; this included ethical and moral qualities of an urbane person. *Adab* material had been growing in Arabia before Islam, but after Islam its content became quite diverse. Some of the classics of *adab* literature are contained in the works of Ibn Muqaffaʿ (d. 760), al-Aṣmaʿī (d. 828), al-Jāḥiẓ (d. 868), and al-Mubarrad (d. 898).

61 Also translated as *The Precious Necklace*. I quote from the translation *The Unique Necklace* by Issa J. Boullata, Reading: Garnet Publishing Limited, 2007.

> him; how needy he is of a compassionate companion, a kind friend, an eye that foresees consequences, and a heart that fears others."[62]

However, more systematic and philosophical accounts of friendship in the pre-modern period are rare. One such account can be found in Miskawayh's tenth-century work *Tahdhīb al-Akhlāq*.[63] Abū 'Ali Aḥmad ibn Muḥammad ibn Ya'qūb Miskawayh's treatise on philosophical ethics is one of the most influential and important books on Islamic ethics'. It contains six discourses of which the fifth discourse is on love and friendship. In his preamble to the whole work, Miskawayh writes that the object of the book is to "acquire for ourselves such a character that all our actions issuing therefrom may be good, and at the same time, may be performed by us easily, without any constraint or difficulty . . . The way to this end is to understand first of all, our souls: what they are, what kind of thing they are, and for what purpose they have been brought into existence within us."[64] The human goal should be to perfect and refine individual character. Miskawayh dwells both on the different kinds of love between people and the various forms of friendship in the one discourse. Though he addresses love and friendship in discourse number five, it is necessary to look at his conclusions at the end of discourse number four on justice to acquire a better sense of the relationship between justice and love. Miskawayh has just concluded with two points. Firstly:

> While the Law prescribes universal justice, it does not prescribe universal benevolence. It only urges people to practice benevolence, and this in particulars which cannot be specified because they are endless. On the other hand, law is definitive in prescribing universal justice because it is limited and can be specified.[65]

For Miskawayh, justice and just relations lie at the core of the ideal society. If people are just towards themselves, they will be just towards others, not just towards friends and relatives but towards those who are remote as well.[66] But justice is the essential component of the good society mainly because citizens do not love each other enough:

62 Ibn 'Abd Rabbiḥ, *Unique Necklace*, p. 30.

63 Aḥmad ibn Muḥammad Ibn Miskawayh, *Tahdhīb al-Akhlāq: The Refinement of Character*, trans. Constantine K. Zurayk, Chicago: Great Books of the Islamic World Inc., 2002. All references will be to this translation, beginning *Refinement*. For a comparative view of friendship between al-Ghazālī and Miskawayh Oliver see Lenn Goodman, "Friendship in Aristotle, Miskawayh and al-Ghazālī", in Leaman, ed., *Friendship East and West: Philosophical Perspectives*, Richmond: Curzon, 1996, pp. 164–91.

64 Miskawayh, *Refinement*, p. 1.

65 Miskawayh, *Refinement*, p. 116.

66 Miskawayh, *Refinement*, p. 118.

> There are those who have said that the good order of all existence and the soundness of all their conditions depend upon love. They have also said that man is forced to acquire this virtue, i.e. the disposition from which justice in dealings proceeds, only because he fails to achieve the dignity of love, and that if those who deal with one another are bound by love, they will be fair to one another and no disagreement will take place among them. For a man loves his friend and wishes for him what he wishes for himself.[67]

If citizens loved each other then they would act with benevolence towards each other. It is on the note of love where he ends his discourse on justice and begins the discourse on love and friendship. He begins by stating clearly that there is no way for a single individual to become complete by themselves and that as individuals each of us finds completion in our friends.[68] Love in its various forms is the basis of society:

> Friendship is a kind of love, but it denotes something more particular than love. It is affection in its very essence, and it does not take place among a large group, as is the case with love. Passionate love is the excess of love and more particular than affection because it takes place between two persons only.[69]

Miskawayh contrasts the friendship of the young with the friendship of the old. For the young, friendship is motivated largely by pleasure. Among the young, friendships form quickly and fade quickly. Among the old (or those who are old by nature), friendships arise because of mutual benefit. Then there are the virtuous:

> Friendship among virtuous people is for the sake of the good and is caused by the good. Since the good is something stable and has an unchangeable essence, the affections of those who are bound by such friendship are lasting and unchangeable.[70]

Like Aristotle, Miskawayh places emphasis virtue ethics in friendship, on seeking the good oneself and in another:

> The mutual love of virtuous people is not motivated by an external pleasure or any benefit but is due to their essential similarity, namely at aiming [at] what is good and seeking virtue. They exchange advice and agree to be just and equal in their desire of the good. This is why a friend is defined as another person who is yourself but is other than you in person, and this is why he is so rarely found.[71]

[67] Miskawayh, *Refinement*, p. 118.
[68] Miskawayh, *Refinement*, p. 123.
[69] Miskawayh, *Refinement*, p. 125.
[70] Miskawayh, *Refinement*, p. 125.
[71] Miskawayh, *Refinement*, p. 126.

The friend is an alter ego. Following a similar argument to Aristotle, Miskawayh regards human fellowship as the innate good in each of us, for in fellowship resides all different manners of love. He enters a lengthy discussion about the virtues of congregational prayer as a way of developing fellowship, which custom and the law enjoin:

> Possibly the Law made it an obligation on people to meet five times a day in their mosques and preferred communal prayer to individual prayer in order that they may experience this inborn fellowship which is the origin of all love and which exists in them in potency. In this way, this inborn fellowship would become actual and would become strengthened by the right beliefs which bind them together.[72]

For Miskawayh, public worship including the obligation of the *ḥajj* (pilgrimage to Mecca) is devised by law to foster human fellowship and sentiments of community. Religion through law encourages humanity to come together. Miskawayh agrees with the Aristotelian idea that one needs actual practice to give substance to the good life. Before entering a more systematic analysis of friendship Miskawayh returns to the subject of love. The one love that is unlike any other love is the love of the divine:

> Such a love is tied up with obedience and veneration. A man's love of his parents, and the veneration and obedience he renders to them, come near to this love, but no other love rises to the rank of these except the love of disciples for the philosophers.[73]

The love of God "is beyond any other love, its causes are beyond any other cause, and the blessings which come from it are beyond comparison with any other blessings".[74] The love of the disciple for the philosopher is nobler and superior to the love of parents because the philosophers have nobility and rank reflected in our souls making them the 'causes of our real existence, [by whose] help we can attain perfect happiness'.[75]

At times, Miskwayh writes similarly of both love and friendship, keenly quoting Aristotle:

> Whoever adulterates love or friendship is in a worse position than he who counterfeits silver or gold coins.

[72] Miskawayh, *Refinement*, p. 127.
[73] Miskawayh, *Refinement*, p. 134.
[74] Miskawayh, *Refinement*, p. 134.
[75] Miskawayh, *Refinement*, p. 134.

The intelligent person seeks good, does good, and acts in a good way towards his friends and family. The wicked person seeks companionship only to run away from the evil that lies within him.[76] Doing good for the soul is a matter of choice, but one who acts with goodness in his soul 'allots to his friends more than is within the power of those who lead the other lives, and he will thus come to be honoured by everybody and especially by his friends'.[77]

Miskawayh returns to the essence of friendship that results from the civic and social nature of human beings and claims that 'man's complete human happiness is realized through his friends'. He quotes Aristotle and agrees with Socrates:

> I am greatly astonished at those who teach their children the tales of kings and the fighting among them, and the stories of wars, hatred, revenge and rebellion, but who forget the subject of affection and the benefits which all people gain through love and fellowship. For no man can live without affection, even though the world may favour him with all its attractions.[78]

Miskawayh is in total agreement with the Greek philosophers who saw in friendship not just fellowship but a relationship that is essential to the well-being of our human souls. We need friends in good times as well as bad times, but it is important to distinguish what makes a good friend. For Miskawayh, a person should show gratitude for favours and kindness from others, he should not have a love of authority or be eager for excessive praise, nor should he show arrogance. Nevertheless we should overlook small defects in friendship:

> You must rather overlook slight defects from the like of which no human being can be free, and consider the defect that you find in yourself and tolerate its equivalent in others. Beware of the enmity of your friend or of one whom you have intimately treated as a friend.[79]

Once we have made a friend, we have a moral responsibility to look after the friend. Utmost in this mutual understanding is the show of pleasure when two friends meet each other. Furthermore, if it is important to share good news with a friend, it is even more important to share a friend's bad fortune:

> Do not wait until he asks you either explicitly or implicitly, but know what is in his heart, be quick to catch what is in his soul and share with him the pain of what has befallen him so that it may be easier for him to bear.[80]

[76] Miskawayh, *Refinement*, p. 136.
[77] Miskawayh, *Refinement*, p. 139.
[78] Miskawayh, *Refinement*, p. 140.
[79] Miskawayh, *Refinement*, p. 143.
[80] Miskawayh, *Refinement*, p. 145.

Miskawayh considers carefully the necessity of cultivating and maintaining a friendship. He sees neglect in friendship as resulting in possible harm to the individual whereby the friend might turn into an enemy. Miskawayh does not see neglect turning into indifference, but neglect making a friend into a possible enemy, which can only lead to harmful effects. His perspective on friendship demands honesty and generosity to the point where one should be able to display in front of a friend one's learning and accomplishments:

> The men of learning do not look upon one another as do the men of the world. For the goods of the world are few in number; thus when people compete for them, some hurt others and each one diminishes the other's lot. But in knowledge the reverse is true, for one's lot is not diminished by what another takes from him; instead it grows with spending, thrives on beneficence and increases by being given and freely imparted.[81]

For Miskawayh friendship is something we need for the flourishing of human civilisation, and yet he argues 'friendship and the kinds of love, by which the happiness of man as a civic being by nature, is achieved, have been subject to differences and to all kinds of corruption, have lost the character of unity, and have met with dispersion'.[82] Human nature being imperfect needs temperance and order to achieve the just society, and this demands hard work. To this end, Miskawayh clarifies his own position:

> It is for this reason that we have censored those who lead an ascetic life when they seek solitude away from other men, live in mountains and caves, and choose the state of savagery which is the opposite of civilisation, for they become deprived of all the moral virtues which we have enumerated. How is it possible for a person to be temperate, just, generous, or courageous, if he forsakes other men, keeps away from them, and loses moral virtues? Would he not be then in the rank of the inanimate or the dead?[83]

We cannot be moral citizens without people around us. Friendship is the context in which virtues are embodied. Our moral life struggles, indeed cannot exist outside of us opening ourselves to others and cultivating virtuous relationships, indeed virtuous friendships. Towards the end of this discourse, Miskawayh quotes Aristotle increasingly with a view to narrowing the gap between human aspirations and the highest ranks of good character:

[81] Miskawayh, *Refinement*, p. 147.
[82] Miskawayh, *Refinement*, p. 149.
[83] Miskawayh, *Refinement*, p. 150.

> Aristotle said, "Man's aspirations should not be human, though he be a man; nor should he be satisfied with the aspirations of the animal which is destined to die, though he himself also may be so destined. He should rather aim with all his capacities to live a divine life. For though man is small in body, he is great by his wisdom and noble by his intellect."[84]

Miskawayh's analysis of friendship is based on love as the ideal basis for society. It is in the absence of love that justice is needed and needs to prevail through just beings, just works, and just relationships; friendship is one such relationship. However, like Aristotle, Miskawayh sees friendship not just as important for the happiness of the individual but as fundamental to the well-being of society.

Miskawayh, unlike Bacon or Montaigne, does not write with an ardent passion about personal friendships or a personal friendship. His concern is with the necessity of friendship in cultivating personal good and the wider good of society. His style is more that of the classical philosophers who saw friendship as intrinsic to virtue ethics. Miskawayh does not betray any secret friendship or passion which has touched his soul and made him see friendship in any particular way. Nor is his language overly concerned with Qur'ānic and other references to brotherhood or feelings of communal solidarity. Miskawayh does not speak of friendship as promoting religious solidarity amongst believers or say that true friendship is cultivated only for the sake of God. His arguments are close to Aristotle where friendship is a state of being but also a cultivation of the self and others for the moral good of society.

Some of the writers discussed here talk of an ideal of friendship for the individual and society where friendship is seen as a good in a cultural context. Others, like Montaigne and to some extent Bacon, discuss how they were touched by a very real friendship and its influence on their lives. For most, it is affection and the unifying force effects of friendship between people that are emphasised. Here, the otherness of the friend is not dissolved in the excesses of friendship but remains the distinctive feature to that which we are drawn.

It seems to me that whether we consider friendships conceptually or structurally, friendships are good for society and for the individual because of the distinct moral good they can bring to us as individuals. Yet it is difficult to be precise as to what exactly draws us to one another as friends. We may list commonalities of hobbies, gender, race, background, and religion but still not come any closer to why certain people develop close and intimate friendships, similar to a love relationship. Furthermore, from certain religious perspectives,

[84] Miskawayh, *Refinement*, p. 152.

true friendships can only be had with those who share the same faith or at the very least a similar understanding of God. For to love for the sake of God, to find God in the friendships we form, may theoretically become a major primary determinant of whom we choose as friends and whose friends we choose to become. And yet, it seems to me that for most of us a true friendship does not emerge or become deeper based on such factors. Those who have faith in God see God working through their friendship whoever their friends become. If anything friendship demands that we accept the other clearly as the other and not simply as a reflection of our self or our interests. Friendship becomes a model for the moral life which insists that the self is social and relational, not autonomous and solitary.[85] When we stand in the presence of another we have a moral choice to make, that of extending and receiving the gift of friendship. Herein lies the essential mystery of friendship.

In our globalised world where different cultures, races, and religions are coming together, even colliding in private and public spaces, friendship assumes a new significance. There are risks involved in the cultivation of new friendships. A fundamental question of the modern era is: who are our friends in fragmented and divided communities? For some, this becomes a political question of self-identity but for many, the ambiguity of otherness does not create tension but rich opportunities of care and concern for those with whom friendships may not have been possible only a few years ago. In the modern age, with the processes of migration and renewed interest in identity formation, in complex urban societies of today, concepts of friendship have assumed a new significance and say as much about our attitudes to cultural boundaries as they do about our desires and preferences as human beings.

Time and distance are also new components of modern friendships. Despite less routine interaction and face-to-face contact, modern-day technologies allow for people to sustain a friendship even if they do not share the same world. The changing nature of human relationships through new media has also affected the concept of friendship, which in recent years has become a broader but contested issue through the huge explosion of social networking sites. Sites such as Facebook and MySpace allow one to make fast and instant 'friends' and the ability to add or delete 'friends', but they remain ambivalent tools. Emailing or instant messaging do not in themselves create deep friendships; deep friendships, friendships of the soul, need a spiritual dimension, they need loyalty and commitment, but most of all they need passion.

[85] Wadell, *Friendship*, p. 152. Wadell bases this analysis on Enda McDonagh, *Gift and Call*, Meinrad, IN: Abbey Press, 1975, pp. 29–30. 'Our primary moral experience is what happens to us when we stand in the presence of another.'

Many of us would admit that a deep friendship is one of the rarest gifts of life. A single friend, with whom we can be ourselves and yet more than ourselves, can be the most important person in our life. Even if we do not see this person regularly or share with them the daily banalities of life, such a friend may be as dear as, or even dearer than those with whom we are bound by blood ties. This can create its own problems of loyalty and fulfilment. In writing on the ambiguity of friendship, Mark Vernon says that at one stage in his life he relied heavily on friends for company but found that 'notwithstanding the occasional exception, friendship simply cannot bear the demands and intimacies great and small, that are the very stuff of these other relationships of love and blood'.[86] It may be that in the end many friendships are simply not strong enough for all the vicissitudes of life and can not be sustained. But most of us would not wish to end a friendship that speaks to our souls just because others saw a problem in the relationship. Yet, as I began with Emerson, so let me end with Emerson. Emerson said that when friendships are real, 'they are not glass threads or frostwork but the solidest thing we know'. The two elements that go into a friendship are truth and tenderness. Emerson speaks eloquently of the friendship that draws us through tenderness:

> We are holden to men by every sort of tie by blood, by pride, by fear, by hope, by lucre, by lust, by hate, by admiration, by every circumstance and badge and trifle, but we can scarce believe that so much character can exist in another as to draw us by love. Can another be so blessed and we be so pure that we can offer him tenderness? When a man becomes dear to me, I have touched the goal of fortune.[87]

To feel transformed in this remarkable way is where the true essence of a meaningful friendship lies. In the end, however, too much dwelling on the value and significance of friendship has its own dangers and may be self-defeating. It is not by focusing on the logic of how and why a friendship works and becomes fruitful in society that we attain a valuable relationship; a valuable relationship happens only when we reflect less on the friendship and instead concentrate more on the friend. For most of us today that requires a generosity of spirit that exceeds the boundaries often set by religious discourse.

86 Vernon, *Philosophy*, p. 1.
87 Emerson, 'Friendship'.

Glossary

'abd (pl. *'ibād* and *'abīd*) 'slave'. It can also mean 'servant' and 'worshipper' in the Qur'ān, for example, in the term *'abd Allāh*, 'worshipper/servant of God'.

'abd mamlūk a slave who is possessed or owned by someone.

'aqd a contract; can also refer to a legal transaction or agreement.

'aql 'sense, understanding intelligence'.

'awra 'genitals'; refers more widely to the parts of the body that should be covered.

'azl 'removal, withdrawal', used as the term for *coitus interruptus* as a means of birth control.

'idda 'waiting period', required of a woman before she may remarry following divorce or widowhood.

'ilā an oath to cease sexual relations with one's wife.

'illa the reason or cause of something.

'innīn to be impotent.

'ishq-i haqīqī love directed to God.

'ishq-i majāzī love directed to human beings.

'itāq 'freeing, liberation', in particular the setting free of slaves.

'udwan 'enmity, hostility'.

'uqr a compensatory dower paid for illicit sexual activity with a woman slave.

Abū Ḥanīfa (d. 767) Also known as Nu'mān ibn Muḥammad, Abū Ḥanīfa. He was an Iraqi jurist and the eponymous patron of the Sunnī Ḥanafī school of *fiqh*.

adab As a literary term it is used to refer to the elegant prose and poetry of belles-lettres. In a wider sense it refers to ettiquette, including ethical, moral, and cultural refinment.

afhash 'monstrous, loathsome'.

ahl al-kitāb 'People of the Book'; communities who had received the earlier scriptures, most commonly denoting Jews and Christians.

Aḥmad b. Muḥammad al-Qudūrī (d. 428/1037) Ḥanafī *faqīh* who was born and who died at Baghdād. His most famous work is the *Mukhtaṣar*.

al-bāri' one of God's names, meaning 'the Creator'.

al-muḥṣanāt min an-nisā 'all married women'.

al-qadar wa-l-qadā' 'God's power and decree', refers to the complex issue of predestination.

al- Dhahābī (d. 1348) Muḥammad b. Aḥmad al-Dhahābī a Shāfiʿī historian and theologian, who was an expert in canonical law.

al-Ashʿarī (d. 935) the main branch of Sunnī kalām. ʿAlī ibn Ismāʿīl Abū al-Ḥasan al-Ashʿarī: he was a theologian from Baṣra, after whom was named a school of theology,

al-Azhar University a prestigious university in Cairo, a centre of learning for Arabic language and Sunnī Islam.

al-ghafūr one of God's names, meaning 'the forgiver'.

al-ghayb that which is hidden or unseen.

al-ḥalīm one of God's names, meaning 'the gentle'.

al-ḥubb al-Ilāhī God's love for man, as defined by Ibn ʿArabī.

al-hurr A free person.

al-kabāʿir the major sins.

al-laṭīf one of God's names, meaning 'the Kind'.

Almohad caliphs The Almohad dynasty was a Moroccan Berber dynasty which was founded in the twelfth century and ruled parts of North Africa and al-Andalus.

al-murīd a spiritual aspirant.

al-raʿūf one of God's names, meaning 'the Merciful'.

al-raḥmān one of God's names, meaning 'the most compassionate'.

al-Rāzī (d. 1209) One of the most influential Sunnī theologians of the medieval period. Aside from his commentaries on the Qur'ān, he also wrote a critical commentary on Ibn Sīnā (d. 1037).

al-ṣaghā'ir 'minor sins'.

al-Tirmidhī (d. 892) Abū ʿĪsā Muḥammad ibn ʿĪsā bin Sawrah ibn Mūsā ibn al Ḍaḥḥāk al-Sulamī al-Sulamī al-Tirmidhī; he was the compiler of one of the six canonical collections of *ḥadīth*.

al-walī one of God's names, meaning 'the friend'.

al-wudūd one of God's names, meaning 'one who loves'.

ama a female slave.

anhār min khamr the 'rivers of wine'.

aqbah morally bad.

Ashʿarites A school of early Muslim speculative theology founded by the theologian Abū al-Ḥasan al-Ashʿarī.

aṣnām 'idols'.

awdāj 'jugular veins'.

awliyā' al-shaytān 'friends of Satan'.

ayāt 'signs'.

azwāj 'spouses'.

bā'in either 'irrevocable' or 'definite'.

bāṭil 'futility'; can also confer 'falsehood' or mean 'void'.

Bedouin an ethnic group of Arabs who were traditionally nomads or desert-dwellers.

birr 'righteousness'.

bismillah 'in the name of Allāh (God)'; said as a blessing before eating food or praying, to give thanks to God.

bita' a drink made from wheat and barley.

bitāna 'that which is inside', sometimes used to refer to a confidant.

Bukhārī (d. 870) Muḥammad ibn Ismā'īl Bukhārī, major *ḥadīth* scholar and author of one of the two most famous collections of *ṣaḥīḥ ḥadīths* with extensive *isnāds*.

dhabīḥa 'slaughter animal, sacrificial blood'; an animal that has undergone ritual slaughter in accordance with Islamic law.

dhaka 'to sacrifice an animal', the ritual of pouring out of blood from the slaughtered animal.

dhanb (pl. *dhunūb*) 'sin, offence, crime'.

dhauq 'aqli 'intellectual taste'.

dhimmī a non-Muslim member of the People of the Book living under Muslim rule, who benefited from protected status in exchange for paying special taxes.

diya a compensatory payment.

fa'l ma'qūl a rational act.

falsafa philosophy.

fāsid bad or foul; but when used in Islamic law, refers to a contract that is defective.

fāsiq an offender or sinner.

fatā a term for a slave, used predominantly in the Qur'ān as a term for a youth.

Fatāwā 'Alamgīrī A collection of Muslim law compiled by the order of the Moghul emperor Abu'l-Muẓaffar Muḥammad Muḥyi 'l-Dīn Awrangzīb 'Ālamgīr (d. 1707), during the years 1662–72. It remains an authoritative guide to traditional Ḥanafī doctrine in India. It is also known as the *Fatāwā Hindīyya*.

Fatāwā al=Qāḍīkhān The *fatāwā* of the Transoxanian jurist, Fakhruddīn Ḥassan b. Mansūr al-Uzjandi al-Farghāni Qāḍīkhān (d. 1196).

fatwā (pl. *fatāwā*) a legal opinion formulated by a *muftī* in reply to a particular question.

fiqh 'understanding, knowledge', the technical term for Islamic jurisprudence.

fisq 'sinfulness'.

fuqahā' (sing. *faqīh*) legal jurists, experts in *fiqh*.

furqān 'proof, 'evidence', also one of the names of the Qur'ān.

furū' 'branch', 'section'; the elaboration of religious law.

furū' al-fiqh literary genre (branches of jurisprudence).

ghafūr al-raḥīm 'most Merciful' applied to God.

ghawā'il al-shahwa 'dangers of lust'.

Ghazālī (d. 1111) Abū Ḥāmid Muḥammad bin Muḥammad a hugely influential Muslim jurist, theologian, and mystic. Among his most prominant works is *Iḥyā' 'Ulūm al-Dīn*, which consists of forty individual books and addresses every aspect of religious life for the devout Muslim.

ghufūr al-wudūd 'the forgiving, the loving', names of God.

ghulām a term for a slave, also a youth.

ḥadd (pl. *ḥudūd*) a punishment for a crime against religion.

ḥadīth 'tradition or report', being the source material for the *sunna* of the Prophet Muḥammad.

ḥadīth qudsī 'divine sayings', God's thoughts expressed by the Prophet.

ḥalāl 'permissible, lawful'; that which is allowed in Islamic law. It is popularly used amongst Muslims to refer primarily to meat that has been slaughtered according to ritual prescription.

Hallāj (d. 922) Abu 'l-Mughīth al-Ḥusayn b. Manṣūr b. Maḥammā al-Bayḍāwī al-Hallāj was a mystic theologian.

Ḥanafī follower of the Sunnī legal school of Abū Ḥanīfa.

ḥaqq absolute 'truth'.

ḥarām 'forbidden', 'prohibited'; that which is not permitted in Islamic law.

ḥasan 'good'.

Ḥasan al-Baṣrī (d. 728) A famous theologian and mystic who defended the freedom of the will.

ḥasanāt (sing. *ḥasana*) good deeds or acts.

Hidāya A classic book of Islamic jurisprudence by Sheikh 'Alī ibn Abī Bakr al-Marghīnānī (d. 1197). It is a commentary on the *Jami' al-Saghīr* and the *Mukhtaṣar* of Aḥmad ibn Muḥammad Qudūrī (d. 1037).

ḥubb 'love'.

ḥukm an Islamic commandement or legal judgment.

hurrīya 'freedom'.

ḥusn 'good, excellence'.

ibāq a slave who runs away from his master.

Ibn 'Abd Rabbb of Cordova (d. 940) Andalusian scholar, writer of *adab*, and poet.

Ibn 'Arabī (d. 1240) A brilliant Andalusian Ṣūfī scholar, philosopher, and poet famous for his works on cosmology and Muḥammad as the Perfect Man.

Ibn ʿAbbās ʿAbd Allāh ibn al-ʿAbbās: a cousin of the Prophet, renowned as an outstanding authority on *ḥadīth* and *tafsīr* during the early period.

Ibn Kathīr (d. 1373) ʿImād al-Dīn Ismāʿīl b. ʿUmar b. Kathīr, scholar, expert in *fiqh*, a historian, and traditionalist.

Ibn Miskawayh (d. *c.* 1030) Aḥmad ibn MuḥammadIbn Miskawayh: philosopher and historian, who wrote systematic ethics.

Ibn Qutayba Ninth-century teacher and philologist a theologian and a writer of *adab.*

Ibn Rushd (d. 1198) Muḥammad ibn Aḥmad Ibn Rushd, also known in the Western world as Averroes. He was a renowned philosopher, physician, and jurist. Among his most celebrated legal works is the *Bidāyat al-Mujtahid wa-Nihāyat al-Muqtasid.*

Ibn Sīnā (d. 1037) Abū ʿAlī al-Ḥusayn b. ʾAbd Allāh Ibn Sīnā, also known in the West as Avicenna. A famous physician and philosopher seen as a key figure in the Islamic Golden Age.

iḥsan 'performance of good deeds', also used to denote 'excellence' or 'virtue'; one of the three central tenets of Islam, along with *islām* and *imān.*

iḥṣan in Islamic law 'of an unblemished reputation'.

ijtihād independent scholarly effort or exertion used in Islamic law to understand God's law.

ikhtilāf 'difference of opinion'; among scholars and jurists in the elaboration of arguments.

imām In Sunnī Islam, leader of a congregational prayer or leader of a community. In Shiʿī Islam, the title of the renamed leaders of Shīʿism who are the source of authority in that community.

Imāmī Name given to the largest group of the Shīʿa, "The Twelvers'.

imān 'faith'.

isnād a chain of named authorities through whom a *ḥadīth* has passed.

istīlād a slave bearing the child of a master.

istiqāl the sense of doing something in the future.

ithm 'sin' or 'crime'.

jāhilīyya the pre-Islamic period, known as the age of ignorance.

jāriya a slave girl.

jihād striving in the name of faith, in particular towards a religious path. It can also mean 'holy war'.

jumaʿ Friday, or a shorthand to refer to Friday prayers.

Kaʿba the main Islamic sanctuary in Mecca.

kadīʿa 'deception'.

kafāʾa the concept of equality between husband and wife in a variety of criteria in a marriage contract.

kaffāra 'expiation, penance'.

kalām literally 'speech', 'words'; in religious matters it refers to theological debate and argument.

kasb 'appropriation', also 'acquisition', 'earnings.'

kashrūt Jewish dietary laws.

khādim a domestic servant or employee.

khalīl 'friend'.

khalwa any period of 'seclusion' (referring to husband and wife).

khamīr al-'aql 'veiling the intellect'.

khamr wine, specifically made from grapes.

khatī'a (pl. *khatāyā*) 'mistakes, crimes, sins'.

Khawārij A sect of early Islam emerging from the battle of Ṣiffin. They emphasised good works over faith and made all forms of sinning analogous to unbelief.

khayr 'good'.

khinzīr 'swine'.

khiyār 'choice', 'option' in Islamic law.

khiyār al-'ayb in contracts of sale, the option of defect.

khiyār al-bulūgh 'option of puberty'.

khudī 'ego', referring specifically to an awareness of the self.

kināya indirect expression or obliqueness.

kitābī Adherent of a divinely revealed religion. Often refers to the People of the Book, namely, the Jews and Christians.

kufr 'unbelief' or denial of God.

laqīt 'foundling'.

lawḥ al-maḥfūẓ the Preserved Tablet, on which is written all that has happened, and will come to happen in history.

li'ān In Islamic law this refers to a sworn allegation of adultery.

ma akala l-sabu'u animals killed by other animals.

mā malakat aymānuhum 'those whom your right hands possess,' meaning those whom you rightfully possess – often referring to female slaves.

ma'dhūn slaves who have been given authority by their masters to carry out certain types of transactions.

mabsūṭ 'extended, outstretched, large, elaborate': in Islamic law, it refers to a larger and more sophisticated tome of work.

madhhab a Muslim school of law.

mafātīḥ al-ghayb 'the keys to the unseen'.

maḥārīm that which is forbidden or taboo, in law it refers to the boundaries of 'legal consanguinity'.

māḥīya 'quiddity': to erase/wipe out something.

mahr a dower that a groom owes or gives the bride on the completion of a marriage contract.

mahr al-mithl An implicit dower, when an amount of dower has not been formally agreed upon. This applies in every marriage.

majāz a figurative expression.

makr 'deception'.

makrūh 'loathsome', 'hated'; in Islamic law, it refers to something that is generally disliked and discouraged but which is not forbidden.

malaka to rule over, or to be the owner of something.

Mālik b. Anas (d. 795) Anas b. Mālik Abū Ḥamza; one of the most prolific traditionists, a Companion of the Prophet, after whom is named one of the four schools of Sunnī law.

Mālikī The Mālikī school is one of the four main schools of *fiqh* in Sunnī law, named after its Medinan jurist founder, Mālik b. Anas.

Mamlūk a dynasty that ruled Egypt and Syria from 1250 to 1517.

mamlūk a soldier of slave origin, often of Turcvic ancestry.

mansik a sacred ceremony or ritual, in particular as part of a pilgrimage.

maqqūdha Animals that die by being beaten to death.

matanza the ritual public slaughter of pigs.

matn the main text in a *ḥadīth* report, as opposed to the chain of transmitters.

mawadda 'love, friendship'.

mayta 'carrion'.

mithāqun ghalīdūn a solemn covenant.

mizr a drink made from wheat and barley.

mu'allaq literally means 'pending', 'conditional'; in legal terms it refers to a contract that is dependent on a condition.

mu'min a believer, someone who has faith.

Mu'tazila A major rationalist school of theology which dominated 'Abbāsid circles. They stressed human free will, the unity of God, and the createdness of the Qur'ān.

mudabbar a word for slave in classical Arabic.

muḍāf literally means 'added'; in legal terms it refers to a contract of marriage or divorce.

muftī a scholar learned in the legal sciences who has the authority to give legal opinions (*fatwās*).

muḥṣana literally a 'woman who is fortified [against unchastity]' and carries three meanings; a married woman, a chaste woman and a free woman.

muḥṣanāt 'free', can also refer to married women.

mujtahid a legal scholar who uses independent reasoning to explain or clarify a point of law.

mukallaf a person who is legally capable (of sound mind), and thus obliged to fulfil religious duties.

mukātab a word for slave in classical Arabic (fem. *mukātaba*).

mukhtaṣar epitomes of the law, more condensed and succint than the *mabsūṭ*

multikh a fool/ass.

munāfiqūn 'hypocrites'.

munkar 'wrongdoing'.

munkhaniqa strangled or suffocated animals.

Murji'a Sometimes refered to as the 'Postponers'. they were an early school of *kalām*, who left the decision of what constituted grave sins to God.

murtadd an apostate.

mushrik an idolator or polytheist (pl. *mushrikūn*).

muskir 'intoxicating drink'.

Muslim (d. 875) Ḥusayn Muslim ibn al-Hajjāj Qushayri al-Nishapūrī; he authored a major collection of *ḥadīth*, thought to be second only to the collection by Bukhārī.

musta'min someone under temporary protection.

mutaraddiya animals killed by falling.

nabīdh A fermented fruit drink common among the Arabs, made from dates, barley, or honey. It can imply both intoxicating and non-intoxicating drinks (pl. *anbidha*).

naḥr the slaughter of a camel by cutting the jugular vein at the base of the neck.

najas 'impure'.

najasa something that is considered impure.

nakaḥa 'to marry'.

naṣīr 'helper'.

nāṭiḥa animals gored to death by other animals.

nikāḥ 'marriage; a marriage contract'.

nīyya 'intention'.

nuzūl 'to come down, or be sent down'.

qabīh 'disgraceful, shameful, vile or bad'.

qadhf defamation and in, Islamic law, and explicit accusation of unlawful intercourse by the husband against his wife.

qadar 'predestination'.

Qadarites An early school of theology, championing human free will. Often thought to be the forerunners of the Mu'tazila.

qāḍī a judge in a court of law.

qalb 'heart'.

qayna a word for slave in classical Arabic.

qibla the direction of Mecca, towards which Muslims pray.

qinn a word for slave in classical Arabic.

qiṣāṣ 'retaliation or punishment'.

qiyās the use of analogical reasoning as the third principle in *fiqh* to determine God's law.

qiyās mursal an analogy that does not rely on a specific rule.

Qurṭubi Abū 'Abd Allāh Muḥammad b. Aḥmad b. Abī Bakr b. Faradj al-Anṣārī al-Khazradjī al-Andalusī al-Qurṭubī; a thirteenth-century Mālikī exegete and an expert on ḥadith. Famous for his commentary on the Qur'ān.

ra'ūf al-raḥīm the description of 'the most compassionate, the most merciful' applied to God.

raghban 'desire'.

raḥīq 'drink', usually referring to a most exquisite wine.

raḥma mercy or loving compassion.

raḥma Allāh the mercy of God.

raj'ī 'revocable'.

raqīq a word for slave in classical Arabic.

rijs 'unclean'.

rizq ḥasan 'good nourishment'.

rūḥ 'spirit'.

Rūmī (d. 1273) Jalāl ad-Dīn Muḥammad Rūmī, perhaps the most celebrated Ṣūfī poet and the author of the *Mathnawī.*

sabb 'cursing/insulting'.

ṣabr 'patience'.

sādiq 'friend'.

sadr chest or breast.

saghā'ir minor sins.

ṣaḥīḥ 'valid'. 'complete', 'correct'. Also refers to some of the collections of *ḥadīths.*

Saḥnūn (d. 855) Abū Sa'īd 'Abd al-Salām b. Sa'īd b. Ḥabīb b. Ḥassān b. Hilāl b. Bakkār b. Rabī'a al-Tanūkhi Saḥnūn a Tunisian jurist from the Mālikī school.

sakira to be drunk or intoxicated.

sakrātihim a state of intoxication.

ṣāliḥ 'good'.

ṣāliḥāt 'good deeds'.

Sarakhsī (d. fifth century) Muḥammad ibn Aḥmad Sarakhsī. He was a Transoxanian Muslim jurist of the Ḥanafī school.

ṣarīḥ direct, or clear, expression.

ṣayd 'hunting'.

Shāfi'ī A Sunnī school of *fiqh*, named after the jurist Abū 'Abdullāh Muḥammad ibn Idrīs al-Shafi'ī (d. 820).

shahāda literally, 'testimony' the declaration of belief for a Muslim in the oneness of God and the messengership of Muḥammad. The first pillar of Islam. The *shahāda* will also be uttered by one wishing to convert to Islam.

sharīʿa In general refers to all of the religious law as contained in the Qur'ān and *ḥadīths*.

sharr 'evil'.

shaytān Satan, demon; the name given to Iblīs after his expulsion from paradise.

Shiʿites Followers of the Shīʿī sect of Islam, the second largest after the Sunnī school. They championed the righful succession of ʿAlī, the Prophet's cousin and son-in law after the Prophet's death. They also recognise the authority of their *imāms* as having righful claim to leadership of the community.

shirk associating another with God, idolatry.

siḥr 'sorcery'.

sūʾ (pl. *aswāʾ*) ill, misfortune, bad deed.

ṣubḥa 'Friendship, companionship'.

Ṣūfī one who follows one of the many mystical paths of Islam.

sukr nafsihi la al-ʿain 'the intoxication itself, not the source'.

sukran an intoxicated person.

sunna A term originally used to refer to the custom of a community. It came to mean the way the Prophet acted and which is subsequently to be emulated by Muslims.

Sunnī The largest form of Islam, distinct from the Shīʿī.

Sūra a chapter of the Qur'ān.

ṭaʿam 'food'.

ṭaʿlīq al-ṭalāq an intention to divorce.

taʿzīr a discretionary punishment in Islamic law.

tadbīr the setting free of slaves on the death of a master.

tafsīr 'interpretation'; exegesis of the Qur'ān.

tafwīd 'delegation'.

ṭalāq Commonly translated as divorce, separation between husband and wife, which is normally instigated orally by the husband.

tamlīk the transfer of ownership.

taqwa 'piety'.

taṣawwuf the mystical path in Islam, or Ṣūfism.

tashbīh 'simile'.

tasmiya To pronounce God's name, often used synonymously with the Bismillah.

tasnīm a paradisiacal spring.

tawakkul trust; more specifically, trust in God.

tawba 'repentance'.

tawḥīd The doctrine of the oneness of God.

tazwīj 'to marry off'.

umm walad A slave woman who gives birth to her master's child and becomes free on his death.

wadd 'love'.

waḥy inspiration or revelation.

wājib 'obligatory', a duty.

walā' 'clientage'.

walad a male child or son.

walī (pl. *awliyā*) 'friend'.

yuwaffiq 'reconcile'.

Ẓāhirī an early school of thought in Islamic law.

zakāt 'alms giving'; one of the five pillars of Islam.

ẓihār A pre-Islamic formula of divorce or repudiation by the husband. It consisted of words such as 'You are to me like my mother's back' and resulted in making the wife prohibited to her husband with regards to sexual intercourse.

zinā illicit intercourse between two unmarried people; can also refer to adultery.

ẓulm 'injustice or darkness'.

Bibliography

The Holy Qur'ān, trans. Yusuf Ali. Beltsville, M.D: Amana Publications, 2003.

Asad, Muhammad. online *tafsīr* at http://www.archive.org/details/TafsirUlAsad.

al-Ash'arī, 'Alī ibn Ismā'īl Abū al-Ḥasan. *Kitāb al-Luma' fī al-Radd 'ala Ahl al-Zaygh wa'l-Bida': The Theology of al-Ash'ari*, ed. and trans. Richard Joseph McCarthy. Beirut: Imprimerie Catholique, 1953.

al-Bāqī, Muḥammad Fu'ād 'Abd, ed., *Kitāb al-Sunan*. Cairo, 1953.

Baydāwi, 'Abd Allāh ibn 'Umar. *Tawāli'al-Anwār min Matāli'al-Anzār*, ed. and trans. E. Calverley and James Pollock. Leiden: Brill, 2002.

Bukhārī, Muḥammad ibn Ismā'īl. *Ṣaḥīḥ al-Bukhārī: The Translation of the Meanings of Ṣaḥīḥ al-Bukhāri: Arabic–English*, trans. Muḥammad Muḥsin Khān. Saudi Arabia: Maktaba Darrussalām, 1997.

Burhānpūr, Nizām. *Fatāwā 'Alamgīrī*, 3rd edition, vol. 3, Beirut, 1973.

al-Dhahābī, Muḥammad b. Aḥmad. *Kitāb al-Kabā'ir (The Major Sins)*, trans. M. al-Selek. Beirut: Dār al-Fikr, 2007.

al-Ghazālī, Abū Ḥāmid Muḥammad b. Muḥammad. *Iḥyā' 'Ulūm al-Dīn*. Damascus: Ālim al-Kutub, 1992.

Ibn 'Abd Rabbih, Aḥmad ibn Muḥammad. *The Unique Necklace*, trans. Issa J. Boullata. Reading: Garnet Publishing Limited, 2007.

Ibn Anas, Mālik. *al-Muwaṭṭa*. Cairo: Dār al-Ḥadīth, 1999.

Ibn 'Arabī, Muḥammad ibn 'Alī Muḥyī al-Dīn. *al-Futuhāt al-Makkiyya*. Cairo: 1972–89.

Tarjumān al-Ashwāq: A Collection of Mystical Odes by Muḥyiuddīn ibn al-'Arabī, ed. and trans. Reynold A. Nicholson. London: Oriental Translation Fund, 1911.

Ibn Ḥanbal, Aḥmad ibn Muḥammad. *al-Musnad*, Ed. *Aḥmad Muḥammad Shakir*, Cairo: Dār al-Ma'ārif, 1946.

Ibn Kathīr, Ismā'īl ibn 'Umar. *Tafsīr Qur'ān al-'Aẓīm*. Cairo: Dār al-Ḥadīth, 1994.

Ibn Miskawayh, Aḥmad ibn Muḥammad. *Tahdhīb al-Akhlāq: The Refinement of Character*, trans. Constantine K. Zurayk. Chicago: Great Books of the Islamic World Inc., 2002.

Ibn Rushd, Muḥammad ibn Aḥmad. *Bidāyat al-Mujtahid wa-Nihāyat al-Muqtasid*. Beirut, 1992.

Ibn Sa'īd, Saḥnūn. *al-Mudawwana al-Kubra l-il-Imām Mālik*. Beirut, 1999.

Iqbāl, Muḥammad. *The Reconstruction of Religious Thought in Islam*. Lahore: Ashraf Press, 1954; reprinted 1960.

Tulip in the Desert: A Selection of Poetry, trans. Mustansir Mir. London: Hurst & Company, 2000.

al-Jāḥiẓ, Abū 'Uthmān 'Amr b. Baḥr. *The Epistle on Singing Girls*, ed. and trans. Alfred F. L. Beeston. Warminster: Aris & Philips Ltd, 1980.

al-Kisā'i, Muḥammad ibn 'Abd Allah. *Qiṣaṣ al-Anbiyā'*, trans. Wheeler Thackston. Great Books of the Islamic World, 1997.

al-Marghīnānī, 'Alī ibn Abī Bakr. *al-Hidāya*, vol. 2, Maktabāt al-Tawfiqīyya, n. d.

Nu'mān ibn Muḥammad, Abū Ḥanīfa. *Kitāb al-Āthār of Imām Abū Hanīfah*, ed. Muhammad ibn al-Hasan ash-Shaybāni. London: Turath Publishing, 2006.

Qāḍī Khān, Fakhruddīn Hassan b. Mansūr al-Uzjandi al-Farghāni. *Fatāwā al-Qāḍī-Khān*, ed. and trans. Mahomed Yusoof Khan Bahadur and Wilayat Hussain. New Delhi: Kitab Bhavan, 1994.

al-Qudūrī, Aḥmad ibn Muḥammad. *The Mukhtaṣar al Qudūrī*, trans. Tahir Mahmood Kiani. London: Ta-Ha Publishers Ltd, 2010.

al-Qurṭubī, Muḥammad ibn Aḥmad. *al-Jāmi' al-Aḥkām al-Qur'ān*. Cairo: Dār al-Hadīth, 1996.

al-Ṣan'ānī, Abū Bakr 'Abdarrazzāq b. Hammām. *al-Muṣannaf*, ed. Ḥabibarraḥman al-A'ẓamī. 1970.

Sarakhsī, Muḥammad ibn Aḥmad. *Kitāb al-Mabsūṭ*, vol. 5. Beirut: Dār al-Ma'rifa, 1993.

Sijistānī, Abū Dawūd Sulaymān bin Ash'ath. *Sunan Abū Dawūd*, vol. 2, Lahore: Ihsān, 1987.

al-Rāzī, Fakhr al-Dīn Muḥammad ibn 'Umar. *al-Tafsīr al-Kabir*. Beirut: Dār Iḥyā' al-Turāth al-'Arabī, 1999.

Ṭabarī, Muḥammad ibn Jarīr. *Jāmi' al-Bayān 'an Ta'wil āy al-Qur'ān*. Beirut: Dār al Kutub, 1995; also Beirut: Dar al-Fikr, 1990.

al-Tirmidhī and Ibn Māja: see http://www.muttaqun.com/alcohol.html.

SECONDARY SOURCES BIBLIOGRAPHY

Abrahamov, Binyamin. 'A Re-examination of Al-ash'ari's Theory of "Kasb" According to "Kitāb al-Luma"'. *Journal of the Royal Asiatic Society of Great Britain and Ireland*, (1989), pp. 210–21.

'Fakhr al-Dīn al-Rāzī on the Knowability of God's Essence and Attributes'. *Arabica* (2002), pp. 204–30.

Divine Love in Islamic Mysticism. London: Routledge, 2003.

Al-Azhary Sonbol, Amira. 'Rethinking Women and Islam', in Yvonne H. Haddad and John Esposito, eds., *Daughters of Abraham: Feminist Thought in Judaism, Christianity and Islam*. Gainesville: University Press of Florida, 2001, pp. 108–46.

Ali, Ameer. *Muḥammadan Law*, vol. 2. Calcutta: Thacker, Spink, 1917.

Ali, Kecia. *Marriage and Slavery in Early Islam*. Cambridge, MA: Harvard University Press, 2010.

Allison, Henry E. 'Reflections on the Banality of Radical Evil', in María Pía Lara, ed., *Rethinking Evil*. London: University of California Press, 2001.

Aquinas, Thomas. *Summa Contra Gentiles, Books 1–111*, in Joseph Kenny, ed., *Christian-Islamic Preambles of Faith*. Washington: The Council for Research in Values and Philosophy, 1999.

Arendt, Hannah. *Eichmann in Jerusalem: A Report on the Banality of Evil*. New York: Penguin Books, 1994.

The Origins of Totalitarianism. New York: Harcourt, Brace & Co,. 1951.

Aristotle. *Nichomachean Ethics*, trans. Sarah Broadie and Christopher Rowe. Oxford: Oxford University Press, 2002.

Augustine. *The Confessions*, IV:4, trans. John K. Ryan. New York: Image Books, 1960.

Austin, John L. *How To Do Things with Words*. Oxford: Clarendon Press, 1965.

Babić, Jovan. 'Toleration vs Doctrinal Evil in our Times'. *Journal of Ethics* 8:3 (2004), pp. 225–50.

Bacon, Francis. *The Essays*, ed. John Pitcher. Harmondsworth: Penguin, 1985.

Banani, Amin and Vryonis, Speros, eds. *Individualism and Conformity in Classical Islam*. Wiesbaden: Harrassowitz, 1977.

Baudrillard, Jean. *The Intelligence of Evil or the Lucidity Pact*, trans. Chris Turner. Oxford: Berg, 2005.

Bearman, P. J., Bianquis, T., Bosworth, C. E., van Donzel, E., and Heinrichs, W. P. et al. *The Encyclopaedia of Islam*, 2nd edition. Leiden: Brill, 1960–2005.

Bell, Richard. 'Muḥammad and Divorce in the Qur'ān'. *Muslim World*, 29:1, pp. 55–62.

Bennett, John C. 'The Problem of Evil'. *Journal of Religion*, 18:4 (1938), pp. 401–21.

Bennett, Merrill K. 'Aspects of the Pig'. *Agricultural History* 44:2 (1970), pp. 223–36.

Brockopp, Jonathan. *Early Mālikī Law: Ibn 'Abdal Ḥakam and his Major Compendium of Jurisprudence*. Leiden: Brill, 2000.

'Slaves and Slavery', in J. McAuliffe, ed., *Encyclopaedia of the Qur'an*, vol. 5, Leiden: Brill, 2006, pp. 56–60.

Brunschvig, Robert. 'Averroès juriste'. *Études d'Orientalisme dédiées à la mémoire de Lévi-Provençal*, 1, (1962), pp. 35–68.

Burrell, David. 'Transforming Love', in Miroslav Volf, Ghazi bin Muhammad, and Melissa Yarrington, eds., *A Common Word*. Grand Rapids, MI: Eerdmans Publishing Co., 2010, pp. 153–6.

Calder, Norman. '*Hinth, Birr, Tabarrur, Tahannuth*: An Inquiry into the Arabic Vocabulary of Oaths'. *Bulletin of the School of Oriental and African Studies*, 51 (1989), pp. 214–39.

Islamic Jurisprudence in the Classical Era, ed. Colin Imber. Cambridge: Cambridge University Press, 2010.

"Method and Theory in the Study of Religion". *Journal of the North American Association for the Study of Religion* (1997), pp. 47–73.

Studies in Early Muslim Jurisprudence. Oxford: Clarendon Press, 1993.

Cantor, Norman F. *Antiquity: From the Birth of Sumerian Civilisation to the Fall of the Roman Empire*. Harper Perennial, 2003.

Chittick, William. *Ṣūfism: A Short Introduction*. Oxford: Oneworld Publications, 2000.

Cicero, Marcus Tullius. *De Amicitia*, trans. E. S. Shuckburgh: http://ancienthistory.about.com/library/b/b1_text_cicero_deamic.htm.

Clarence-Smith, William Gervase. *Islam and the Abolition of Slavery*. Oxford: Oxford University Press, 2006.

Coelho, Paul. *Like the Flowing River*. London: HarperCollins, 2007.

Cook, Maeve. 'Moral Evil and Moral Identity', in María Pía Lara, ed., *Rethinking Evil*. London: University of California Press Ltd, 2001.

Cook, Michael. 'Early Islamic Dietary Law'. *Jerusalem Studies in Arabic and Islam*, 7 (1986), pp. 217–77.

Commanding Right and Forbidding Wrong in Islamic Thought. Cambridge: Cambridge University Press, 2001.

Forbidding Wrong in Islam. Cambridge: Cambridge University Press, 2003.

'Magian Cheese: An Archaic Problem in Islamic Law'. *Bulletin of the School of Oriental and African Studies* 47:3 (1984), pp. 449–67.

Cooper, John M. 'Aristotle on Friendship', in Amelie Oksenberg Rorty, ed., *Essays on Aristotle's Ethics*. Berkeley: University of California Press, 1980, pp. 301–40.

Den Uyl, Douglas J. 'Friendship and Transcendence'. *International Journal for Philosophy of Religion*, 41:2 (1997), pp. 105–22.

Derin, Suleyman. *Love in Ṣūfīsm*. Istanbul: Insan Publications, 2008.

Dews, Peter. '"Radical Finitude" and the Problem of Evil', in María Pía Lara, ed., *Rethinking Evil*. London: University of California Press Ltd, 2001.

Diener, Paul and Robkin, Eugene. 'Ecology, Evolution and the Search for Cultural Origins: The Question of Islamic Pig Prohibition'. *Current Anthropology*, 19:3 (1978), pp. 493–540.

Dotoli, Carmelo. *The Christian Revelation: Word, Event and Mystery*, trans. Cavallo Domenica. Aurora, CO: Davies Group Publishers, 2006.

Douglas, Mary. *Purity and Danger: An Analysis of the Concepts of Pollution and Taboo*. London: Routledge & Kegan Paul, 1996.

Dziob, Anne Marie. 'Aristotelian Friendship: Self Love and Moral Rivalry'. *Review of Metaphysics*, 46 (1993), pp. 781–801.

Emerson, Ralph Waldo. 'Friendship', in *Essays: First Series*. Boston: J. Munroe & Co., 1841 (http://www. emersoncentral.com/friendship.htm).

Emon, Anver M. 'Natural Law and Natural Rights in Islamic Law'. *Journal of Law and Religion*, 20:2 (2004–2005), pp. 351–95.

Fierro, Maribel. 'The Legal Policies of the Almohad Caliphs and Ibn Rushd's *Bidāyat al-Mujtahid*'. *Journal of Islamic Studies*, 10:3 (1999), pp. 222–48.

Firmage, Edwin B., ed. *Religion and Law: Biblical, Jewish and Islamic Perspectives*, Winona Lake, IN: Eisenbrauns, 1989, pp. 159–91.

Frank, Richard M. 'The Structure of Created Causality According to al-Ash'ari: An Analysis of the *Kitāb al-Luma*''. *Studia Islamica*, 25 (1966), pp. 13–75.

Gadamer, Hans-Georg. 'The Ethics of Value and Practical Philosophy (1982)' in trans. *Hermeneutics, Religion and Ethics*, Joel Weinsheime. New Haven: Yale University Press, 1999.

Gaiman, Neil. *Sandman: Season of Mists*, 1992, online quote

Glassé, Cyril. *The New Encyclopaedia of Islam*. Walnut Creek, CA: AltaMira Press, 2002.

Goitein, Shelomo. 'Formal Friendship in the Medieval Near East'. *Proceedings of the American Philosophical Society*, 115:6 (1971), pp. 484–9.

Goldziher, Ignaz. *Muslim Studies*, ed. S. M. Stern. London: Allen & Unwin, 1967.

Goodman, Lenn. 'Friendship in Aristotle, Miskawayh and al-Ghazālī', in Oliver Leaman, ed., *Friendship East and West: Philosophical Perspectives*. Richmond: Curzon, 1996, pp. 164–91.

Avicenna. Ithaca, NY: Cornell University Press, 2006.
Goodrich, Peter. 'Laws of Friendship'. *Law and Literature*, 15:1 (2003), pp. 23–52.
Graham, William A. *Beyond the Written Word: Oral Aspects of Scripture in the History of Religion*. Cambridge: Cambridge University Press, 1987.
Haddad, Yvonne H. and Esposito, John, eds. *Daughters of Abraham: Feminist Thought in Judaism, Christianity and Islam*. Gainesville: University Press of Florida, 2001.
Harris, Marvin. *Cows, Pigs, Wars and Witches: The Riddles of Culture*. New York: Random House, 1974.
Hawting, Gerald Richard, Mojaddedi, Jawhid Ahmad, and Samely, Alexander, eds. *Studies in Islamic and Middle-Eastern Texts in Memory of Norman Calder*. Oxford: Oxford University Press, 2001.
Hidayatullah, Aysha. 'Māriyya the Copt: Gender, Sex and Heritage in the Legacy of Muhammad's *umm walad*'. *Islam and Christian–Muslim Relations*, 21:3 (2010), pp. 221–43.
Hofstadter, Albert. 'Reflections on Evil'. *The Lindley Lecture*, University of Kansas, 1973.
Hourani, Albert. 'Averroes on Good and Evil'. *Studia Islamica*, 16 (1962), pp. 13–40.
Hourani, George F. 'Ethical Presuppositions of the Qur'an'. *The Muslim World*, 70 (1980), pp. 1–28.
Hyamson, Albert Montefiore. *Jewish Quarterly Review*, 9:2 (January 1897).
Ibrahim, Ezzeddin and Johnson Davies, Denys. *Forty Hadith Qudsi*. Cambridge: Islamic Texts Society, 1999.
an-Nawawi's Forty Ḥadīth. Damascus: Holy Koran Publ. House, 1976.
Imber, Colin. *Ebu's-Su'ud: The Islamic Legal Tradition*. Stanford: Stanford University Press, 1997.
Izutsu, Toshihiko. *Ethico Religious Concepts in the Qur'an*. Montreal: McGill University Press, 2002.
Jamal, Mahmood, ed. and trans. *Islamic Mystical Poetry: Ṣūfī Verses from the Early Mystics to Rūmī*. London: Penguin Books, 2009.
Jeanrond, Werner. *A Theology of Love*. London: T&T Clark International, 2010.
Jeffrey, Arthur. *The Foreign Vocabulary of the Qur'ān*. Baroda: Oriental Institute, 1938.
Julian of, Norwich. *Showings*, trans. Edmund Colledge and James Walsh. New York: Paulist Press, 1978.
Juynboll, T. W. 'Islam and Slavery in General', *Encyclopaedia of Islam*, 1st edition, vol. 1, Leiden: Brill, 1913, pp. 16–17.
Kant, Immanuel. *Religion Within the Limits of Reason Alone*, trans. Theodore M. Greene and Hoyt H. Hudson. New York: Harper Torchbooks, 1960.
Karic, Enes. 'Intoxicants', in Jane Dammen McAuliffe, ed. *Encyclopaedia of the Qur'ān*. Leiden: Brill, 2002 vol. 2, pp. 555–7.
Keddie, Nikki. 'Symbol and Sincerity in Islam'. *Studia Islamica*, 19 (1963), pp. 27–63.
Khan, Ruqayya Yasmine. *Self and Secrecy in Early Islam*. Columbia: University of South Carolina Press, 2008.
Komroff, Manuel, ed. *The History of Herodotus*. New York: Tudor Pub. Co., 1956.
Kueny, Kathryn. *The Rhetoric of Sobriety*. Albany: State University of New York Press, 2001.
Lara, Maria Pia, ed. *Rethinking Evil*. London: University of California Press, 2001.
Lazarus-Yafeh, Hava. 'Some Differences between Judaism and Islam as Two Religions of Law'. *Religion*, 14 (1984), pp. 175–91.

Leaman, Oliver. 'Secular Friendship and Religious Devotion', in Oliver Leaman, ed., *Friendship East and West: Philosophical Perspectives*. Richmond: Curzon, 1996, pp. 251–62.

Lerner, Pablo and Rabello, Alfredo Mordechai. 'The Prohibition of Ritual Slaughtering (Kosher, Shechita and *ḥalāl*) and Freedom of Religion for Minorities'. *Journal of Law and Religion*, 22:1 (2006–7), pp. 1–62.

Lewis, Bernard. *Race and Slavery in the Middle-East*. Oxford: Oxford University Press, 1990.

Lewis, C. S. *The Four Loves*. New York: Inspirational Press, 1991.

Lobban, Richard A. Jr. 'Pigs and their Prohibition'. *International Journal of Middle East Studies*, 26 (1994), pp. 57–75.

Marmon, Shaun E. 'Concubinage, Islamic', in Joseph R. Strayer, ed., *Dictionary of the Middle-Ages*, Vol. 3, New York: Scribner, 1983, p. 528.

Slavery in the Islamic Middle-East. Princeton, NJ: Markus Wiener Publishers, 1999.

Massignon, Louis. *The Passion of Hallāj*, trans. Herbert Mason. Princeton, NJ: Princeton University Press, 1982.

Mathewes, Charles T. 'Original Sin and the Hermeneutics of Charity: A Response to Gilbert Meilaender'. *Journal of Religious Ethics*, 29:1 (2001), pp. 35–42.

McAuliffe, Jane Dammen. 'Exegetical Identification of the Ṣābi'ūn'. *Muslim World*, 72 (1982), pp. 95–106.

Encyclopaedia of the Qur'an. Leiden: Brill, 2002.

McCord Adams, Marilyn and Merrihew Adams, Robert, eds. *The Problem of Evil*. Oxford: Oxford University Press, 1990.

McDonagh, Enda. *Gift and Call*. Meinrad, IN: Abbey Press, 1975.

McGrath, Alistair E. *Christian Theology: An Introduction*. Oxford: Blackwell, 1994.

Middleton, Paul, ed. *The God of Love and Human Dignity: Essays in Honour of George Newlands*. London: T&T Clark, 2007.

Milgrom, Jacob. 'Ethics and Ritual: The Foundations of the Biblical Dietary Laws', in Edwin B. Firmage, ed., *Religion and Law: Biblical, Jewish and Islamic Perspectives*. Winona Lake, IN: Eisenbrauns, 1989, pp. 159–91.

Montaigne, Michel de. *The Complete Essays of Montaigne*, trans. Donald Frame. Stanford: Stanford University Press, 1965.

Mourad, Suleiman A. *Early Islam between Myth and History*. Leiden: Brill, 2006.

Muhammad, Ghazi bin, Volf, Miroslav, and Yarrington, Melissa, eds., *A Common Word*. Grand Rapids, MI: Eerdmans, 2010.

Murata, Sachiko and Chittick, William. *The Vision of Islam*. London: I. B. Tauris, 1996.

Nygren, Anders. *Agape and Eros*, trans. Philip S. Watson. New York: Harper & Row, 1969.

Obermann, Julian. 'Political Theology in Early Islam: Hasan al-Basri's Treatise on Qadar'. *Journal of the American Oriental Society*, 55:2 (1935), pp. 138–62.

Pannenberg, Wolfhart. *The Apostles' Creed*. London: SCM Press Ltd, 1972.

Patrides, Constantinos A. 'The Salvation of Satan'. *Journal of the History of Ideas*, 28:4 (1967), pp. 467–78.

Patterson, Orlando. *Slavery and Social Death: A Comparative Study*. Cambridge, MA: Harvard University Press, 1982.

Peters, Rudolph. *Crime and Punishment in Islamic Law*. Cambridge: Cambridge University Press, 2005.

Plantinga, Alvin. "The Logical Problem of Evil". in William Rowe, ed., *God and the Problem of Evil*. Oxford: Blackwell, 2001.

Rapoport, Yossef. *Marriage, Money and Divorce in Medieval Islamic Society*. Cambridge: Cambridge University Press, 2005.

Ricoeur, Paul. *Evil, A Challenge to Philosophy and Theology*, trans. John Bowden. London: Continuum, 2007.

Rippin, Andrew and Knappert, Jan. *Textual Sources for the Study of Islam*. Chicago: University of Chicago Press, 1990.

Rodinson, Maxime. *Mohammed*. New York: Pantheon Books, 1974.

Rorty, Amelie Oksenberg. *Essays on Aristotle's Ethics*. Berkeley: University of California Press, 1980.

Rosenthal, Franz.'"I am You" – Individual Piety and Society in Islam', in Amin Banani and Speros Vryonis, Jr., eds. *Individualism and Conformity in Classical Islam: Fifth Georgio Levi Della Vida Biennial Conference*. Wiesbaden: Harrassowitz, 1977, pp. 33–60.

Rowe, William, ed. *God and the Problem of Evil*. Oxford: Blackwell, 2001.

Safran, Janina M. 'Rules of Purity and Confessional Boundaries: Mālikī Debates about the Pollution of the Christian'. *History of Religions*, 42:3 (2003), pp. 197–212.

Schacht, Joseph. 'Umm al-Walad', in *Encyclopaedia of Islam*, 1st edition, Leiden: Brill, 1934, p. 1014.

An Introduction to Islamic Law. Oxford: Clarendon Press, 1964.

The Origins of Muḥammadan Jurisprudence. Oxford: Clarendon Press, 1967.

Schuon, Frithjof. *Dimensions of Islam*, trans. P. Townsend. London: Allen & Unwin, 1970.

Islam and the Perennial Philosophy. London: World of Islam Festival Publishing Company Ltd, 1976.

Schwarz, Michael. 'The Letter of Ḥasan al-Baṣrī'. *Oriens*, 20 (1967), pp. 15–30.

Shah-Kazemi, Reza. 'God, "The Loving,"', in Miroslav Volf, Ghazi bin Muhammad and Melissa Yarrington, eds., *A Common Word*. Grand Rapids, MI: Eerdmans, 2010, pp. 88–109.

Siddiqui, Mona. 'Between God's Mercy and God's Law: Human Dignity in Islam', in Paul Middleton, ed., *The God of Love and Human Dignity: Essays in Honour of George Newlands*. London: T&T Clark, 2007, pp. 51–64.

'The Concept of Wilāya in Hanafi Law'. *Yearbook of Islamic and Middle-Eastern Law* (1998–9), pp. 171–85.

"The Defective Marriage in Classical Ḥanafī Law: Issues of Form and Validity", in Gerald Richard Hawting, Jawhid Mojaddedi and Alexander Samely, eds., *Studies in Islamic and Middle-Eastern Texts in Memory of Norman Calder*. Oxford: Oxford University Press, 2001, pp. 271–86.

"The Juristic Expressions of the Rules of Marriage as Presented in the Fatāwā'Alamgīrī". Unpublished Ph.D. thesis, Manchester University, 1992.

Singer, Irvine. *The Nature of Love, Plato to Luther*, 2nd edition. Chicago: University of Chicago Press, 2009.

Smith, Robertson. *Kinship and Marriage in Early Arabia*. Cambridge: Cambridge University Press, 1885.

The Religion of the Semites. New York: Meridian, 1957.

Sozomenus, Salaminius Hermias. *The Ecclesiastical History of Salaminius Hermias Sozomenus*, Book VI, Chapter XXXVIII: eng.orthodoxonline.org/early_church_fathers/volume 25/ECF 00014.htm.

Spectorsky, Susan Ann. *Women in Classical Law: A Survey of the Sources*. Leiden: Brill, 2010.

Stiles, Erin.'When is a Divorce a Divorce? Determining Intention in Zanzibar's Islamic Courts'. *Ethnology*, 42:.4 (2003), pp. 273–88.

Stoddart, William.'Lossky's Palamitism in the Light of Schuon': www.sacredweb.com/online_articles/sw6_stoddart.pdf.

Swinburne, Richard."Some Major Strands of Theodicy", in William Rowe, ed., *God and the Problem of Evil*. Oxford: Blackwell, 2001, pp. 240–64.

Telfer, Elizabeth. 'Friendship'. *Proceedings of the Aristotelian Society*, NS, 71 (1970–71), pp. 223–41.

Thomas, Laurence. "Friendship." *Synthese*, 72:2 (1987), pp. 217–36.

Trakakis, Nick. "Is Theism Capable of Accounting for Any Natural Evil at All?" *International Journal for Philosophy of Religion*, 57:1 (2005), pp. 36–66.

Troeltsch, Ernst. *The Christian Faith*. Minneapolis: Fortress Press, 1991.

Valīuddīn, Mīr. *The Qur'ānic Sūfism*. Delhi: Motilal Banarsidass, 1997.

van Gelder, Geert Jan. *Close Relationships: Incest and Inbreeding in Classical Arabic Literature*. London: I. B. Tauris, 2005.

Vernon, Mark. *The Philosophy of Friendship*. New York: Palgrave Macmillan, 2005.

von Grunebaum, Gustave E. "Observations on the Muslim Concept of Evil". *Studia Islamica*, 31 (1970), pp. 117–34.

Wadell, Paul. *Friendship and the Moral Life*. Notre Dame, IN: University of Notre Dame Press, 1989.

Wensinck, A. J. "Khamr", in *The Encyclopaedia of Islam*, 2nd edition, ed. P. J. Bearman, T. Bianquis, C. E. Bosworth, E. van Donzel, and W. P. Heinrichs et al., Leiden: Brill, 1960–2005.

The Muslim Creed. Cambridge: Cambridge University Press, 1932.

'Wine in Islam'. The *Muslim World*, 18:4 (1928), pp. 365–73.

Wheeler, Brannon. "Good and Evil", Jane Dammen McAuliffe, ed., *Encyclopaedia of the Qur'ān*. Leiden: Brill, 2002, vol. 2, pp. 335–9.

Wiesel, Elie. *Night*. London: Penguin, 2006.

Wild, Stefan, ed. *The Qur'ān as Text*. Leiden: Brill, 1996.

Wolfson, Harry A. *The Philosophy of the Kalām*. Cambridge: Cambridge University Press, 1976.

Zaman, Muhammad. "Sin, Major and Minor", in Jane Dammen McAuliffe, ed., *Encyclopaedia of the Qur'ān*. Leiden: Brill, 2006, vol. 5 pp. 19–27.

Žižek, Slavoj. *Violence*. London: Profile Books, 2009.

Index

For EU product safety concerns, contact us at Calle de José Abascal, 56–1°,
28003 Madrid, Spain or eugpsr@cambridge.org.

www.ingramcontent.com/pod-product-compliance
Ingram Content Group UK Ltd.
Pitfield, Milton Keynes, MK11 3LW, UK
UKHW012150180425
457579UK00015B/181

* 9 7 8 0 5 2 1 7 4 0 1 2 8 *